'It is a significant creative challenge to develop, implement and bring a successful
Didau manages to offer a practical field guide to conquer that very challenge with this invaluable book. It is jam-packed full of useful insights and resources. It feels both challenging and celebratory, pragmatic and uplifting. English leaders and teachers will find countless gems in this essential book'.

Alex Quigley, Author of *Closing the Writing Gap*, *Closing the Reading Gap* and *Closing the Vocabulary Gap*

'*Making Meaning in English* provided us with the purpose and reasons for teaching English. *Bringing the English Curriculum to Life* provides a blueprint as to how we can transform the subject, through gapless instruction. "Success must **precede** struggle". For too many years, this has been the other way around. Why shouldn't students study modules like the 'Ancient Origins' in Year 7? Knowing that some may have access, this book argues that we should be making such topics and texts accessible to all – that is inclusion.

There's always talk about intent, implementation and impact but do we spend time as individuals or departments ruminating over what that actually looks like? This book provides clear definitions for each. It also continues the notion that the English curriculum is a conversation between students and the subject.

Didau and OAT's English Lead Practitioner Team have curated a text that gets us thinking about the breadth of the English curriculum and the depth in which topics can be explored. This is another insightful book that is a must for all those involved in the teaching of English!'

Paul Bell, English Teacher and Senior Leader

'The assembling of an English curriculum that engages, inspires and allows our students to flourish is difficult. Equally, designing a curriculum that engages the enactors of that curriculum – our teachers – can be an onerous task. *Bringing the English Curriculum to Life*, however, equips English Teams and their leaders with the tools to build an engaging yet challenging curriculum that connects various threads – intent, implementation, assessment and outcomes – enabling our students to experience the joys English has to offer. The voices of David Didau and his team's collaborative efforts shine through powerfully; their guidance, expertise and sense of overarching purpose is a sure-fire way to kick-start your approach to English teaching'.

Gaurav Dubay, Director of English at Windsor Academy Trust

'As English teachers, it's easy to state that we want an ambitious curriculum for our students. But mapping out a comprehensive, knowledge-rich English curriculum is another thing entirely. Does it have a clear intent? Is it logically sequenced? Is it based on a thorough interrogation of the subject's overarching concepts? In *Bringing the English Curriculum to Life*, David Didau and colleagues manage to put forward a curriculum that answers these questions and much more.

Considering the fundamental role of challenging texts from the canon, and how these can be partnered with more diverse modern texts, Didau's ideal curriculum adds to the stimulating debate of *what* we should teach in KS3 English. Yet it also offers a convincing argument about *how* we should be teaching key concepts. Both theoretically invigorating yet very accessible, this is a compelling book full of highly practical strategies for the busy English teacher'.

Mark Roberts, Author, English Teacher, and Director of Research at Carrickfergus Grammar School

'*Bringing the English Curriculum to Life* is an inspirational read that addresses how a curriculum brimming with powerful knowledge can be successfully put into practice across a Trust of schools, with multiple examples of effective classroom implementation. The book emphasises curriculum entitlement by focusing on empowering all students to access the same level of challenge and academic rigour. Functioning as a handbook for implementing an ambitious and rigorous English curriculum, this is not only a must-read for those with an investment in the teaching of English but for all of us involved in curriculum thinking. *Bringing the English Curriculum to Life* shows how educational theory looks in practice, explaining the "what", "why" and "how" with the perfect blend of seminal evidence and practical classroom examples. No aspect of curriculum implementation is overlooked: from the importance of sequencing and retrieval to reading and vocabulary strategies; from granular writing and meaningful classroom discussion to mastery assessment.

While Didau's *Making Meaning in English* explains the thinking behind curriculum intent, this natural next step answers questions those readers may have about applying powerful knowledge in a purposeful, inclusive way. Now, more than ever, we need to be challenging all students, making social mobility possible and narrowing ever-increasing gaps in education: this book shows us how an English curriculum can do just that'.

Helen Howell, Author and Assistant Headteacher

'In this comprehensive book filled with well-explained approaches, David Didau sets out a compelling and detailed vision of how to optimise curriculum sequencing, pedagogy and assessment in English. Building upon his previous book *Making Meaning in English*, this text is essential reading for all English teachers'.

Tom Needham, Author of *Explicit English Teaching*

'The experience of reading David Didau on teaching and the curriculum can be a bit strange; there's a kind of easy and gentle déjà vu, then you begin to doubt yourself: did I think that already, or is it just such an obviously good idea? However, whether you always thought this way, or are right now being slowly enlightened with each turn of the page, you do find yourself arriving somewhere new: a deeper appreciation of what we do in every lesson, every day – that is, teaching English.

It's only when you find yourself disagreeing with Didau that you can get a better sense of what he's about – because he is changing your mind, the way you have always thought about teaching, and you find yourself wondering, re-evaluating and imagining: what if I did it this way instead? And surely that is why we read any book: not to deepen our convictions, but to begin thinking in a new way. And if that is not why we read books about education and curriculum, I think it really should be.

Didau's *Bringing the English Curriculum to Life* does just that. It nudges, it cajoles, it chips away, it changes the furrow we so steadily and earnestly plough every day. It might even breathe new life into us jaded and cynical English teachers, freeing us from what we thought we should be doing, fearing we weren't doing it, and forever looking over our shoulders when really, what we should have been doing all along is little more than loving our subject and sharing the joy we take in it.

Will this book have a profound impact on my teaching? On our curriculum? The answer is 'yes' to both. There are few books in education that have the potential to have such far-reaching changes to the manner in which a subject is taught'.

Peter Ahern, Head of English Department in a large comprehensive school in the North West

'It's impossible for me to capture here everything that I think about this book, so broad and rich is its scope. It's a joy. What David Didau and his team have created is remarkable. Not only are we treated to the gorgeous curriculum they've curated, we're taken by the hand and guided through five core pedagogical principles – approaches to teaching English that are easy to implement and have an identifiable impact on pupils' ability to learn. And these "basics", as Didau and his team call them, are the ways in which we can ensure our kids can master speaking, listening, reading and writing. But more than that, they can lead to the ability to *make meaning* from language and literature, so it sings in our classrooms and echoes forward into our children's lives. It's also one of the best – if not *the* best – books I've read about assessment in English. Not only do I want to teach this curriculum with the principles it recommends, I also want to be taught it. It's exciting and exhilarating and everything that's beautiful about English, the best of subjects'.

Claire Stoneman, Principal and English Teacher, AET Academies

'When we are working on the curriculum, we are holding in tension the big picture for a subject, with the nitty gritty of making it work in the classroom. Too often, there's a gap between the lofty ambitions and the quality of what lands on pupils' desks. In *Bringing the English Curriculum to Life* David Didau and colleagues show how they go about tackling this and they offer it to the rest of us in a spirit of humility and an invitation to engage. There is so much here, from the teaching of fluency, to getting proper talk in place, to the clever "Couch to 5k writing", that all educators, whatever their phase or specialism, will find masses of takeaways and the odd wakeup call. Absolutely marvellous!'

Mary Myatt, Co-author of the Huh Curriculum series of books and founder of Myatt & Co

'While the last few years in education have seen something of an explosion in cognitive science and curriculum-related research, we have had very few models that help teachers to see what the theory could look like in practice, and this is especially true of English. David and his team at OAT start with the contention that every child can achieve their potential through a knowledge-rich, concept-led curriculum which is deep in meaning and broad in scope. We are presented with a thorough walkthrough of the whole OAT curriculum, but the book is packed with easily digestible takeaway ideas. It is a joyful curriculum, but a realistic one – the authors share not just their successes, but the lessons learnt. *Bringing the English Curriculum to Life* is a genuine gift to the English teaching community'.

Sam Gibbs, Co-author of *The Trouble with English and How to Address It: A Practical Guide to Designing and Delivering a Concept-Led Curriculum*

Bringing the English Curriculum to Life

Bringing the English Curriculum to Life builds on David Didau's groundbreaking book *Making Meaning in English* by showing how the principles of the original book can be applied in schools and classrooms. Drawing together experiences of designing, teaching, supporting and assessing English across the schools within Ormiston Academies Trust (OAT), this book demonstrates what an ambitious, coherently sequenced, broad and balanced English curriculum with successful adaption for students with SEND can look like in practice.

Designed around the explicit teaching of the powerful conceptual knowledge students need to master the discipline, the book offers a fully resourced English curriculum packed with teaching suggestions and examples of high-quality practice. Covering intent, implementation and assessment, and outlining in detail what is included in each module for KS3 and 4, the curriculum can be adopted in its entirety, but is also flexible enough for departments to take modules and slot them into their own curriculum.

Providing an inspiring model for teaching English that enables all students to succeed, this is an essential resource for all English teachers and school leaders responsible for curriculum development.

David Didau is Senior Lead Practitioner for English at Ormiston Academies Trust as well as the author of several books covering a wide range of education topics.

Bringing the English Curriculum to Life

A Field Guide for *Making Meaning in English*

David Didau

with contributions from Daniel Blackburn, Emma Levins, Kate Moloney, Tom Pinkstone, Amy Rose, Claire Woozley and James Hibbert

Routledge
Taylor & Francis Group

LONDON AND NEW YORK

Designed cover image: © Dani Pasteau

First published 2024
by Routledge
4 Park Square, Milton Park, Abingdon, Oxon OX14 4RN

and by Routledge
605 Third Avenue, New York, NY 10158

Routledge is an imprint of the Taylor & Francis Group, an informa business

© 2024 David Didau

British Library Cataloguing-in-Publication Data
A catalogue record for this book is available from the British Library

Library of Congress Cataloging-in-Publication Data
Names: Didau, David, author.
Title: Bringing the english curriculum to life : a field guide for making
  meaning in english / David Didau with additional material from Claire
  Woozley, Amy Rose, Tom Pinkstone, James Hibbert, Emma Levins, Kate
  Moloney & Dan Blackburn.
Description: Abingdon, Oxon ; New York, NY : Routledge, 2024. | Includes
  bibliographical references and index.
Identifiers: LCCN 2023036297 (print) | LCCN 2023036298 (ebook) |
  ISBN 9781032596587 (hardback) | ISBN 9781032596563 (paperback) |
  ISBN 9781003455622 (ebook)
Subjects: LCSH: English language—Study and teaching (Middle school) |
  English language—Study and teaching (Secondary) | Language arts—
  Correlation with content subjects. | Language arts—Curricula.
Classification: LCC LB1576 .D464178 2024 (print) | LCC LB1576 (ebook) |
  DDC 428.0071/2—dc23/eng/20231005
LC record available at https://lccn.loc.gov/2023036297
LC ebook record available at https://lccn.loc.gov/2023036298

ISBN: 978-1-032-59658-7 (hbk)
ISBN: 978-1-032-59656-3 (pbk)
ISBN: 978-1-003-45562-2 (ebk)

DOI: 10.4324/9781003455622

Typeset in Berling
by Apex CoVantage, LLC

Contents

Preface

I wrote *Making Meaning in English* in the middle of the first national lockdown after having been out of the classroom for almost ten years. Whilst this had given me lots of time to think, read and refine my ideas about the English curriculum it also meant I was fairly out of touch with the reality of working full-time as an English teacher. When schools reopened after the first lockdown in September 2020, I started teaching again. Much to my surprise and relief, I found that teaching is at least somewhat similar to riding a bike. An even more pleasant discovery was that so much of the pontificating and theorising of the previous decade had made me a more effective teacher.

After a term spent back at the chalk face, I was persuaded to work at Ormiston Academy Trust by the improbably named Tuesday Humby. After a decade of being independent, I needed some convincing, but I eventually started as OAT's Senior Lead Practitioner for English in January 2021, just as schools went into a second lockdown for three months. The silver lining in this particular cloud was that I was able to spend time talking – via Teams – to the heads of English at all 32 of our secondary academies about their curriculum offer.

As a Multi-Academy Trust, OAT is the polar opposite of those MATs which prescribe the detail of what happens in schools; our academies have almost complete autonomy to approach curriculum and teaching in whatever way they decide best suits them. Whilst this can sometimes feel frustrating – getting academies to agree to anything as a group can feel a lot like herding cats – it does mean that there is huge freedom for teachers and school leaders to do potentially amazing things. It also means that whatever the Trust produces must be of the highest quality to persuade anyone that it's worth

adopting. There was – and still is – a huge variety of different curriculum offers in our English departments. While most have gone down the route of creating their own curriculum from scratch, a significant minority had bought in commercially available English curriculums from outside providers.

My brief was to oversee the creation a KS3 English curriculum which would fulfil three different functions. First, it had to be at least as good (if not much better) than the commercially available alternatives. Second, it had to provide a benchmark of what an ambitious English curriculum could look like for schools to measure their own curriculum against. And third, it had to be flexible enough for departments to take modules and slot them into their own curriculum.

Having spent the previous decade thinking hard about the English curriculum, I had a clear idea of what I thought was right, but the challenge was to persuade not just the curriculum leaders in our academies but also the fantastic team of English lead practitioners I'd inherited. I knew the curriculum I envisaged would be outside the comfort zone of many English teachers and that if I was to convince anyone that students in our schools could rise to the challenge, we'd need to produce really high-quality resources and training.

So, over these first three months I listened, made suggestions and recommendations when asked, and offered respectful challenges when appropriate. The starting point came when each member of the Lead Practitioner team (Amy Rose, Claire Woozley, James Hibbert, Tom Pinkstone and I) wrote a pilot module to be ready for the summer term of 2021 and approached teachers in our schools to see if any would be willing to give them a go. At that point, I had only the sketchiest idea of what our materials should look like (although we were clear that writing detailed lesson slides was not the way we intended to go) but the Lead Practitioner team responded brilliantly to my vague directions on what we should be producing. Obviously, on such short notice there were relatively few takers, but – thankfully – enough that we were able to learn a lot about what worked and what didn't. We combined the best of the five different approaches to writing materials and took advice from the teachers that had piloted our modules about what needed to improve.

After reaching final agreement as a team about what should be included in our KS3 curriculum, we went about the process of putting together a long-term plan. At this point, Holly Hammond, Head of English at Cliff Park Ormiston Academy in Great Yarmouth, got in touch to say she wanted to teach the entirety of our brand-new, untested curriculum for all three KS3 year groups starting the following September. This was both thrilling and terrifying. Apart from our five pilot modules and some vague plans, we had nothing tangible to offer. And so, with reckless optimism and naïve determination, we set about creating resources for the first three modules to be ready for September 2021 and committed to having the rest ready in advance of when they'd be needed.

This was the best thing that could have happened. Done is always better than perfect and, as Voltaire put it, 'perfect is the enemy of good'. We definitely had no time to make things perfect, but we could strive to make them good. OAT's marketing team did a superb job in helping us design professional-looking resources and getting them printed and delivered to Cliff Park ready for the new academic year. Claire Woozley (the Lead Practitioner based at Cliff Park) and I spent a day with the English department training them in the core pedagogical approaches we were advocating and trying our best to alleviate their concerns about the huge project they were about to undertake.

At the same time, Rikki Cole, Assistant Principal at Victory Academy in Norwich, began piloting our Couch to 5k writing programme with his classes. Victory was one of the first OAT schools I visited when the second lockdown was over in April 2021. I modelled teaching a Couch to 5k writing lesson to Rikki's Year 9 class and we were all very impressed with the work they produced in the lesson. He has gone on to be instrumental in developing and refining the process over the following two years. The results his students produced in the 2022 exam series were nothing short of remarkable.

As with all the best-laid plans, things did not unfold as smoothly as anyone would have wished. The staff at Cliff Park were without a headteacher for much of the year and the English team faced huge and unanticipated challenges. Inevitably, the implementation of the curriculum diverged from our expectations. But although many mistakes were made (most of them mine) important lessons were learned. Through a process of trial and error, we honed our understanding of what our resources needed to include and what training and support were required to make the curriculum a success. And through it all, Holly and Claire (who spent two days per week deployed at the school throughout the year) were the rocks that kept everyone's heads above water.

I can't express emphatically enough how grateful I am to Holly and the English team at Cliff Park. What they achieved that year was simply extraordinary. Finding out that not only did the students enjoy their experience of studying our curriculum but that they knew more and could do more as a result has been the most marvellous proof of concept. Speaking to students who were able to converse enthusiastically about texts and writers as diverse and challenging as *The Odyssey*, *Beowulf*, the King James Bible, Chaucer, Aphra Behn, Chinua Achebe and Zora Neale Hurston has been both humbling and a huge vindication of everything I believe the study of English can and should be. Hearing from students that they 'loved' reading *Oedipus Tyrannus*; how viscerally they'd felt the tension of the final act of *Journey's End*; how much they'd enjoyed reading and writing sonnets; how much they knew about language change (and how much more they wanted to know) and that they were requesting even more Shakespeare, has been the proudest experience of my career.

At the time of writing, there are five OAT schools that have embraced teaching our curriculum in its entirety, with many more including one or more of our modules as part of their own curriculum offer. We feel that what we've produced is as good as anything out there and, even if you disagree with the principles that underpin our work, the effect it is having on students is hard to argue with.

This book is an attempt to explain and exemplify the process of designing, teaching, supporting, assessing and iterating the ideas in *Making Meaning in English* into a living, breathing curriculum being taught in real schools to actual students. I very much hope you find it useful and that even if you don't want to teach it, you can at least use it as a point of comparison for making your own English curriculum the best it can be.

David Didau, Backwell, March 2023

An introduction to OAT's English Lead Practitioner team

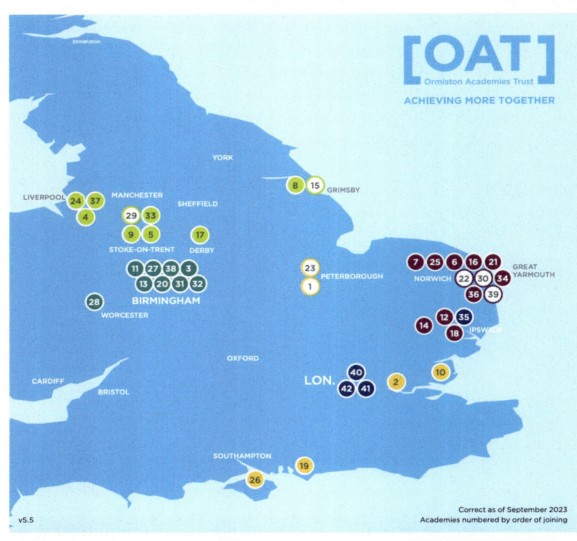

[OAT]
Ormiston Academies Trust

ACHIEVING MORE TOGETHER

v5.5

Correct as of September 2023
Academies numbered by order of joining

NORTH

- 4 Ormiston Bolingbroke Academy
- 24 Ormiston Chadwick Academy
- 9 Ormiston Horizon Academy
- 17 Ormiston Ilkeston Enterprise Academy
- 8 Ormiston Maritime Academy
- 33 Ormiston Meridian Academy
- 37 Sandymoor Ormiston Academy
- 5 Ormiston Sir Stanley Matthews Academy

WEST

- 38 Brownhills Ormiston Academy
- 13 Ormiston Forge Academy
- 11 George Salter Academy
- 32 Ormiston NEW Academy
- 3 Ormiston Sandwell Community Academy
- 27 Ormiston Shelfield Community Academy
- 31 Ormiston SWB Academy
- 28 Tenbury High Ormiston Academy
- 20 Wodensborough Ormiston Academy

EAST

- 38 Broadland High Ormiston Academy
- 25 City of Norwich School, An Ormiston Academy
- 21 Cliff Park Ormiston Academy
- 16 Ormiston Denes Academy
- 12 Ormiston Endeavour Academy
- 34 Flegg High Ormiston Academy
- 18 Stoke High School – Ormiston Academy
- 14 Ormiston Sudbury Academy
- 6 Ormiston Venture Academy
- 7 Ormiston Victory Academy

PRIMARY

- 39 Ormiston Cliff Park Primary Academy
- 30 Edward Worlledge Ormiston Academy
- 22 Ormiston Herman Academy
- 23 Ormiston Meadows Academy
- 29 Packmoor Ormiston Academy
- 15 Ormiston South Parade Academy

ALTERNATIVE PROVISION AND SPECIAL

- 40 Ormiston Beachcroft Academy
- 41 Ormiston Bridge Academy
- 42 Ormiston Latimer Academy
- 35 Thomas Wolsey Ormiston Academy

We, the English Lead Practitioner team at Ormiston Academies Trust, have worked on this curriculum together over the past two and a half years. We are:

- David Didau, Senior English Lead Practitioner
- Amy Rose, Regional Lead Practitioner for the West
- Tom Pinkstone, Regional Lead Practitioner for the North
- Claire Woozley, Regional Lead Practitioner for the East
- Emma Levins, Regional Lead Practitioner for the South
- Kate Moloney, Regional Lead Practitioner for the South
- Dan Blackburn, Regional Lead Practitioner for the East

During that time, James Hibbert, one of the original 'fab four' (Amy, Tom and Claire are the others) left us to become a Vice Principal in August 2022, and we have been joined by three wonderful new members of the team.

OAT is made up of 43 academies (32 secondaries, six primaries and five special schools) and covers a geographical spread from Cowes on the Isle of Wight up to Grimsby in the North, and from Tenbury in the West to Great Yarmouth in the East. You can find an interactive map of our academy's locations here: www.ormistonacademiestrust.co.uk/our-academies/interactive-network-map/

Here we are in our own words:

Amy Rose

When I look back over my teaching career and consider change, even just in the past decade, it forces me to consider Deepak Chopra's line, 'All great changes are preceded by chaos'. It is safe to say that during my time in education, there has been plenty of chaos!

When I joined Ormiston Academies Trust over four years ago, it was the most exciting yet daunting change I ever made. Back then, there were only two other Lead Practitioners and English teaching seemed to be in a very different place. We were still focusing on the 'jazzy'; funky activities in lessons with sprinkles of magic to make lessons 'outstanding'. However, OAT was passionate about stripping everything back, and asking two of the most powerful questions: What are we going to teach to challenge and inspire? How are we going to do this?

David joining the Trust was the addition we needed as an English team to drive these questions forward. A refreshing, very well-read set of ambitious eyes looking at a curriculum that needed to change. Without careful managing, this change could well have resulted in chaos. Together, we have created a highly ambitious and diverse curriculum offer for our schools. Instead of causing chaos, it has been met with relief.

Reflecting now on the past two years of this process leaves me quite emotional. I work with a team of highly driven, caring and knowledgeable individuals and together we have created something magical. A curriculum that is interesting, challenging and engaging and will leave students with an in-depth knowledge of concepts and characters they may otherwise never have encountered. It has been a delight to be a part of this process and I am forever grateful for being in the role I am with such a passionate team. I remain excited for the journey this curriculum will take us on, teachers and students alike.

Tom Pinkstone

Working on the OAT curriculum, with the best practitioners in my field, has been the most beneficial CPD I could have hoped for. It has continually pushed my thinking and made me evaluate not just what students are capable of learning, but also how they best go about learning it. I am proud to have contributed towards the design of a curriculum which offers our schools high-quality teaching materials and guidance on the best ways to implement them in the classroom. I believe these modules will, at the very least, ensure our students have access to culturally rich knowledge and the opportunity to master skills which will enable them to compete with anyone, anywhere.

Claire Woozley

April 2023 marks my third anniversary of joining OAT, after some 20+ years in a diverse range of classrooms and nigh on 15 years since I first became a Head of English. In that time, the subject of English has been through many and various iterations: from mini plenaries (remember those!) to discovery learning to, now, a subject far more literary and knowledge-rich than when I first started teaching. Our curriculum represents for me the very best of our combined experience, wisdom and thought, balancing high challenge and ambition with texts which we love, and which staff and students enjoy. And whilst it's our names on the front cover, I'm entirely indebted to the English teams I work with for their patience, insight and willingness to take a chance on something that, at first glance, can seem fairly terrifying. There have been countless conversations, questions and observations from the fantastic Heads of English and their departments, without which my own thinking on the curriculum would be all the poorer. Walking the corridors at our schools and hearing Year 7 classes loudly declaiming lines from the Odyssey, arguing with Year 9 students about whether or not they're on 'Team Heathcliff', and observing reluctant Year 8s cracking 'the sonnet code' have been the very best moments of my career. As one of our Heads of Department aptly put it, 'I wish I'd had the opportunity to do this when I was at school'. I will be forever grateful to David that I could have a role in bringing this curriculum to life and providing that chance to the students in our schools.

Emma Levins

Having joined the team in September 2022, I am still in complete awe at the wealth of experience that this team, and OAT as a wider Trust, encompasses. Part of what encouraged me to join was the opportunity to provide the help and support I would have loved as a Head of Department. When I became Head of Department, I could not have predicted the turbulence that would characterise my time as a leader. With radical changes to the educational landscape, from shifting inspection priorities to managing school closures and teaching online during the pandemic, the ground at times felt as if it was shifting under my feet. However, a well-planned and sequenced curriculum thoughtfully implemented goes a long way to ensuring stability in uncertain times. That, to me, is what this book offers.

Kate Moloney

The landscape of education has changed considerably since I first set foot in a classroom in 2005. In English, this has been evident through what continue to be pertinent questions: what texts should be taught? When should they be taught? How should we teach them? For me, this ongoing interrogation is the very debate which makes the subject I love so varied and so brilliant, albeit at times frustrating! From viewing English as a primarily skills-based subject, to a now much greater focus on knowledge, it's endlessly fascinating to reflect on the ways in which our approaches have evolved. Throughout my career, as teacher and Head of Department, in the UK and abroad, I have been fortunate to work with teams of people who share a passion for English, and the relentless drive to deliver the very best education possible for our students. Working as a teacher at Cowes Enterprise College, and more recently as

part of the OAT Lead Practitioner team, has provided me with so many opportunities to reflect on, and indeed to challenge, my own thinking about curriculum and teaching; I genuinely do view the role I have as an absolute privilege. The OAT curriculum represents a culmination of the very best of our subject; texts which are endlessly interesting, which challenge and entertain, and which introduce students to complex concepts. To have played a small role in bringing this to life has been (and continues to be) an absolute joy and I am hugely grateful to David and the team for the chance to be part of something so amazing.

Something I am particularly passionate about is the ambitious nature of what has been produced here. In this level of challenge is the unequivocal belief that all students deserve to experience the joys of great literature and the opportunity to express themselves. I am immensely grateful for all the hard work that has gone into this, and it is a privilege to support its evolution.

Dan Blackburn

As the newest addition to the team, it has been a real joy to join an ongoing discussion about what English should look like as a subject in a knowledge-rich curriculum. When I was a Head of English, I was fortunate to work with a wonderful team of English teachers in my department who totally embraced the challenge of developing a curriculum filled with knowledge, rigour and enjoyment. I feel very fortunate to have the opportunity to bring my experience to this team and help to develop and deliver a challenging curriculum, which lifts the experience of every student. It's a real privilege to see students engaging with such valuable, literary knowledge and grow in confidence as they begin to see the evolution and connections that run throughout literature. I am really grateful to everyone in the team – and in OAT as a whole – for making me feel so welcome and valued so quickly.

*

Our English curriculum is by no means a finished, polished product. It continues to be updated and iterated on as we find new connections, spot gaps in our instructional sequences and respond to feedback from the teachers and students in our schools. We hope you find this account of the principles that underpin how we approached designing, planning, teaching, supporting and assessing the curriculum as useful as we've found it to write.

Intent

Specifying the curriculum

1.1 WHAT WE MEAN BY 'INTENT'

Before we consider anything else, we need to be clear about what we intend students should learn.

The word 'intent' has had an unfortunate effect on the work of curriculum. Someone in Ofsted Towers got overexcited when they realised that finding three words beginning with 'I' would be a catchy way to integrate the work being done on setting out how they would inspect curriculum in schools. Confusingly, the intent of a curriculum was not *intended* to have anything to do with *why* schools had decided to teach certain topics. Neither is it about coming up with vague mission statements on getting all children to fulfil their potential and become life-long learners, or whatever. The intent of the curriculum is the content children are expected to learn. More simply, the intent of the curriculum *is* the curriculum, or as Chief Inspector Amanda Spielman has put it, 'what [school leaders] expect pupils to know by certain points in their life'.[1] As Ofsted have made clear, 'Intent is about what leaders intend pupils to learn. It's as simple as that. Intent is everything up to the point at which teaching happens'.[2]

Good intent, according to Ofsted's Inspection Handbook, means a curriculum that is:

- ambitious for all pupils
- coherently planned and sequenced
- successfully adapted, designed and developed for pupils with special educational needs and/or disabilities (SEND)
- broad and balanced for all pupils.[3]

And if an English curriculum can balance ambition for all with successful adaption for students with

SEND, if it can be at once coherently sequenced as well as covering the breadth of what the subject offers, and intelligently balanced between the needs of reading, writing and speaking, it will be more than merely good.

At a more basic level, the purpose of a curriculum is to communicate with students and, as American educator Siegfried Engelmann put it, 'the curriculum is supposed to convey information about concepts that the learner does not possess'.[4] How these concepts are selected and communicated is the focus of this first section.

If you can explain why you've chosen to teach *this* and not *that*, if you know why the curriculum is ordered and taught in the way that it is, then you probably have a good grasp of what you intend students to learn.

NB. If you have already read *Making Meaning in English* you will be familiar with some of the arguments made in sections 1.2–1.4. If this is the case, you might prefer to skip straight to section 1.5.

1.2 CURRICULUM AS CONVERSATION

If the English curriculum is conceptualised as a conversation between students and the subject, then we should consider the quality of that conversation.

Of course, despite inveighing against 'intent statements', there's a clear rationale behind all the choices we've made. Our curriculum is designed to induct students into an ongoing conversation about the place of language and literature in the world. The philosopher of language, HP Grice, determined that the principles of cooperative conversation are

DOI: 10.4324/9781003455622-1

those of **quality**, **quantity**, **manner** and **relatedness**.[5] These then are the principles to which the curriculum should conform.

Quality – Not only must curriculum materials be clear and accurate, the texts studied must also be complex and challenging enough to provoke interesting conversations. The curriculum will be of sufficient quality if we ensure it consists of both **powerful** and **shared** knowledge (see section 1.3.)

Our curriculum is designed around the explicit teaching of the powerful conceptual knowledge students need to master the discipline. For knowledge to be powerful it should provide reliable explanations, a sound basis for making judgements and generalisations about the world beyond students' direct experiences, be developed systematically by specialists within subject disciplines, have the capacity to change students' perceptions, values or understanding, and provide a language for engaging in political, moral and other kinds of debates. We've chosen to divide the powerful concepts on which mastery of English depends into six broad areas of study: metaphor, story, argument, pattern, grammar and context. Each of these is explored further in section 1.6.

In choosing texts as vehicles for studying powerful conceptual knowledge, we have considered the following points:

- lexical challenge – how demanding are texts' vocabulary and syntax?
- the appropriateness of its content for the age group we're teaching
- the extent to which it has had 'conversations' backwards and forwards with other texts, that is to say, how influential it has been
- its quality – whether it introduces a broad range of literary conventions and offers sufficient stylistic merit to repay careful study
- to what extent it fulfils a role or niche within a broad and coherent curriculum
- and lastly, personal preference – there's little point teaching texts we feel are inferior to other, possible choices that could fulfil the same purpose.

Our choice of texts matters. While reading modern young adult fiction might give us a feeling of fulfilment as students identify with the characters, mastery of the subject comes from knowing how language and literature has evolved and how it has been influenced. **Texts should be chosen because they're worth studying, not just worth reading.**

Quantity – Clearly a curriculum must be sufficiently broad to introduce those aspects of the domain deemed essential, but it should not be so extensive as to overwhelm the opportunity to challenge assumptions; in this way, the breadth of our curriculum is held in tension with the depth in which topics are explored. In order to understand topics in depth, students need a breadth of literary and linguistic knowledge; our curriculum exposes students to sufficient breadth to enable them to develop a broad schema of what is meant by **language and literature**.

Manner – For students to make meaning they must be given opportunities to argue, debate, challenge, question and critique the knowledge they are taught. By possessing shared, culturally rich knowledge, students gain the ability to share ideas with a community of minds, living and dead. And by knowing what others know, students have a language to ask questions and make objections; they are orientated towards a tradition beyond the thin slice of the present and encouraged to use it to locate themselves in the here and now.

Relatedness – For a curriculum to be meaningful it must be carefully sequenced with each aspect chosen for its connection to every other topic as much as for its individual value. The sequence in which topics are studied should be inherently meaningful. Whatever is studied first should lead to subsequent study and subsequent topics should depend on and refer back to those previously encountered. As such, the curriculum attempts to relate a coherent narrative. This narrative is structured conceptually, chronologically and thematically.

1.3 THE 'KNOWLEDGE TURN' IN ENGLISH

To prepare all students, regardless of the starting points, to appreciate the depth and richness of the English language and its literature, we need to think carefully about the knowledge we need to teach.

Curriculum design has taken a swerve in the past few years. Happily, most schools have moved away from an 'edutainment' approach to learning – with the endless card sorts, carousels and hot-seating this entails – to instead focus on implementing a 'knowledge-rich' curriculum. This 'knowledge turn' is in part a reaction to GCSE reforms which were first proposed in 2013 and implemented from 2015 onwards, and to Ofsted's 'Key Stage 3: The Wasted Years'.[6] This has led to a widespread rethinking of what should be taught in schools and, particularly, in English.

Academic arguments around the role of knowledge in education tend to fall into two camps: constructivism and realism. Constructivists argue that knowledge is unique to individuals and will be independently discovered one way or another during compulsory education, and that schools shouldn't impose a corpus of knowledge upon an individual. Realists take the view that culture consists of knowledge, accumulated over the span of time, and that children can be taught that knowledge in order to better access the world once they leave school. There are, of course, many positions that fall between these poles.

There is also an argument about the responsibility of schools to impart 'cultural capital' to their students. The notion of cultural capital comprises the knowledge and customs of a locality, be it a family, village, city, nation or the shared knowledge of a global society.[7] However, what is considered to be the valuable knowledge children need in order to get ahead is that of the middle classes. A knowledge of fine art or classical music is more highly prized than the knowledge of popular artists or musicians. Just look at the questions asked on *University Challenge* for an indication of what is considered to be valuable. However, without every child in the country having a similarly broad background, knowledge inequalities are only likely to become further entrenched.

The following extract is taken from the now-infamous 2016 Key Stage 2 SATS reading paper:

> Then, in 2005, a team of scientists unearthed thousands of dodo bones in some mud flats in Mauritius. The remains date back to over 4,000 years ago, when the island was suffering from a lengthy drought. The mud flats would have formed a freshwater oasis in an otherwise parched environment. It is thought that most of the animals, while trying to reach the slowly receding waters of the lake, became stuck and died of thirst or suffocation. However, clearly some dodos survived as they did not become extinct until much later.[8]

Read it over a couple of times and consider what children would need to know to truly understand this piece of writing.

A reader would probably need to know:

- what a dodo was (and credit where it's due, this was explained in the paper)
- what mud flats are
- what Mauritius is and where it is located
- what a drought is
- A secure understanding of metaphor to recognise that the island itself wasn't in pain, but the flora and fauna were physically suffering
- what a freshwater oasis is and why it is special
- what the words 'parched', 'receding' and 'extinct' mean
- that animals can die of thirst.

No doubt there's much more knowledge which children would need to be familiar with to fully understand what's going on, and this is just for one paragraph! The demands on the knowledge of an 11-year-old child for them to understand a SATs paper is enormous. Those cognitive demands grow as they move into secondary school and the subjects they study become increasingly discrete and academic.

Without explicit introduction to shared, culturally rich knowledge, children who are unlikely to be exposed to art, literature, history or science at home will tend to have a less well-developed understanding than their more fortunate peers. Whilst this makes understanding a piece of writing about dodos a struggle, the ability to understand the rich allusions of a Shakespeare play or grasp the criticism of the class system in Dickens' novels will be frustratingly out of reach.

Without this grasp of the context and allusion which lie behind a subject, a cycle of intellectual deprivation ensues, through a process of 'social reproduction' resulting in a shared cultural knowledge becoming the reserve of the most fortunate in society.[9] This being the case, we argue that providing students with the knowledge they need, rather than relying on them to discover it for themselves, is both sensible and morally right. The children who most depend on teachers to make explicit the knowledge they need tend to be those from the most disadvantaged backgrounds. If we deny them this, we further widen social divides.

Regardless of one's views, the turn towards knowledge-rich curriculum planning is everywhere. Knowledge organisers pervade classrooms, frantic conversations about what factual information best constitutes a particular subject fill department meeting agendas and lunch time staff-room conversations. But in many English departments the part of the conversation which frequently seems to be missing is about how to transform the subject – which for so long has been a pastoral exploration of feelings and pure self-expression – into something more rigorously academic.

Professor Michael Young posited his ideas of 'powerful knowledge' as forming the centre of a school's curriculum.[10] In this paradigm, powerful knowledge is presented as abstract and far removed from what is likely to be learnt at home. What might powerful knowledge be in English? For us, it includes a grounding in the conventions of poetry, novels and plays. This grounding is then challenged as students are introduced to texts which subvert or defy those conventions. Merely knowing the definitions of language devices is a shallow approximation of subject specialism. Such knowledge becomes powerful when students can apply it to interrogate *why* devices have been used and the effects they may have.

Clearly, Young's ideas – and the approach to the conceptual knowledge of language and literature presented in this book (section 1.6) – align strongly with the realist view of knowledge. The approaches we recommend are intended to give students of all backgrounds and abilities the same in-depth knowledge of English as an academic subject. Our texts have been chosen for their cultural richness and to be vehicles for the conceptual knowledge required for students to critique and question the ideas they will encounter. We want our students to understand the context in which the texts were written but also realise that modern readers will interpret things differently. By combining a carefully sequenced curriculum with regular and thorough instruction on how to read, write and speak, students acquire the knowledge to build and defend arguments, and to communicate clearly and precisely.

1.4 THE PROBLEM WITH THINKING OF ENGLISH AS 'SKILLS BASED'

It is better to think of 'skills' in English as being composed of items of knowledge which can be taught and practised until they become skill.

One of the biggest barriers to the successful implementation of an English curriculum is that all too often students are assessed on their ability to do things they haven't actually been taught. This may sound bizarre, but it is an inevitable product of the belief that English is a 'skills-based subject'. Let's say you teach students a unit on 'Greek myth', 'a background to Shakespeare', or Malorie Blackman's YA novel *Noughts and Crosses*. How will you assess students' progress? Typically, some theme or aspect covered in the unit is brought to the fore and then students are asked to write some sort of analytical essay in response to a prompt. Alternatively, they might be asked to use an aspect of the topic studied to produce a piece of transactional or descriptive writing. This then would be assessed using a mark scheme which – in most cases – will be something similar to the marking criteria used to assess GCSE reading or writing. Students are then awarded a grade or sometimes a grade masquerading as a description of their progress, such as 'emerging' or 'secure'. These labels or grades are then fed into the data machine for everyone to mull over the 'progress' students appear to be making.

The trouble is teachers seldom teach the actual things they go on to assess. Let's take a selection of performance descriptors to see how this might happen:

1. Learners spell and punctuate with consistent accuracy, and consistently use vocabulary and sentence structures to achieve effective control of meaning
2. Some awareness of implicit ideas/contextual factors
3. Makes sophisticated and accurate use of subject terminology
4. Shows clear understanding of structural features[11]

Now let's detail some of the difficulties with teaching the students to do the things they are commonly assessed on:

- What does 'consistent accuracy' look like? How do you actually go about teaching spelling and punctuation? Is it clear to students how vocabulary and sentence structures achieve 'effective control of meaning'? How have you taught them to do this?
- How much awareness is 'some'? What is an implicit idea? How have you taught students to demonstrate awareness of them?
- Although English teachers regularly teach students to use subject terminology – and being

accurate in the application of this terminology is relatively straightforward – how do we teach 'sophisticated use'?

- As all English teachers will be painfully aware, there's a world of difference between knowing what a structural feature is and demonstrating 'clear understanding' of how one is being used. Although we may have a reasonable idea of what this understanding will look like, do we have an equally clear idea of how to teach it?

The same sorts of challenges can be made of any type of descriptor statement; what it all boils down to is *what* do students actually need to be able to do, and *how* are we *explicitly* teaching them to do it? The answer to these questions is – or should be – the curriculum. Perhaps the most important purpose of curriculum planning documents is that they will specify everything that students should learn. What is not specified is far less likely to be taught, let alone taught well.

One of the difficulties with designing a five-year curriculum in English is the divide between KS3 and KS4. Assessment at GCSE forces the subject through some interesting contortions. To do well in Literature at KS4, students need to know a small number of texts in detail; they benefit from learning quotations and the minutiae of character, plot and theme. To be successful in Language, students need to be widely read, possess large vocabularies, have an encyclopaedic knowledge of 'what the examiner is looking for' on particular questions, and to have had extensive practice at writing in a very narrow range of forms.

Surprisingly little of this transfers naturally between key stages. During KS3, there is very little reason for students to memorise the details of specific texts and none in their learning quotations, beyond the inherent value in being able to bring beautiful language to mind at will. What students are expected to learn is the generalised ability to write analytically about *any* text, as if all texts are essentially the same, and to compose their own writing on *any* topic, as if all topics were the same. To this end, while there is a clear reason to master the components of the critical essay, there is almost no reason at all to learn most of the information that finds its way onto knowledge organisers. Similarly, the topics about which students may be expected to write in KS3 will have no bearing on the topics on which they will be assessed in their GCSE exams.

On this basis, deciding to teach a five-year GCSE course focusing only on those aspects of English assessed at the end of KS4 is entirely rational. If all we care about is exam success, this can seem like an obvious solution. But of course, with the advent of Ofsted's focus on 'quality of education', schools are no longer allowed to do this, whatever teachers' personal feelings on the matter. Whether or not you concur, we *have* to show that students are being exposed to the breadth of what English has to offer.

An English curriculum should seek to encompass two distinct aspects: the *experiences* we want students to have and the *knowledge and skill* we want them to acquire. So, at OAT, the experience we have curated for our students allows them to see the broad sweep of literature and language, to read wonderful texts and to have opportunities to think, discuss, write and present in a range of different forms. The experience of reading matters. And *what* children get to read *really* matters. **The experience of reading works of literature does more to induct children into what it means to study English than any other single thing**. But alongside these experiences, there's a whole heap of stuff students need to learn. The texts we read in KS3 are (part of) the experience we want our students to have, but they cannot be the sole focus of what we want students to know, remember and do more of. Knowledge organisers which dwell on the recall of plot minutiae, contextual information and quotes miss the point. Further, although we know that to prepare students for the rigours of GCSE, they're going to have to practise a host of different 'skills', we're often unsure how to plan a curriculum around their acquisition. This tension is what leads us to insert vaguely worded assessment objectives into the curriculum and to shoehorn GCSE-style tasks into lessons.

The ideas in this guide rest on three crucial principles:

1. You can't teach skill directly; you can only teach knowledge. Knowledge turns into skill through practice. This means we must think carefully about how to break down what we see as 'skills' into teachable components of knowledge which can then be recombined, through practice, as skill.
2. Anything you can't specify is much harder to teach; if we're not able to identify the components of skill then we are likely to miss teaching them. Conversely, anything we *can* specify is much more likely to be taught.

3. We should never assess students on things that we have not, specifically, taught them to do. This means there should be a through line between what we specify in curriculum planning documents, what is actually taught in the classroom and the assessment students experience.[12]

So, for instance, although every English teacher wants students to be able to select appropriate textual references to support their arguments, the selection of evidence often gets subsumed into the wider business of analytical writing. Students have a go at writing an essay, or part of an essay, and we assess, amongst other things, how well they go about it. But analytical writing is not selecting evidence. If we use an assessment of one thing to assess another, we end up assessing students on something we've not specifically and explicitly taught.

So, what if we assessed students' ability to select appropriate quotations by giving them a passage from a text they had studied and asked them to pick out what they believe to be the best quotation with which to explore a particular prompt and then to write a short commentary on why they had made their choice? Although this looks nothing like the assessments students will face in their GCSE exams, it might be a much better way to sequence the teaching of how to judiciously select quotations and therefore ensure that students have learned what we have actually taught them.

The important work is to specify and sequence the concepts upon which mastery of English depends and then teach and assess students' ability to know, remember and be able to do things with these concepts.

1.5 WHY DO SO MANY STUDENTS FAIL TO MAKE PROGRESS?

Because English curriculums tend not to specify what students should learn with enough clarity and precision, it becomes a matter of chance as to whether they learn what is intended.

As will be restated throughout this guide, the curriculum should be the model of progression: students are making progress if they are learning the curriculum. Superficially, this sounds straightforward and self-evidently true, but the most pressing obstacle to using the curriculum as a progression model is that – all too often – the curriculum isn't good enough. There are two main reasons why a curriculum might

not lend itself to effectively assessing students' progress. First, the curriculum is often not *specific* enough about what students need to know, remember and be able to do. This inevitably leads to students not being taught crucial knowledge and then, to compound the error, assessing students on things they have not been taught. This is far more widespread in English than you might imagine. In fact, it has been the norm for many years.

The second major failing of the curriculum is that it's not coherently sequenced to ensure students are able to make progress. Again, the inevitable result is that students don't possess the requisite knowledge to be able to do what is being assessed. A good question to ask of your curriculum is whether it would make a difference to move a unit from one term or year to another. If the answer is that it *wouldn't* make a difference, then that might indicate that the sequencing of your curriculum is not coherent. While the order of precedence in which areas of the curriculum are taught varies widely and matters more in some subjects than it does in English, it should be the case that what is taught in Term 2 depends in some way on what was taught in Term 1. If it doesn't, maybe what you intend students to learn in Term 1 isn't worth learning?

In both cases, some students – usually the more advantaged – will be successful *despite* the poor curriculum. They come to school with enough background knowledge to make sense of our vague explanations and assumptions and have enough support outside of school to cope with any deficits. The students who suffer will be the most disadvantaged who possess neither the required background knowledge we've failed to teach nor the external support required to recover from our failures. If these students are getting good outcomes, we can be reasonably sure it will be *because* we've done a good job.

This is, perhaps, the most important lens through which to judge the success of our endeavours. When thinking about students' outcomes, always consider who might have been successful despite us and who is only likely to have been successful because of us.

1.6 SPECIFYING CURRICULUM CONCEPTS

The conceptual knowledge of English can be usefully organised using a number of 'organising concepts'.

David's book, *Making Meaning in English* (2021), theorised that mastery of English depends on acquiring knowledge in six overlapping areas as shown in Figure 1.1.

These 'organising concepts' are 'boxes' in which the disciplinary knowledge of the subject can be contained. As you can see in Figure 1.2, the 'shape' of knowledge in English is very wide and shallow (unlike, say, maths which is very tall and thin). It's important to recognise that each of the six conceptual areas has equal importance. In maths, students need to master number before moving to other areas of the curriculum, but English has a much less strict order of precedence. Each conceptual area can and should be taught alongside every other. Despite this, there may be a useful order of precedence within each organising concept.

Metaphor	Understanding language, as a way to analyse literature and think about the world
Story	The primary means of describing the world; plot, narrative, form and genre
Argument	Formal structures of thought and expression to enable students to communicate, discuss and persuade with force and clarity
Pattern	The ways we use similarity and difference to create meaning in texts (repetition, sounds, structures)
Grammar	Noticing, understanding and experimenting with morphological and syntactic structures
Context	The broad sweep of knowledge which enables students to interpret individual texts and authorial choices

FIGURE 1.1 Organising concepts of English

The following diagrams are an attempt to map out the shallow hierarchies which exist in English. The items at the top of each box will, we believe, enable students to better grasp the items which follow beneath. The organising concepts are intended to be used as a tool to ensure that an English curriculum is covering all of the most important concepts on which mastery of literature and language depends.

1.6.1 Metaphor

As you can see in Figure 1.3, the prerequisite for thinking well about metaphors is understanding that they are made of different components. We suggest that metaphors are composed of a tenor (the subject of the metaphor) and a vehicle (the language used to describe the tenor) and that the ground is the effectiveness of the connection between the two. We'll go into more detail in section 2.11 about how to go about teaching this idea, but for now we'll just say that if students don't have terms for these components of metaphor, it's easy for them to become confused and struggle to articulate their understanding of language.

Beneath that are two strands: the linguistic and literary approaches to metaphor. The linguistic approach is contained in the idea that metaphor is a fundamental feature of language and thought. Abstract concepts can only be grasped by reference to concrete items in the real world – once we can visualise what an abstraction is 'like' we can start

Metaphor	Story	Argument	Pattern	Grammar	Context

FIGURE 1.2 The 'shape' of conceptual knowledge in English

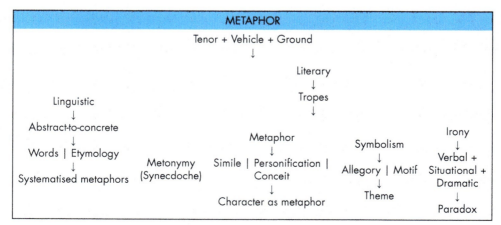

FIGURE 1.3 The structure of Metaphor

to appreciate how it goes beyond its concrete tenor. For instance, as teachers in order to think of an abstraction like 'progress' we tend to visualise it as a set of steps or an ascending arrow. The metaphors we think with constrain how we see the world; in the example above, we can fall into the trap of thinking progress is a smooth linear ascent rather than a messy ebb and flow (note the metaphor) that it usually is.

We can see this idea at play in the etymology of words. Abstract words tend to have their origins in some concrete thing. In polysemous words (words with more than one meaning) this is visible, if unnoticed. For instance, the word 'root' is using the vehicle of plant roots to help us grasp the tenor of any kind of origin. In words loaned from other languages, metaphors are often concealed behind a layer of Latin or Greek (metaphor comes from the Greek for 'transfer' – *meta* 'over or across' and *pherein* 'to carry'). Seeing the 'fossil poetry'[13] in everyday words can open up new vistas of meaning.

This then leads to conceptual metaphor where whole domains of thinking are systematically circumscribed by metaphor. For instance, argument is usually conceived as war (we *win* or *lose* arguments, claims must be *defended* etc.) and time is often expressed as currency (we *spend* time with friends and *waste* it in various ways). 'Grasping' this allows students to 'see' how language shapes the way we think (grasping and seeing are two different systematised metaphors for understanding).[14]

The literary approach to metaphor is much more familiar to English teachers but will still benefit from being taught in a more systematic way which attempts to ensure that students encounter multiple examples and learn agreed definitions, so they are better able to notice their effects in the work of others and use them with increasing facility in their own writing.

1.6.2 Story

The concept of story, or narrative, has its root in the notion that even though stories seem like the most natural thing in the world, they are artificial ways of holding meaning and are deliberately created. This is as true of the most basic stories – the story of our day – as well as the most elaborate and sophisticated. On the left of Figure 1.4, the strand that leads from 'Sense making' to 'Mythology' is an attempt to introduce the concept that, from our earliest origins, storytelling seems an innately human activity. We have always told stories in order to make sense of what happens to us and around us. Over time, these stories about why the natural world behaves as it does have been systematised into complex mythologies, many of which have informed some of the most well-known and influential stories students will encounter.

The rest of the diagram is an attempt to tease out the various concepts contained within story that make up how narratives are constructed and populated. Most of these labels will be familiar but a quick note about the ideas that follow from characterisation: thought, speech and action are the three main ways in which character is established – how their thoughts are described, how their speech is transcribed and the description of their behaviour. The concept of 'façade and flaw' helps students think about the arc of a character over a text. A tragic character would begin with their façade intact only to have it peel away to reveal their flaw as the story progresses. A comic character would experience the opposite; at the start of a story the façade would represent a false belief which is preventing them from achieving their objectives. What is initially perceived as a flaw – a character trait buried beneath their façade – is revealed to be what they must embrace to achieve fulfilment.[15]

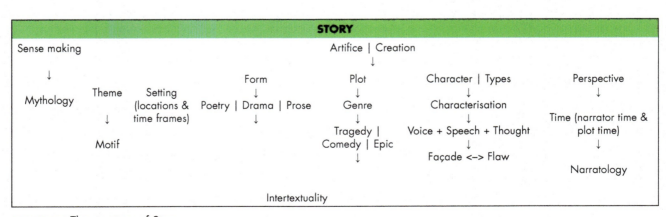

FIGURE 1.4 The structure of Story

1.6.3 Argument

Figure 1.5 attempts to map argumentation by showing that dialectic (conversation) and rhetoric (persuasion) are the starting points which feed into the different modes of writing students need to master. Although students should be introduced to various formal components of rhetoric, more weight should be given to the practical aspects of constructing arguments. How written and spoken arguments are systematically taught and practised is unpicked in sections 2.8 and 2.10.

The concept of summarising is more of an adjunct and is left to one side. Speaking & Listening runs down the left of the diagram to show that it pertains throughout.

1.6.4 Pattern

Pattern contains the concept of structure but is also concerned with other patterns that exist in English. Of these, the most important are the sound patterns in phonemes and how vowels and consonants can be used to make meaning through alliteration and assonance.

When we think about the ways texts are organised, the big split is between the different ways poetry, prose and drama are structured. As shown in Figure 1.6, poetry has a host of structural techniques and conventions that are absent from prose, but prose is far more structurally cohesive than students sometimes think. Poetry uses rhyme and metre to reinforce meaning, but within other longer texts, which aim to feel a little closer to reality, attention has to be bound in different ways. The idea of 'binding time' is concerned with the ways writers create an itch and

then the means to scratch it through sequences of problem and resolution, question and answer, call and response.

1.6.5 Grammar

Grammar is an aspect of Pattern but is broad enough to warrant its own diagram. Figure 1.7 reveals the divide between the two aspects of grammar: morphology (patterns in words) and syntax (patterns in sentences). The other aspect – which often goes unaddressed in schools – is that of semantics (meaning) and pragmatics (language in context). As we will discuss in section 2.8, the point of grammatical instruction is not to burden students with lists of metalinguistic terminology but to allow them to answer these three questions:

1) What choices are available?
2) Why is one choice preferable to another?
3) What is the effect of the choice selected?

1.6.6 Context

Finally, Figure 1.8 attempts to organise the ideas which come under the label 'Context'. Obviously, this includes all the knowledge which comes alongside and opens up a deeper understanding of the texts being studied, but also includes some of the major theoretic approaches to literary criticism as well as disciplinary knowledge of how to include contextual information in students' own analysis of texts.

For a more detailed explanation of each of these concepts see the relevant chapters of *Making Meaning in English*.[16]

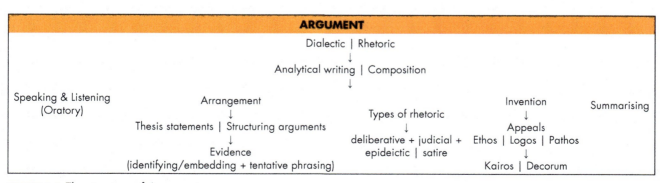

FIGURE 1.5 The structure of Argument

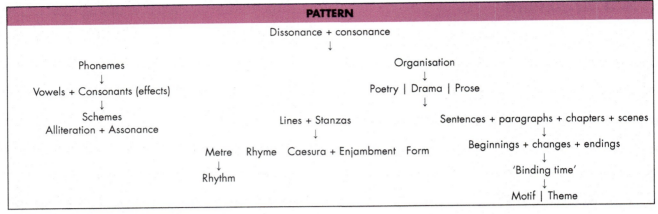

FIGURE 1.6 The structure of Pattern

```
GRAMMAR
Morphology                    Syntax
    ↓                           ↓
                            Word class
                                ↓
                          Subjects + Verbs          Meaning
                                ↓                       ↓
Spelling   Roots + Fixes   Phrases | Clauses |      Semantics
   +           ↓           Sentences + Fragments        +
Decoding    Etymology              ↓                Pragmatics
                            Punctuation
                                ↓
                          Complexity | Purpose
```

FIGURE 1.7 The structure of Grammar

```
CONTEXT
Classical       Specific
+ Biblical      background
Allusions |     knowledge        Theory          Analysis
Elizabethan |       ↓               ↓               ↓
Romantic |      Historic |     Feminist | Marxist  Embedding
Victorian |     Social |       | Psychoanalytical  into literary
20th century    Literary (the                      essays
                Canon)
```

FIGURE 1.8 The structure of Context

1.7 AMBITIOUS FOR ALL

For a curriculum to be ambitious for all it must introduce students to knowledge which allows them to think outside the scope of their personal experience.

With every student being introduced to some of the major figures of the canon of English literature, as well as many less well-known writers who have been affected or influenced by the canon, the curriculum we have developed at OAT is certainly ambitious. This is intended to ensure our students have access both to the most powerful concepts in English, but also to the cultural richness which children from more advantaged backgrounds take for granted. Figure 1.9 shows the range of texts our students study.

At first glance, it may seem that many of these texts are unrealistically challenging and that expecting KS3 students to read them is unrealistic. That would be true if we expected students to read these texts independently or to approach them like set texts for GCSE Literature. However, the emphasis is very much on teachers reading to students and focusing on meaning and enjoyment rather than analysis.

We start with the canon because that's central to our subject. If children have no knowledge of canonical texts, they are simply ignorant. Instead, we view the canon as a springboard to include modern writers from diverse backgrounds as part of that fundamental conversation between writers and texts. Although the canon is the starting point, it's not where we finish. For instance, in the Year 7 Romance module we move from Chaucer to Shakespeare (via Patience Agbabi) but also include N.K. Jemisin and her modern feminist response to the tropes of the quest narrative. We are seeking to create literary critics; scholars, who are able to engage with and argue against the literary establishment.

The point of this survey of language and literature is to endow our students with an experience of the subject that is immersive, enjoyable and diverse. But although each module has been crafted with care, the texts are not presented as objects of study which should be learned and analysed so much as vehicles for teaching the powerful concepts of English. Our aim is that through reading such a rich variety of texts, the abstract, esoteric-seeming conceptual knowledge will find a roost in students' minds. (See section 1.10.)

Year 7	Ancient Origins	Links to Legends	The Art of Rhetoric	Romance
	• Epic of Gilgamesh, the Iliad • Greek mythology • **Homer's Odyssey**, Simon Armitage	• Beowulf (Heaney & Headley) • **Sir Gawain and the Green Knight** • Arthurian Legend • Journey to the West	• Shakespeare, **Julius Caesar** • Famous speeches (Paradise Lost, Lincoln, MLK Jr, Obama) • Cicero & Aristotle	• Chaucer, **'The Knight's Tale'** • Patience Agbabi • Shakespeare, Romeo & Juliet and A Midsummer Night's Dream • 'La Belle Dame Sans Merci', 'The Lady of Shalott'
Year 8	The Sonnet Form	The Bible as Literature	Comedy through Time	The Story of the Novel
	Petrarch to Shakespeare to Donne to Wordsworth to Duffy and Dharker	• Medieval mystery plays (Noah) • Tyndale and the King James Bible • Paradise Lost, Pilgrim's Progress • Blake, Dickinson & Marley	• Aristophanes, Lysistrata • Chaucer, 'The Miller's Tale' • **As You Like It** • Restoration comedy • Oscar Wilde	• Extracts from Oroonoko, Robinson Crusoe, Gulliver's Travels, Pamela, Pride and Prejudice, Catcher in the Rye, Purple Hibiscus • Dickens, **Great Expectations**
Year 9	The Gothic Tradition	War Writing	Tragedy through Time	Women in Literature
	• Gothic anthology • Emily Brontë, **Wuthering Heights**	– A selection of war poetry (including Owen & Sassoon) – R.C. Sherriff, **Journey's End**	• Oedipus the King • 'The Monk's Tale' • The White Devil • Shakespeare, **Othello** • A View from the Bridge • Things Fall Apart	• A feminist 'retelling' of the story of English • Charlotte Perkins Gilman, **The Yellow Wallpaper**

FIGURE 1.9 Texts studied in the OAT KS3 English curriculum

1.8 COHERENT PLANNING AND SEQUENCING

A coherently sequenced curriculum should seek to tell a story that unfolds over time.

As well as encountering ambitious texts, the aspiration of our curriculum is for students to become familiar with the six organising concepts. Each of these areas are 'boxes' which contain distinct constructs which can be coherently sequenced. Although the order of precedence in which concepts should be taught is far less clear in English than in subjects like maths and science, we can still make some logical arguments about which ideas it is sensible to introduce first and which depend on this prior knowledge.[17]

These concepts can then be plotted against the aspects of language and literature we want students to experience, in a way which ensures each is encountered on multiple occasions with the intention that on each subsequent encounter, students' understanding becomes ever deeper. Figures 1.10 to 1.12 show how we have gone about this.

Our KS3 curriculum, the rationale for each year's programme of study and the details of individual modules are all discussed in Part 4.

Much of the sequencing in our curriculum is chronological, with students beginning their survey of language and literature with the earliest known literary texts and moving forward through time. The idea is that as students experience new writers and texts, they will see how these link back to what has gone before. Some of the modules are 'mini-chronologies'

which show the development of particular forms (such as the sonnet) or genres (such as comedy or tragedy) over time. By the time students arrive in Year 9, they begin to apply different theoretical perspectives to the broad sweep of the curriculum, and the final module, Women in Literature, is a synoptic retelling of everything students have experienced through a particular lens.

One criticism of the curriculum outlined above is that it's *too* ambitious, *too* demanding, *too* far out of the reach of KS3 students from working-class backgrounds. We reject this. The educational psychologist Jerome Bruner dismissed the idea that some kinds of knowledge could be developmentally inappropriate. He said, 'Any subject can be taught effectively in some intellectually honest form to any child at any stage of development'.[18] ED Hirsch Jr refers to this as the 'Bruner Principle': that any topic can be taught appropriately to any age of child, as long as they are taught the necessary background knowledge.[19] Bruner saw the learning of *structure*, rather than the mastery of facts and techniques, as the central concern of education. He believed that if children were able to understand the structures of different subjects at an early age, then they would find it easier to incorporate new ideas within these domains.

Bruner's much misunderstood and mangled idea of the 'spiral curriculum' sought to introduce the structure of disciplines in a carefully sequenced and logically coherent way. Children should first encounter a simple iteration of an idea and then, on re-encountering it, the complexity should be incrementally increased. This makes intuitive sense and would seem to be supported by what we know about learning and forgetting. This should remind us that simply putting culturally rich, powerful knowledge in front of children is not enough. It must be carefully sequenced, introduced and reintroduced, piece by careful piece. This is precisely the approach we have adopted with students being introduced to the disciplinary structures of language and literature from the outset.

Year 7: The origins of English				
Content	**Ancient Origins** - *Epic of Gilgamesh*, the *Iliad* - Greek mythology (heroes) - Creation myths - **Homer's *Odyssey***, Simon Armitage	**Links to Legends** - *Beowulf* (Heaney & Headley) - *Journey to the West* - King Arthur - **Sir Gawain and the Green Knight** (Armitage)	**The Art of Rhetoric** - Shakespeare - *Julius Caesar* - Famous speeches (*Paradise Lost*, Lincoln, MLK Jr, Obama) - Cicero & Aristotle - Extracts from Forsyth, Heinrichs & Leith	**Romance** - Chaucer, **'The Knight's Tale'** - Patience Agbadi, *Telling Tales* - Shakespeare, *Romeo & Juliet* and *A Midsummer Night's Dream* - Keats, 'La Belle Dame Sans Merci' - Tennyson, 'The Lady of Shalott'
Metaphor	- Definition of metaphor - Tenor, vehicle, ground - Homeric epithets	- Tenor, vehicle, ground - Abstract to concrete - Metaphors in words - Kennings	- Tenor, vehicle, ground - Flowers of rhetoric (antithesis, hyperbole, metonymy, transferred epithets)	- Tenor, vehicle, ground - Symbolism - Characters as vehicle - Theme as tenor
Story	- Sense making - Mythology - Plot: five act structure - Heroes; the epic	- Epic - Heroes - Plot: five act structure - Characterisation	- Genre: tragedy - Drama - Character & plot – façade/flaw	- The romance; quests - Tragedy & comedy - Poetry
Argument	- Debate: Is Odysseus admirable? - Thesis statements - Summarising	- Debate: What makes a good ruler? - Thesis statements - Topic sentences - Summarising	- Ethos, logos, pathos - Thesis statements - Topic sentences - Selecting evidence - Arrangement (Act 3 scene 2)	- Summarising - Thesis statements - Topic sentences - Selecting & embedding evidence - Tentative phrasing
Pattern	- Beginnings, changes and endings: in medias res - Morphology - Creative sentence structures	- Phonemes - Schemes: Alliteration - Caesura - Creative sentence structures	- Metrical feet: iambic pentameter - Acts & scenes - Anaphora, alliteration, assonance, isocolon, tricolon - Creative sentence structures	- Rhyme, alliteration; metre - Binding time: theme & motif - Lines, stanzas - Form - Creative sentence structures
Grammar	- Syntax: subject-verb agreement - Fragments & phrases - Nouns & adjectives - Complex sentences - Subordinating conjunctions - Commas as pivots	- Morphology – roots and fixes (spelling & decoding) - Changing word classes; matching suffixes to word class - Noun phrases - Clauses & sentences	- Changing word classes; matching suffixes to word - Complex sentences - Subordinating conjunctions - Commas as pivots - Semantics & pragmatics	- Changing word classes; matching suffixes to word - Sentence types & complexity - Semantics & pragmatics
Context	- Literary timeline - Aristotle's poetics - Development of writing (cuneiform) & literature (*Gilgamesh*)	- Identifying relevant context - Old English - Christianity	- Using context to support arguments - Origins of rhetoric - Elizabethan anxieties	- Find connections between contexts - Middle English - Courtly love

FIGURE 1.10 Year 7 curriculum

Year 8: The development of form				
Content	**The Sonnet Form** 6 weeks Petrarch to Shakespeare to Donne to Wordsworth to Duffy and Dharker	**The Bible as Literature** 8–10 weeks - Medieval mystery plays (Noah) - Tyndale and the King James Bible - Extracts from *Paradise Lost*, *Pilgrim's Progress* - Poetry: Blake, Dickinson & Marley	**Comedy through Time** 10–12 weeks - Aristophanes, *Lysistrata* - Chaucer, 'The Miller's Tale' - *As You Like It* - Restoration comedy - Oscar Wilde	**The Story of the Novel** 11–12 weeks - Extracts from *Oroonoko, Robinson Crusoe, Gulliver's Travels, Pamela, Pride & Prejudice, Catcher in the Rye, Purple Hibiscus* - Dickens, **Great Expectations**
Metaphor	- Tenor, vehicle, ground - Systematised metaphor - Irony	- Biblical imagery - Allegory - Symbolism	- Analysing metaphors - Motif	- Extended metaphors - Motif - Irony
Story	- Can sonnets tell stories, or are they arguments? - Theme	- Mythical bases for stories - Narrative perspective - Characterisation	- Genre - Comic plot: disorder to order - Comic archetypes - Dialogue - Theme	- Narrative voice - Narrative structure (frames, cyclical structures etc.) - Characterisation; dialogue - Epistolary writing ('found' narratives)
Argument	- Volta as crux of argument - Analysing writers' use of language, structure & form - Comparative statements - Summarising	- Analysing writers' use of language, structure & form - Evaluating writers' intentions - Summarising	- Analysing writers' use of language, structure & form - Evaluating writers' intentions - Summarising	- How does the novel try to persuade us? - Analysing writers' use of language, structure & form - Evaluating writers' intentions - Summarising
Pattern	- The sonnet form - Rhyme - Metre - Creative sentence structures	- Tyndale's style - Diachronic change - Iambic pentameter; rhyming couplets - Creative sentence structures	- Epigrams - Comic structure - Form - Caesura + enjambment - Creative sentence structures	- Serialisation; chapters - Form - Beginnings, changes & endings - How prose 'binds time' - Creative sentence structures
Grammar	- Adverbs & adverbials - Sentence combining - Sentences (subjects & verbs; fragments; run-ons)	- Uses and effects of conjunctions - Embedding and moving clauses - Varying subordinating conjunctions for effect	- Planning and drafting essays; writing purposes - Morphology - Using pronouns; sentence combining	- Semantics & pragmatics - Paragraphing - Serial sentences - Understanding the effects/uses (disinterest/avoiding responsibility etc.)
Context	- Conventions of Petrarchan & Shakespearean sonnets - History of the sonnet - Elizabethan; Romanticism	- The influence of King James Bible on English - Lyric poetry - William Tyndale	- Embedding context - Literary: How comedy has evolved - Satire - Conventions of comedy over time	- Caxton & mass literacy; letter writing - Historical: 18th century - Feminism

FIGURE 1.11 Year 8 curriculum

Year 9: Into the world				
Content	**The Gothic Tradition** - Gothic anthology (The Castle of Otranto, Vathek, The Monk, The Italian, Northanger Abbey) - *Dracula, Frankenstein* - Emily Brontë – **Wuthering Heights** - Angela Carter, *The Werewolf*	**War Writing** - A selection of war poetry (including Owen & Sassoon) - RC Sherriff, **Journey's End**	**Tragedy through Time** - *Oedipus the King* (Sophocles) - *The Monk's Tale* (Chaucer) - *The White Devil* (Webster) - **Othello** (Shakespeare) - *A View from the Bridge* (Miller) - *Things Fall Apart* (Achebe)	**Women in Literature** A feminist 'retelling' of the story of English - Sappho; Chaucer, 'The Wife of Bath's Tale'& Zadie Smith's *The Wife of Willesden.* - Aphra Behn, *Oroonoko,* Mary Wollstonecraft, Virginia Woolf, The Brontës - Charlotte Perkins Gilman, **The Yellow Wallpaper**
Metaphor	Conceptual metaphors, and symbols systematised metaphors, motifs	Irony Symbolism Language analysis	Symbolism & motif: definition, identification and effect	Comparing metaphors Types of irony Symbolism & motif Language analysis
Story	Characterisation, narrative perspective, narrative structure, narratology, theme, setting	Thought Perspective Theme: concrete (object in text) to abstract (idea external to text)	Themes: Fate, morality, reputation, justice Characteristics of the tragic hero Structure: prologue, parodos, stasima, exodus	Narratology Perspective Intertextuality
Argument	Debate/thesis statements/structuring arguments: Dialectic (they say/I say) analysis of language Focus on the effects of the whole text & controlling ideas	Debate/thesis statements/structuring arguments: War as argument Focus on the effects of the whole text & controlling ideas Comparing texts in relation to literary concepts, ideas and methods Linking to context	Debate/thesis statements/structuring arguments: How should we live? Pity or fear? What is our fascination with human suffering? Victim or hero? Private vs public justice? Comparing texts in relation to literary concepts, ideas and methods Linking to context Extend: recognising different arguments	Debate/thesis statements/structuring arguments: Arguments for equality Ethos, pathos, logos Comparing texts in relation to literary concepts, ideas and methods Linking to context Extend: recognising different arguments
Pattern	Periodic sentences Beginnings, changes & endings Binding time Creative sentence structures	Noticing poetic patterns (figures and schemes) Scenes and acts Creative sentence structures	Noticing patterns in plays/novels: structural patterns (acts, scenes, chapters – rising action, climax, denouement); motifs; theme; character arcs Creative sentence structures	Noticing patterns in novels How prose writers 'bind time' Creative sentence structures
Grammar	Summarising; explaining; discussing; describing	Thesis statements; introductions & conclusions	Semantics and pragmatics: Direct meaning vs intentions Complexity: The deconstructed essay/structuring arguments	Multi-paragraph compositions
Context	Romanticism, Gothic conventions, Victorian social anxieties (science, religion, the supernatural, women, race), psychoanalytic theory	20th century drama (the 'well-made' play) 'The Great War' Realism; Modernism; Aristotle's unities	Venice/Ottoman empire; attitudes to race in Renaissance era; patriarchal hierarchy; religious conflict. Conventions of Greek tragedy/Aristotelian unities; conventions of medieval, Renaissance/revenge tragedy & modern tragedy (modest and ordinary)	Feminist literary theory First, Second and Third Wave feminism Embedding into essays

FIGURE 1.12 Year 9 curriculum

Obviously, this macro level of planning in the curriculum outlined in Figures 1.10 to 1.12 reveals nothing about the specificity of the curriculum. At each stage, we have carefully planned what we want students to know and be able to do.

All of our curriculum resources can be found at sites.google.com/view/oat-english/home.

1.9 DESIGNED FOR STUDENTS WITH SEND

A curriculum that balances ambition with accessibility lays the foundations of disciplinary equity.

What works best for children with SEND? That, of course, depends upon the precise nature of children's particular needs. That said, we can draw some generalisable conclusions by thinking about some of the more common areas of special educational need. For instance, a child with a working memory deficit is likely to benefit from having information carefully sequenced and instruction broken into manageable chunks. *But all children have limited working memory capacity.*[20]

Dyslexic children have the best possible chance of learning to read fluently if they are given carefully sequenced systematic synthetic phonics instruction followed by extensive exposure to a broad range of texts. However, *this is equally true of children who are not dyslexic.*[21]

Students with an attachment disorder are likely to benefit from a structured environment, consistent rules, professional distance and focusing feedback on behaviour not the child. A child with an autistic spectrum disorder is likely to benefit from orderly routines and a calm environment. And a child who has ADHD is likely to benefit from clear boundaries and consistent, proportional consequences, *but so is every other child.*[22]

While there will always be exceptions, by and large, the types of pastoral support and instructional practice that work best with children with SEND will almost certainly be most likely to get the best results with *all* children. While not all children are equally able, all children are more likely to achieve well if their teachers have high expectations of what they are capable of achieving. Those with educational disadvantages need explicit instruction, clear modelling, well-designed scaffolding which is taken down as rapidly as is possible and lots of guided practice. But this is what is likely to be most beneficial for *all* children. The children who are most educationally disadvantaged (including many children with SEND) are the most at risk of failing and those who most need their teachers to be aware of effective practice. Advantaged children are more likely to thrive regardless of what their teachers do but they too will benefit from the kinds of practice children who are educationally disadvantaged *need*.

Although the texts selected for our curriculum are unapologetically ambitious and challenging, we have ensured that they are accessible both through carefully selecting appropriate versions of older texts, and by focusing on reading for meaning and enjoyment. We recommend regular reading fluency lessons where students get to perform readings of the texts they are studying (see section 2.9.1), and the 'Couch to 5k' approach to writing (see section 2.8) ensures that all students can achieve the highest standards of success.

In order to successfully design an English curriculum for students with SEND we must embrace two essential principles. First, the principle of **gapless instruction** which suggests that if students fail to make progress it's due to gaps in our teaching or in the curriculum. This idea is detailed further in section 2.2.

The second principle is that **success must precede struggle**. This is explored in section 2.3 but, in summary, the message is that introducing struggle is important and valuable but risky. Students need to have a firm foundation of success in order for struggle to be bearable or productive. If we get this wrong, students won't enjoy lessons and will probably give up. But, if we never make them struggle at all they may well develop an unrealistic view of their own ability and end up believing they're better than they actually are.

These principles are embedded into our curriculum planning at every level. Although we have very high expectations of what all students can achieve, we have broken the monumental 'skills' of English into manageable chunks of knowledge which can be practised again and again until they are mastered.

1.10 BROAD AND BALANCED

Breadth of knowledge provides a template for students to explore topics in depth. Balance doesn't have to mean the curriculum is equally balanced between **different components; rather, it should mean that this balance has been carefully considered.**

Sometimes it's easier to explain a thing by showing what it is not. Here are a few things which do *not* represent a broad and balanced curriculum:

- Spending class time on SATs practice papers before Christmas in Year 6
- Neglecting those areas of the Key Stage 2 curriculum that are not examined to concentrate solely on those areas that are
- Starting GCSEs in Year 9 (or earlier)
- Using GCSE exam board specifications as a model for designing the Key Stage 3 curriculum

If a school does any of these things, it is putting its own interests ahead of those of its students.

English at KS3 is fundamentally different from English at KS4. The contentless GCSE English Language specification encourages the impoverishing practice of creating 'Paper 1' and 'Paper 2' units of work and spending two years on extended test preparation. The GCSE English Literature specification, on the other hand, focuses on learning a small number of texts in depth and getting students to memorise characters, plot, themes and lists of quotations.

Neither of these approaches is useful or desirable at KS3. Instead, the KS3 curriculum must be focused on surveying the breadth of language and literature 'out there' and using the texts students read as vehicles for understanding the literary and linguistic concepts that will make GCSE study more meaningful. For the core knowledge – the contents of the organising concepts – that we need children to retain to stick, it needs to be brought to life through a rich tapestry of what Christine Counsell has called 'hinterland' knowledge.[23] This hinterland – anecdotes, curiosities, stories – provides a network, or schema, to which the core takeaways are more likely to stick. Instead of teaching students what they 'need to know', a curriculum that is focused on breadth seeks to teach far more than students *need* – and certainly more than they will retain – in order that the residue has meaning. We'll return to how this works in section 1.8.

While it might feel scary to widen the curriculum and spend less time on exam preparation, this is, counter-intuitively, probably the best way to ensure that children do well in exams. The precious time we have in Key Stage 3 is an opportunity to expose children to those areas of English that are *not* covered by GCSE specifications. **Students are unable to think about anything which they do not know. If knowledge is *over*emphasised, then new ways of thinking are made possible.** Teaching pupils more than they will ever need to know for an examination expands the probability that they will know enough to do well. Teaching them just enough to do well reduces the likelihood that they'll know enough. Just as aiming a dart at the centre of the board increases our chance of hitting the board, so teaching pupils more than they will ever need to know for an examination expands the probability that they will know enough to do well. Conversely, teaching them just enough to do well reduces the likelihood that they will know enough.

The answer is not breath *or* depth but *both*. Breadth of knowledge provides intellectual Velcro: new pieces of the puzzle stick more easily. If we take the time to introduce students to the conceptual understandings that underpin English each time we introduce more breadth, the more quickly and easily they will grasp those aspects studied in depth. The solution is to carefully select a few texts to study in depth, a much wider range of texts to *just* read with little time given over to analysis, and a vast range of satellite extracts connecting these chosen texts together.

Depth requires breath. Without sufficient breadth, topics studied in depth become confusing, arbitrary and meaningless. However, if texts are seen as exemplars of literature, as vehicles for teaching literary concepts as much as objects of study in their own right, we are more likely to see them as parts of a much broader conversation. What if the study of *Macbeth* involved less time analysing the play and more time reading around it? You could include some extracts from Marlowe's *Doctor Faustus*, selections from Holinshed's *Chronicles* on the murders of Duncan and Banquo (surprisingly similar to events in the play) as well as some critical response including some of Dr Johnson's 'Miscellaneous observations of the Tragedy of Macbeth'. Rarely do teachers dip into other lit crit.* You could also add something lighter like James Thurber's short story, 'Macbeth Murder Mystery'. Woven together with

this, constantly compare Shakespeare's verse with that of other poets. Read as many poems as you can, why not? One per lesson (and don't be afraid of reading the same poems over and over; they should be as familiar as songs) to get students used to the cadences of different metres.

By giving students a glimpse of what language and literature actually *are*, we enable students to pursue more in-depth investigations later on. Breadth enables depth.

What of balance? If we aim to make a curriculum 'balanced' we need to state what the balance should be *between*. Our curriculum has been designed to balance between three axes:

1. Reading vs writing (and speaking)
2. Extracts vs whole texts
3. Analysis vs enjoyment & meaning

First, we think lessons should be balanced in favour of reading. There are many cognitive benefits to reading including increased vocabulary, improved concentration, attention and memory, increased empathy, as well as reduced stress and improved mental health.[24] The more reading students do – and the more they enjoy it – the better they are likely to be at everything.[25]

While of course developing students' ability as writers is also essential, the way we approach this focuses on quality over quantity. We intend that students master writing sentences before we ask them to produce more extended pieces of writing. If students cannot write great sentences, they will not write great paragraphs. If we dedicate curriculum time to students producing poor-quality extended writing, we will ensure that they become worse, not better at writing. Instead, our approach to writing is focused on the principle that students shouldn't practise until they can do something, but rather that they should continue practising until they can no longer *not* do it. This means they write so many examples of sophisticated analytical and creative sentences that it becomes unthinkable that they could write a shoddy sentence (see section 2.8). The consequence of removing low-quality writing practice is that there is much more time available to read and let texts come to life.[26] By reading more and analysing less we're able to do *much* more interesting things with the texts.

The second axis asks us to consider the balance between reading a broad range of extracts and reading whole texts. If students only read extracts, then

---

* *Macbeth: Critical Essays* edited by S. Schoenbaum (2015) is an excellent source of critical essays and contains, amongst other treats, L.C. Knight's classic 'How many children had Lady Macbeth?

they never get the experience of seeing texts as complete works of art, and miss out on the hard work and satisfaction of embarking on the journey conceived of by the writer. However, if students only read whole texts, they miss out on seeing how the text being read connects to other equally interesting and important texts that also exemplify the forms, ideas and themes being studied; they miss the experience of seeing that individual texts have relationships with what came before and after. So where should the balance lie?

Because we have carved out more time for reading, our curriculum enables students to eat their cake and have it.[27] Instead of either/or, we read whole texts *and* extracts. Most of our modules are written around a 'focus text', which students read in its entirety, as well as a carefully curated anthology of satellite extracts that introduce connections and breadth. (This is discussed in detail in section 2.15.)

The third axis, analysis vs enjoyment, tips the balance firmly in favour of enjoyment and meaning. While modules will sometimes zoom in on sections of text where we want students to notice specific ideas or techniques, the emphasis is firmly on teachers reading texts aloud and modelling *how* they are read, and then conducting conversations about meaning. We also want to ensure a balance between creative and analytical responses to texts so that students see texts not just as objects of study, but also as models of excellence and inspiration.

On top of all this, there is also the need to address *diversity and inclusion*. First, it is important to note that these terms are not synonymous. Diversity should be concerned with variety; inclusion is about opportunity and access for the most marginalised. We confuse the two at our peril.

A commitment to diversity means we should make students' curricular experience as broad and as varied as possible. We should seek to provide them with experience across the domain of specialisms and refuse to be constrained by specifications. And, of particular importance, we should strive to engender a conversation between 'the canon' and critiques and responses to the canon. If students don't possess canonical knowledge then they are merely ignorant. For instance, they need to experience Chaucer *and* the writers who have responded creatively and critically. Patience Agbabi's *Telling Tales* and Zadie Smith's *The Wife of Willesden* are two brilliant examples of this critical and creative conversation in action. Our curriculum is full of

these connections but in order for them to be meaningful they must start with the canon. **True diversity is represented in the ability to participate in curricular conversations**.

Inclusion is more straightforward: it is essential that all students have equal opportunities to access the full offer our schools provide. This is as important with the academic curriculum as it is the extended curriculum. This should not only apply to 'protected characteristics' (age, disability, gender reassignment, marriage and civil partnership, pregnancy and maternity, race, religion or belief, sex, and sexual orientation) but also to socio-economic status, geographic location, prior attainment, reading ability etc. The challenge is that every single aspect of the curriculum should be accessible (in a meaningful form) to every student.

The breadth of our curriculum, from *Beowulf* to the Brontës, from Aristotle to Achebe, from Shakespeare to Sappho gives students a real sense of what literature is, so that the texts they will study in depth at GCSE can be more firmly rooted in clear traditions and foundations. The conceptual boxes which map out the powerful knowledge students need to be successful ensure that students are fluent in each of these areas, and the Teacher Guides and Student Anthologies for each module provide real balance between reading, writing and discussion, literature and language, analysis and creativity.

1.11 CORE AND HINTERLAND

There's often confusion about exactly where the line between 'core' and 'hinterland' knowledge should be drawn in English. We have tried to keep the distinction simple: core knowledge is represented by the concepts we intend students to learn whereas hinterland knowledge is the texts and examples which exemplify and elucidate these concepts.

One of the key questions to consider about any curriculum is what we want students to remember. What is it we want students to take with them into the next lesson, the next curriculum module, the next key stage, and onwards into the next phase of their lives when they leave school? After all, a relatively small number of the students we teach will go on to study English at A level, and an even smaller number at university. So, what should *all* students have an entitlement to know about the subject by the time they finish compulsory education? This core – the essential knowledge students should retain into adulthood – is at once fairly narrow and too broad to easily specify. Narrow, in that it probably contains few factual items, but impossibly broad in that it includes unquantifiable abstractions such as the ability to 'write well', 'read critically' and 'appreciate literature'.

In our KS3 curriculum, the curriculum-related expectations (see section 3.6) we have specified attempt to capture the core knowledge (rooted in the organising concepts) we want students to retain into GCSE study, but these expectations only scratch the surface of the richness we intend them to experience in lessons. This richness is what Christine Counsell has dubbed 'hinterland knowledge':

> The core knowledge you want your students to remember is supported by an equally important hinterland, the little examples, the stories, the illustrations, the richness, the dwelling on this but not that, and the times when you as a teacher go off-piste with your passion.[28]

This hinterland acts a vehicle for making the core memorable but it's also the very substance of language and literature. Without stories, examples and illustrations, the core knowledge students need to acquire is a dry set of abstractions. By specifying as much of this hinterland as possible, the key concepts are given the opportunity, the possibility, of being brought vividly to life. As discussed in section 1.6, the intricacies of character and plot, language and structure of the texts we teach cannot be the *object* of what we're trying to get students to retain into Key Stage 4 and beyond, but unless they grapple with these things, the core conceptual knowledge will have little meaning. It is the particular that enables the general.

At one level, the hinterland of an English curriculum – especially in KS3 – is the texts we read. For our first module of Year 7, we have specified that students should read not only Simon Armitage's radio script of *Homer's Odyssey* but also a variety of creation myths from around the world, the *Epic of Gilgamesh*, the hero myths of Icarus, Theseus and Perseus, extracts from Robert Fitzgerald's prose translation of the *Iliad*, extracts from Hesiod, as well as classically inspired poetry. All of this is there not only to provide students with a rich, satisfying experience of studying English but also as a focus for teaching the core knowledge we intend them

to learn. Texts are chosen because they are inherently interesting but also because they exemplify the concepts we have specified. Every text students read provides an opportunity to notice, discuss and write about what happens in the story.

Texts should be chosen because they contribute to a bigger, richer picture of what the study of language and literature 'looks like'. Then everything studied in the first three years of secondary schools becomes the vital hinterland for KS4. While students need to learn disciplinary concepts to master the study of English, it is stories which make our subject sing. These stories will, of course, be mediated by teachers in the classroom who will, ideally, supplement the specified hinterland not only with their enthusiasm but also their own rich stock of story and anecdote.

This last – what each individual teacher brings to the enactment of the curriculum – cannot be specified but can only be encouraged. As we'll go on to see in Part 2, a curriculum that is planned as lesson slides tacitly gives permission (whatever is explicitly stated) to teachers to teach only what's on the slides, as if that's the entirety of what can be taught. If core and hinterland knowledge are carefully specified (but not compiled and ordered into ready-made, plug-and-play lessons) teachers are given the opportunity to breathe their own life into the curriculum.

1.12 PERSONAL DEVELOPMENT

The English curriculum should strive to provide disciplinary equity so that all students can access as much of the subject as possible at the highest possible level.

What is personal development and what has it got to do with the English curriculum? As well as teaching academic disciplines, schools are responsible for providing opportunities for students to grow as active, healthy and engaged citizens and to prepare them for life outside of education. This covers spiritual, moral, social and cultural development (SMSC), personal, social, health and economic education (PHSE), and careers education, information and guidance (CEIAG). This can all sound rather removed from the English classroom and it's easy for these things to end up as a set of superficial bolt-ons to which we pay lip service but little else.

Before we look at how our curriculum addresses this personal development agenda, it's worth thinking about the things personal development is *not*. Firstly, it should not be seen as a checklist of one-off lessons or vague nods. Equally, we should avoid conflating personal development with enrichment and extracurricular activities. It's not that these things are bad – creative writing clubs and theatre trips are obviously highly desirable – it's that they do not necessarily represent an entitlement for all students. We should also steer clear of using English lessons as an opportunity for teaching PHSE *instead* of English. To be clear, we should avoid justifying curriculum choices that are neither broad nor ambitious simply because these choices provide an opportunity for teaching a wider life lesson. Neither should we choose texts for study so children can learn how to be nice to each other. The purpose of English in the curriculum is, first and foremost, to teach the academic subjects of language and literature. Students becoming more empathetic is a wonderful by-product of studying English but, if we believe in disciplinary equity, it cannot be the *object* of study.

Above all, we should avoid making sweeping generalisations about 'kids like these' and instead have a solid understanding of the issues in our local areas and know the opportunities and obstacles in our local contexts. We should be aware of the data on employment, levels of education, and levels of deprivation in the community so that instead of saying things like, 'No one at home cares about kids like these', (which is both offensive and incorrect) we can instead say things like, 'We know that 30% of people in the community have no qualifications whatsoever so this is something that will be mitigated by our curriculum'.

The challenge then is to weave our concern for, and understanding of, the context and challenges of the communities we serve into the choices and sequencing of our curriculum. What are typically seen as pastoral concerns – the behaviour and attitudes of students, and the context and challenges school communities face – should bookend our curricular choices, so that what we choose to teach is framed within this larger picture. If curriculum and personal development are properly intertwined, they will drive each other forward; if we know the specifics of our local context – both the barriers and the opportunities – we will understand our students better, which will help us better refine our curriculum to ensure they make excellent progress.

For clarity, when discussing the progress students make in English what we mean is knowing more and being able to do more. At secondary school,

this requires a solid foundation in decoding, reading fluency, orthographic awareness, letter formation, handwriting and specific knowledge of how to read, write and speak in English. Clearly the performance of feeder primaries has a lot of impact here. The same secondary school may take students from primary schools where student outcomes are significantly better than the national average *and* primaries where students do significantly worse. The better we know what our students arrive with, the better we can ensure the curriculum meets the needs of the communities we serve. For instance, because students from more disadvantaged backgrounds are less likely to be exposed to the breadth of language and literature they need to experience in order to be successful, we need to ensure we provide this for them rather than leaving it to chance. The pillars of progress in English – reading, writing and oracy – should both address barriers and take advantage of opportunities to support a broad and ambitious curriculum.

As of 2019, Ofsted, have been asking, 'How does the curriculum address learners' broader development, enabling them to develop and discover their interests and talents'? [29] The key to answering this question is to be clear how the curriculum is a tool for disciplinary equity. We need to think through how the teaching of English enables *every* student, whatever their starting point or background, to access the discipline of English at the highest levels.

For many students, this will be impossible if they don't know enough to make informed choices, or if the foundations are not laid in school. As Doug Lemov argues, 'Social justice... is classrooms that are radically better, classrooms that foster academic achievement and that prepare every student to accomplish their dreams... Equity starts with achievement'.[30] In this way, the curriculum enacts social justice by providing disciplinary equity.

As we move through the subject, at A level, at university, into the professions that English feeds into, there is an eraser at work. Students from more disadvantaged backgrounds or from ethnic minorities are increasingly erased from the picture. Of course, most societal pressures are beyond the scope of schools to address. Equally, studying English at degree level will not be appropriate for all, but if we don't provide students with the means to make a choice, we end up choosing for them based on where they live, who their parents are and what primary school they went to. If a student at the age of 16, after being given every opportunity to explore language and literature in all their beauty, decides they no longer want to pursue their study of English, that's still a success.

Questions to consider:

- What are the local barriers and opportunities for reading, writing and oracy?
- What is happening in feeder primary schools? (Both positive and negative)
- What is the local employment picture?
- What *specific* aspects of the curriculum address these barriers and take advantage of these opportunities?

Only after these questions have been considered should we think about other ways to enact personal development such as intervention, SEND provision and enrichment.

Let's show how all this might work when applied to one of OAT's academies:

- 10% of the local population have a level 4 (degree level) qualification. The national average is 40%
- 23% of the local population have no qualification at all
- The local GCSE pass rate is nearly 15% lower than the regional average (51% vs 65%)
- 30% of the local population are in full-time employment (compared to 70% nationally)
- Local KS2 SATs indicate very wide variations in performance (one feeder school has the highest local average, another has the lowest)
- The borough has a high level of 'elementary occupations' (manual or low-skilled work); this is nearly twice the national level
- However, there is also a relatively high level of skilled employment, especially in the health and leisure sectors
- The average writing age in Year 7 is 9 years 7 months
- 47% of the local community have no access to a car[31]

From this we might infer that there are likely to be poor levels of literacy in many homes but also that there will be a wide variation in reading ability in the Year 7 intake. This being the case, we might conclude that some students will require specific interventions to help them catch up and be able to access our curriculum. Maybe, we might think, this should be addressed by the SEND department rather than the English department. Whilst it should be the case

that those at the bottom end of the distribution will get additional support, the curriculum must also address these needs.

As detailed in section 1.8, the Ancient Origins module which kicks off our Year 7 curriculum is full of texts we should anticipate that many students will struggle to access. Should we swap them out for less demanding texts – thus ensuring disciplinary *inequity* – or should we consider how to make these texts accessible to all? We know that Greek mythology is included in the KS2 National Curriculum so we can be reasonably confident that most students will come with some experience of mythology, but the module begins with some pre-teaching diagnostic questions designed to see what knowledge students arrive with. The myths we've selected link to later elements of the curriculum as well as containing the potential to unlock literary allusions in unfamiliar texts. We also introduce students to Aristotle's story structure to help them understand narrative and reflect on examples of heroes and heroism in various stories. Many students are familiar with the 'story mountain' from primary school and so we deepen and add detail to this familiarity, helping to bridge the gap between descriptive use in KS2 to more analytical understanding in KS3. Instead of selecting a relatively inaccessible translation of the *Odyssey*, we chose Simon Armitage's adaptation because it's earthy and engaging and written as a play, with lots of parts for students to perform. As we'll explore in section 2.9, this performance is supported through fluency lessons which are designed to support all students to be successful readers.

The fact that almost half the families in this community have no access to a car means the scale and scope of students' experiences is likely to be relatively narrow. They are unlikely to know, perhaps, what an outdoor market looks and feels like,[32] and are less likely to have travelled by rail, let alone recognise Grand Central Station in New York. As the AQA English GCSE Examiners Report for Paper 2 in 2019 pointed out,

> 'What characterised the best… responses was the ability to engage with the "big ideas": politics, economics, gender, aesthetics, class, morality, psychology and even philosophy. Students who were confident and familiar with these ideas were able to frame their own perspectives in this larger context and thereby enhance the quality of their argument… it is clear

that providing students with opportunities to encounter and explore these [big ideas] brings benefits across not just this paper but across the entire suite of English assessments'.[33]

If the curriculum isn't explicitly providing these opportunities, then we ensure that the most disadvantaged students have little of interest to write about. If you've never left your local area, when your own experiences are so limited, how are you meant to approach GCSE writing tasks unless the English curriculum seeks to provide proxies for these experiences by explicitly teaching both specific, granular knowledge and abstract concepts?

As well as improving students' ability to read and write, this focus on reading complex and challenging texts and our granular approach to successful writing will help prepare students to read and respond to the texts on which they'll be assessed at GCSE, thus enabling them to access a greater range of employment opportunities and educational options. If students are going to go on to be a senior official in, say, the offshore energy sector, they will need to read difficult texts and write complex reports.

Not only will the stories we've selected help students access later aspects of the curriculum, but also the approaches taken to how these texts are read, how writing is scaffolded and how discussion is placed at the heart of the curriculum will help prepare them for later life. To find out more about how all this works we need to start thinking about the implementation of the curriculum.

INTENT: KEY POINTS

1. **The intent of an English curriculum is likely to be successful if knowledge is carefully specified and sequenced to enable students to achieve mastery of the subject.**
   We need to remember that skill cannot be taught directly. Skill is the product of learning and applying knowledge. So-called 'skills' must be broken down into their component parts so that the requisite knowledge can be taught and practised in the order that is most likely to lead to mastery.

2. **The English curriculum should be ambitious, coherently sequenced, broad and balanced, and adapted for students with SEND.**
   This is a tough balancing act, but ambitious content is made accessible by thinking through how the most vulnerable students will be successful. Coherent sequencing will help ensure the curriculum is accessible. Depth has to be traded off against breath to enable students to experience the widest possible picture of language and literature.

3. **The curriculum should be concept-led: what do we want students to remember?**
   The texts students experience in KS3 should not be studied like GCSE set texts. There is no point and little value to students memorising the details of character and plot. Instead, texts provide the hinterland in which the conceptual knowledge students need to master lives and breathes.

4. **Powerful knowledge in English can be organised into conceptual 'boxes'.**
   The better we organise the conceptual knowledge of English, the more likely we are to sequence it thoughtfully in the curriculum. Although the 'shape' of knowledge in English is very 'wide and shallow' there are important areas of hierarchy where we need to pay attention to optimal sequences for concepts to be encountered. The conceptual boxes of metaphor, story, argument, pattern, grammar and context are broad enough to contain all the knowledge we need students to master.

5. **We must strive for disciplinary equity and organise the curriculum in a way that maximises students' outcomes.**
   All students – no matter our views on their backgrounds or abilities – deserve to be taught an English curriculum that enables them to choose to study the subject at the highest possible level. If we do not intend students to access an ambitious, challenging curriculum we will ensure educational disadvantages are perpetuated.

Implementation

Communicating the curriculum

2.1 WHAT WE MEAN BY 'IMPLEMENTATION'

Implementation covers the way the curriculum you intend students to learn is taught and resourced.

Cracking the intent of the curriculum is a great start, but we all know what the road to hell is paved with. How do we ensure that our wonderful intentions are realised? The implementation of the curriculum is concerned with how intentions become more than hopes and dreams. To think about implementation, we need to ask ourselves how we will go about the business of teaching the curriculum across one, or many, English departments. Clearly there are very many ways to skin a cat, but at the risk of overextending a metaphor, the skin must be separated from the cat. If you find that you're teaching things that you don't care whether students will remember – if you're indulging in activities for their own sake – then you probably haven't got this right.

The thing is, students will always remember *something*, but will it be what you intend? Will they remember your wonderfully zany sense of humour, or your avant-garde taste in ties? Will they remember you standing on desks and reciting Whitman? Or will they retain the nuts and bolts of the subject they need to master if they can be said to have had a good education?

It's reasonable to assume that different areas of the curriculum may benefit from being taught in different ways. It would be rather odd if Year 7 lessons were difficult to distinguish from Year 11 lessons. But then, it seems equally reasonable to suggest that all English lessons will be best taught where there has been thought given to matching curriculum content with pedagogy. And some principles seem so widely applicable and useful – explanation, modelling, scaffolding, practice – that it would be odd if they were absent anywhere. As we'll see, we recommend five core pedagogical approaches to implement our curriculum, each of which is discussed in its own section.

One point to address is that of consistency. Should all teachers teach in the same way? What should be prescribed and where should teachers be given autonomy? From the vantage of designing a curriculum to be used across multiple schools, we have been careful to allow our curriculum materials to be adapted to fit a wide range of different lesson structures. Many, if not most, of OAT's academies mandate that lessons should start with some kind of 'do now' activity, often in the form of retrieval of previously taught content. Similarly, many academies expect all lessons to include teacher modelling and independent practice. As a result, we have ensured that our curriculum materials are flexible enough for teachers to fit into any structure.

We have specified that some of the content in our curriculum is 'core' and that some is optional. Core content is that which we have determined is so useful or important that students will find it useful in their ongoing study of English. Some of this we have tried to codify as curriculum-related expectations – what students should be able to define, what they should know and what they should be able to do at particular points in the curriculum. Within our Teacher Guides we have also designated as 'core' the knowledge that *we expect to be taught* in order for the content to make sense. If it this core knowledge is skipped or neglected, students are less likely to understand later aspects of the curriculum. We've also designated some content as 'expert knowledge'. This is knowledge that goes more deeply into topics and takes students further off-piste. It's interesting

DOI: 10.4324/9781003455622-2

and will deepen students' understanding of topics but is not essential for them to make sense of the curriculum. As such, we intend that teachers should make local decisions about their students, their timetables, the length of lessons etc. to determine how much of this additional content can or should be taught. Additionally, we have made clear recommendations about how teachers should approach the teaching of vocabulary, writing, reading and discussion.

If you can explain why teachers are making pedagogical choices and are able to justify decisions in terms of students' progression through your curriculum, then you will have a good grasp of how to implement your curriculum. The following sections will explore the rationale behind the choices we have made at OAT.

2.2 GAPLESS INSTRUCTION

If we make assumptions about what students know or should be able to do, some of them will inevitably fall into the gaps we leave and fail to meet our expectations.

Teachers are often told to 'teach to the top'. For the most part, this is caveated by included the need to 'scaffold down', but in too many cases, the notion of teaching to the top does more harm than good.

'Teaching to the top' only works if 'the top' refers to outcomes rather than children. If we mean teaching to the top of the ability range, then we will inevitably leave many students behind. But, if we teach all students – regardless of their prior attainment, our perception of their ability, or their own sense of self-belief – to achieve the highest possible standards then maybe all will find it possible to achieve excellence.[1] Getting the most advantaged, the most able, the highest prior attainers to be successful is relatively straightforward. All too often, these students are successful *despite* rather than *because* of what we do in the classroom. If the least advantaged, the least able, the lowest prior attainers are to be successful it will *only* be because of our efforts.

Experiencing success is essential for students to be willing to commit to doing anything difficult. For some students this will inevitably require a huge amount of support. The five teaching strategies which underpin the implementation of our curriculum are all aligned with this ambition. For instance, the focus on reading fluency ensures, through repetition, that all students achieve perfect prosody. Our writing programme, with its relentless focus on

mastering individual sentence structures, attempts to guarantee that every student can compose perfect sentences. Structured discussion, with its emphasis on repetition of academic language, means that all students have the experience of rehearsing the language required for academic success. Because the curriculum specifies small steps repeated over and over, all students can be successful. Obviously, despite this emphasis on mastery, some students will still be more successful than others, but because all students see and feel that they are able to produce something impressive, they come to believe that maybe, just maybe, they might be able to sustain this standard with increasing independence.

The fact that all this is ridiculously optimistic is part of the point. Inevitably, there are still students who, despite every effort, fall through the gaps. But, if we're really serious about all students achieving the highest standards, we need to believe that gapless instruction is possible.

Siegfried Engelmann, the mastermind behind Direct Instruction, says,

> Instructional sequences have the capacity to make children smart or not... If the [curriculum] sensibly counters not merely the content errors that poorly designed programs might induce, but also the more general attitudes about learning and retaining information they promote, children can become impressively proficient in academic skills. **The curriculum will largely determine the extent to which children are smart.**[2] [emphasis added]

Or, to put it another way, **ability is the consequence not the cause of what children learn.**[3] When children fail to achieve the highest standards, we often assume they just aren't up to it, that the fault is theirs. Instead, our default response should be to take responsibility for these inevitable failures and assume that if students haven't been successful, it must be because we've left a gap in our instruction. Whilst it might not *always* be true (there may be some students who, no matter how hard we try, we can't reach) we believe it's a useful fiction. Useful because there's never any point to blaming students.

By taking responsibility and assuming we've inadvertently left gaps we will look more closely at the content and sequencing of our curriculum and reflect more deeply on our teaching. And, if we look carefully and closely enough, we're likely to find areas where we can improve.

In our efforts to make the implementation of our curriculum 'gapless' we certainly cannot lay claim to the kind of 'flawless communication' promoted by Engelmann in his Direct Instruction programs,[4] but we can certainly strive to help teachers understand that if students struggle then the responsibility – if not the fault – lies with us.

2.3 SUCCESS BEFORE STRUGGLE

Most people only persist with something difficult when they believe success is possible. Students are no different. It's pointless having the expectation that students will work hard to get top grades if they are unable to see how this might be achieved. Success and struggle must be balanced in the same way that a challenging and ambitious curriculum must be balanced with accessibility and adaption for the most vulnerable.

Struggle is worthwhile because it's the only way in which we improve. When we stop struggling, we reach a plateau beyond which we stop improving. We may think we're getting better, but we're probably just becomingly increasingly confident. Developing mastery or expertise requires concentration; we must *think* about what we're doing. As soon as we're able to perform a task on autopilot, we're no longer learning.[5]

The problem is that struggling isn't much fun. Most people prefer the feeling of being able to fluently perform a task at a lower level of expertise than pushing themselves to be better. If students struggle too much, or too soon, this will be undesirable. Struggle is only likely to be desirable after success has been encoded. What we mean by this is that most students will find it demotivating to struggle at something if they see little hope of success, but if they have a clear mental representation of what success looks and feels like, they're more likely to persevere in the face of difficulty.

A significant minority of students arrive at secondary school never having experienced success in English. They believe they 'can't read' or 'can't write' and think of themselves as 'rubbish at English'. Why would we ever expect them to be able to struggle with difficult tasks when they have never been successful? If we want students to learn that they can be successful at English, we need to make sure they experience success *before* we ask them to struggle with doing more difficult things. The essence of our approach is encapsulated in Figure 2.1.

A satnav is the perfect assessment for learning machine: it knows exactly where you are; you tell it what your goal is; it gives you step-by-step feedback on your progress until you reach your goal. If you make a mistake, it adapts and provides alternative instructions. It's so well designed that even inept navigators quickly experience success. The downside to this efficiency is that there's little incentive to learn routes.

Using a map is far more demanding. A navigator has to project the two-dimensional image of the map onto three-dimensional reality. For some of us, this requires regularly stopping the car and rotating the map until the roads line up. Needless to say, this is a frustrating way to make progress and so there are clear incentives to memorise landmarks in order to learn routes.

To apply this analogy to English lessons, at the beginning of an instructional sequence students need satnav teaching. If we want students to achieve high standards they need step-by-step instructions, clear models and scaffolds, rapid feedback and lots of support and encouragement. Once they've experienced success, they should be ready to have some of this support removed. We can increase our expectations of what they can achieve independently, reduce our feedback so that we're offering hints and reminders

Explicit instruction with worked examples to encode success

Scaffolds are gradually removed to increase challenge and promote internalisation

Students become increasingly independent and expert

FIGURE 2.1 Success before struggle

instead of solutions and generally incentivising them to remember our instruction. If we remove support too quickly, we can put it back, but the message needs to be that students can have all the support they need to be successful for as long as required but that they are only *really* successful when they can do without the support. That said, if at any point students look to be struggling too much, the best thing to do is to restore some of the support and offer clearer feedback. *The point is not that students should sink or swim, but that they should all swim.*

The most important first step in changing students' beliefs is to let them know what success looks and feels like. Once they have had this experience, the idea of struggling starts to become possible. They will be ready to struggle with increasingly difficult concepts and take on more complex tasks. Once students leave us, they will be more independent. If they're not, that's on us. Anything we have taught them which they can't remember will have wasted their time and ours.

Introducing struggle should always be balanced against students' sense of self-efficacy. Too much struggle is likely to backfire; what they're most likely to learn is that they've reached a limit beyond which they're not capable of improving. They'll either decide to settle for a more achievable-seeming target or give up entirely because they don't want to feel stupid. Instead, they need to believe that improvement is possible through their own efforts. Only when we believe improvement is possible do we put up with having to struggle.[6]

True mastery involves all students achieving at something very ambitious, but which is specified clearly enough to teach gaplessly. At the point where students can be very successful at something very small (such as writing a thesis statement) we can begin to remove scaffolding and increase complexity so that, over time, they can be equally successful at something much more expansive and demanding (such as writing an extended literature essay).

2.4 FIVE CORE PEDAGOGICAL APPROACHES

Approaches to teaching English should be easy to implement and have an identifiable impact on students' ability to learn what's specified in the curriculum.

We have found that the implementation of our curriculum depends on teachers mastering five simple teaching strategies and then committing to using these again and again. The key to each of these 'core pedagogies' is repetition.

We define learning as 'the retention and transfer of knowledge to new contexts'.[7] Retention is concerned with durability whereas transfer is about the flexibility of knowledge. If students cannot remember what we have taught them next week or next term, then it's difficult to argue that they have learned this material in any meaningful sense. Similarly, if students cannot transfer what we've taught from the context of the classroom to other contexts (not least the examination hall) then again, it's hard to claim that they have learned the curriculum we've taught.

Part of the process of designing a curriculum in which all students can be successful is the observation that many students cannot remember what we told them five minutes ago, let alone a couple of lessons later. The trouble is teachers often fail to find this out.

It's axiomatic that we should never assume we have communicated clearly. If anything, teachers would be better off assuming that the default setting for all classroom interactions is that a significant proportion of students are not paying attention at any given time. This has certainly been borne out through observation in our efforts to implement our curriculum. (That said, if students are likely to drift when teachers are speaking, they are even more likely to do so when another student speaks.)

Each of our core pedagogies is predicated on the notion that repetition builds success, that success leads to greater motivation, and that greater motivation leads to greater success.

These five core pedagogical approaches are:

1. Regular retrieval practice
2. Vocabulary instruction
3. Couch to 5k writing
4. Reading for meaning
5. Structured discussion

Together, these approaches to teaching are designed to lead not only to mastery of each of the three modalities of English: speaking and listening, reading, and writing, but also lead to the ability to make meaning from and with language and literature.

To be absolutely clear: we are not suggesting that these five teaching approaches are the be-all and end-all of English teaching. They are the basics. If teachers master these core pedagogies, they will find all the other lovely activities their students might enjoy much easier to implement. An apt analogy is to think of our core pedagogies as the basic food groups needed to create a nutritious meal whereas other activities are the garnish and flavouring which make it delicious.

2.5 MINI-WHITEBOARDS

Mini-whiteboards provide the most straightforward way for both ensuring all students are working and for making their thinking visible.

Before we explore the nuts and bolts of these core pedagogies, we need to consider the importance of mini-whiteboards (MWBs) in implementing an English curriculum. Although we're convinced that MWBs are an essential implementation tool, we've come across lots of objections from English teachers and so it makes sense to think through some of the reasons why teachers may not be keen to take the plunge.

Firstly, let's be clear: MWBs can be a faff. They're one more item of equipment to buy, maintain, distribute and collect. This is one of the reasons why they're gathering dust at the back of cupboards in so many English classrooms. If you're going to use MWBs then you really do have to think carefully about where you will store them, how you will get them in front of students and then returned to storage.

If there's a poor behaviour culture in your school or classroom, then using MWBs will present additional difficulties. Given the opportunity, some children will draw penises on their MWBs. Others might attempt to damage the equipment or each other. The issue is not that MWBs *cause* bad behaviour but that they *expose* it. It's easier to see when children are getting it wrong. This should be viewed as an asset. As always, we need to teach the behaviour we want and embed systems and routines that make it easier for students to make better decisions.

Ideally, after students have been given sufficient time to complete a task on their MWBs, they should be asked to hold them up, using a prompt such as '1, 2, 3, show me'. Such routines should be practised until students know exactly what is expected.

'1, 2, 3, show me' routine

1 = Pens down
2 = Hold MWB with both hands hovering over the table, writing side down
3 = Still holding MWB in both hands, raise in front, writing side towards students

Show me = flip boards so that writing is visible to teacher. Continue holding MWBs until teacher has time to scan answers to spot any obvious mistakes or misconceptions.

What about comparing MWB use to 'no hands up' questioning (cold calling) or getting students to hold up traffic lights (coloured cards)? These options are cheaper, easier to use alternatives for increasing student participation and exposing students' thinking, so what's the point of investing time and money in MWBs? Whilst we'd agree that cold calling should be an essential tool in a teacher's arsenal, cold calling and MWBs should be deployed in different situations and for different reasons.

When a teacher 'cold calls', only one student can participate at a time, whereas when MWBs are used, every student participates. The only real advantage of using cold calling over MWBs is that there is less fuss and answers can be collected more rapidly. But, as well as ensuring all students participate, MWBs enable teachers to see *all* students' thinking instead of just checking a sample.

One issue with MWBs is that writing becomes ephemeral and is wiped away as quickly as it is put down. Surely, if it's worth asking students to go to the time and trouble of writing something down, shouldn't we expect them to write it in their exercise books so that they can reflect on it in the future? No one is arguing that *all* writing should be on MWBs. Of course, some writing should be in students' books. But a lot of what students write in books is definitely *not* worth recording. Very often, students are expected to record answers to retrieval questions which now, in the absence of the question, no longer make any sense. It's difficult to argue there's any merit in this beyond allowing senior leaders to check compliance with ill-judged book scrutiny policies.

There's also the fact that so many English books are filled with low-level comprehension tasks to which students routinely provide poor-quality responses littered with errors. If we're committed to the permanence of writing, then we should be equally committed to upholding the quality of students' writing. What students practise they get better at; if they practise writing badly, they get better at bad writing. This means we are obliged, at a minimum, to read through all students' work and check they are not embedding errors. The costs and benefits of requiring teachers to do this make it problematic at best (see section 2.12).

We should also consider the notion that there might be a benefit to transient writing. One of the uses of MWBs is that they are a 'sandbox' where students can experiment and rehearse ideas before committing to them either orally or in a more permanent written form. The ability to rub away discarded ideas can be constructive in many circumstances.

To help us work out whether we'd be better off writing on a MWB or in a book, the rule of thumb we'd suggest is: if you want students to write it down in their book then you must commit to marking it (see section 2.12). If, on the other hand, the writing is being undertaken to support thinking and you've no intention of valuing the outcome sufficiently to mark it, you're probably much better off using MWBs.

We also need to address the suggestion that using MWBs makes it easier for students to produce sloppy work, littered with errors. Again, as with the faff and behaviour arguments, this is undoubtedly true. However, as with the transience argument, students are as likely to produce untidy error-strewn writing in a book. In either case it's up to us to make our expectations clear and support students in meeting them. The positive *advantage* of students making mistakes on MWBs is that these mistakes are exposed. Teachers get to see, immediately, who's misspelled Priestley, who's doodled in the corner and who's written an unintelligible fragment rather than a beautifully crafted sentence. Because teachers get to see these errors at the time they're made, they can respond rapidly to prevent mistakes, misjudgements or misconceptions from becoming more deeply embedded.

We also often hear that teachers are unable to read every students' answer, especially when practising sentences. Although this may be true to an extent, teachers can still see a much higher sample than with cold calling, and are provided with useful formative feedback without needing to wait to look through exercise books.

As discussed, there are definitely aspects of English for which MWBs will be less appropriate. The question we need to address is whether MWBs in English are useful *enough* to justify their opportunity cost.[8]

There are three main uses to which MWBs should be put in successfully implementing the English curriculum:

1. *Participation*: MWBs are one of the most effective mechanisms for ensuring all students are both participating in an activity and held to account for the quality of their participation. Because they can rapidly see what all students are writing, teachers can intervene as appropriate in the most responsive manner possible. If it's possible to gain insights into all students' understanding then we should.
2. *Visible thinking*: MWBs expose all students' thinking. Teachers are able to scan the room and see at a glance whether an individual requires some bespoke remediation or that whole sections of the class are dangerously wrongheaded. There are other ways of doing this, but these come with other costs and fewer advantages.
3. *Reducing stakes*: When posing a question on which the teacher intends to cold call students, allowing them time to commit a tentative answer, or at least a few thoughts, on their MWB increases the likelihood that all students will be able to respond. This can really support the quality and sophistication of verbal responses.

Whilst we think it's true that most English lessons would benefit from the addition of one or all of these activities, obviously there are aspects of English for which MWBs are not well suited. The following prompts may help determine the opportunity cost associated with both deciding to use and not use them:

- Is the behaviour culture in your school or in a particular class likely to mean you can get rid of the faff and behaviour concerns quickly and easily?
- If you're doing something else that you think is great, would using MWBs force you to stop doing your great thing or might they support it?
- Is all the writing you're asking students to produce something you will value and can give the necessary attention to correct and improve?
- Would using MWBs make it easier or harder to spot students' mistakes and misconceptions than what you're currently doing?
- How else can you hold every student to account for their participation and effort during a lesson?
- How else could you support students to provide fluent academic answers to questions and contributions to discussions?
- And, depending on your answers to the previous prompts, is your alternative quicker and easier to use than MWBs?

2.6 REGULAR RETRIEVAL PRACTICE

Efforts to retrieve knowledge from long-term memory increase the ability of students to recall that knowledge elsewhere and later.

If you're not convinced of the efficacy of retrieval practice by now, there's probably little chance we'll persuade you here.[9] However, although many schools have made regular retrieval practice a non-negotiable expectation of lessons, what students retrieve and how they go about the process of retrieving varies widely. Part of the reason retrieval practice often fails is that teachers are told it is a good thing to do without having the underlying theory explained.

Research has posited that each item in long-term memory has both a 'storage' strength and a 'retrieval' strength. Storage strength is our ability to recall something right now; retrieval strength is our ability to recall something elsewhere and later.[10]

Counterintuitively, attempting to improve retrieval strength in the here and now actually reduces storage strength elsewhere and later, whereas practice that attempts to improve storage strength also results in better retrieval strength in the longer term.[11] Many find this confusing. Essentially, teaching that focuses on students 'demonstrating progress' over the course of a lesson is much less effective than teaching that is concerned with trying to recall previously taught content. This explains why students can produce a slick performance at the end of a lesson by recalling what they have just been taught only to have forgotten it all by their next lesson. The struggle involved in dredging something up from long-term memory strengthens our ability to fluently recall that information again in the future. This is what Robert Bjork called 'desirable difficulty'.[12]

A desirable difficulty is where inducing an element of struggle into current performance results in stronger future recall. But, crucially, **for a difficulty to be desirable it must also result in success.**

This is where a lot of so-called retrieval practice goes wrong: students are asked a question which they fail to answer. In lesson after lesson, students write down 'do now' questions from the board, wait for teachers to reveal the answers and then copy down the answer. There is no struggle and no success, just a meaningless time-wasting exercise. What do they learn from this? All too often, what they learn is: 1) that recall tasks are a piece of mindless box-ticking admin at the start of lessons that they simply have to suffer through or, even worse, 2) that, right at the start of a lesson, they have – yet again – failed. These failures compound, often resulting in the belief that students are 'rubbish' at English. Needless to say, this is in no one's interest.

We offer three simple suggestions for getting the most out of retrieval tasks.

1. Retrieval should be easy

Wait a minute! Surely if we're trying to induce desirable *difficulties*, shouldn't retrieval be *hard*? No.

The last thing we want is to increase the amount of failure students experience. Failure is only ever a useful learning experience when built upon a firm foundation of success. You need enormous self-belief to contend with setbacks; if setbacks are your normal experience, one more is just further evidence you're not good enough. But more than that, retrieval *needs* to result in success in order to be beneficial. The 'difficulty' comes from having to remember something you haven't just been told. If last lesson students learn that Malcolm is Duncan's eldest son and rightful King of Scotland and are then asked next lesson, *Who is Malcolm?* they should have a reasonable chance of remembering *something* about him but many inevitably won't. A better retrieval task might be to ask students to fill in the blank in this sentence: *The name of King Duncan's oldest son is M _ _ _ _ _ _.* Even that momentary pause before remembering the name will help build storage strength. If, when you check students' MWBs and find that some students are still struggling to remember, resist the temptation to just give them the answer. Ideally, you should keep revealing letters (Malc _ _ m.) until the answer is retrieved.

It's also important that we don't go beyond the evidence when designing retrieval tasks. Most evidence for retrieval practice is gleaned from experimentation into 'relatively simple verbal materials, including word lists and paired associates'.[13] Retrieval practice in lessons tends to be most effective when it is fast paced and builds 'fingertips' knowledge. If students can't answer retrieval tasks quickly and easily on an MWB, the task may not be an effective use of lesson time. Of course, that's not to say students shouldn't be asked and expected to tackle challenging tasks, it's just that these are usually not the best way to begin a lesson.[14]

2. The information retrieved should be useful

Arguably, all knowledge is useful but what we mean by this is that the information we ask students to retrieve should be stuff we will ask them to regularly *use*. If *Macbeth* is their set text for English Literature, remembering the name of Duncan's eldest son is useful. But asking Year 11 students to remember plot details of texts studied in Year 7 is almost certainly not useful. Far too frequently, students are asked to recall what amounts to trivia; stuff that's 'nice to know' but not stuff that will be used or useful.

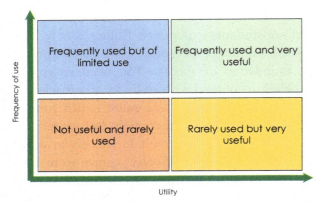

FIGURE 2.2 Matrix to help select information for retrieval practice

When designing retrieval tasks, we should think about both how often students will use the information *and* what utility the information will have if it's successfully recalled. The matrix in Figure 2.2 should help to design better retrieval tasks.

Ideally, retrieval tasks should focus on frequently used and very useful information and avoid information that is not useful and rarely used.

3. Retrieval tasks should be regularly repeated

Once we have selected a body of simple, useful information we want students to fluently recall, we should ask them to recall this information again and again until it is thoroughly embedded. Students need to master currently useful information *and* to recall previously mastered topics in order to keep storage strength high. In the first instance, if some students have struggled to answer a question today, we should definitely ask them the same question tomorrow. Ideally, we should continue to ask the same question until all students are answering it effortlessly.

Once students find it easy to complete a task like 'The name of King Duncan's oldest son is M _ _ _ _ _ _', the next step is to remove the scaffolding until they can reliably answer, 'Who is Malcolm?'

Over time, students begin to forget this mastered information so they will need to be asked again at regular intervals. In a perfect world, it would be amazing to have a package that enabled teachers to flag questions to recur after optimum intervals.[15] Although it can't currently do this, Carousel Learning is probably the most effective tool we have found for helping teachers to use retrieval tasks which conform to these three principles. We have created question banks for each of our modules which can be used to both create quizzes in lessons and to assign homework for students to work on independently (see section 2.13). This allows teachers to be systematic in quizzing students on the

English teaching sits in the fraught space between 'teaching knowledge' and 'teaching skills'. We want students to be able to think deeply and creatively about literature and to be able to produce interesting, insightful and idiosyncratic analysis. But we also know that we first need to break down the text ourselves and model the way that we analyse and dissect it. We have to give students raw material from which to construct their own understandings and interpretations in a way that is both intelligible and memorable, and then support them in consolidating that new knowledge in a way that allows them to deploy it later. Fundamental building blocks must be provided and learnt to enable students to later flourish and go further in their analyses.

When we spoke to English teachers about this issue, they told us that they were in need of a tool that could help them communicate these building blocks and help students commit them to memory in a workload-friendly and efficient way. Because Carousel is designed with issues like this in mind, and via its flashcard, quizzing, marking, feedback and whiteboard functionality, we knew that it could prove to be an enormous help to English teachers.

We **do not** believe that using Carousel is the final word or that students knowing the answers to retrieval questions is the goal of English education. We **do** believe that using our platform will help students gather the raw material needed to think and write creatively, originally and idiosyncratically.

Adam Boxer, Founder of Carousel Learning

knowledge they will need to be successful in our assessments.

NB. We recommend avoiding multiple-choice questions for retrieval tasks as they have been shown to be less effective than short answer tasks.[16]

Although there isn't clear guidance on when in a lesson students should be asked to engage in retrieval practice, many schools expect this to be done at the start of a lesson in a 'Do Now Activity', and because clear routines tend to be supportive of calm, purposeful classrooms, this seems as good a time as any. If teachers are using Carousel to set quizzes, these can be projected very simply so that students can be expected to begin answering as soon as they enter a classroom. We strongly recommend that students use MWBs to record their answers for two important reasons: first, it reduces the stakes of retrieval which has been demonstrated to have a beneficial effect on retention,[17] and second, it makes students much more accountable for their answers.

As students become familiar with the finite number of questions within a module, teachers should reduce the time available for students to write the correct answers to encourage this knowledge to become increasingly automatic and immediately available.

2.7 VOCABULARY INSTRUCTION

If students are to be academically successful, they need to be fluent in the language of academic success.

Teaching academic vocabulary unlocks students' ability to make meaning from the curriculum and to express their own views with clarity and precision.

Vocabulary knowledge and reading skill are mutually dependent; the broader your vocabulary, the easier you'll find it to read. Likewise, the more skilled you are at reading, the more quickly you'll acquire new vocabulary.[18]

The approach to vocabulary instruction we've taken is drawn from the research of Isabelle Beck and colleagues.[19] They estimate that if a new word is encountered in a text, the reader has about a 15% likelihood of making it part of their working vocabulary. If the same word is met in three different contexts, that probability increases to above 50%. However, by using what we've come to call the 'golden triangle' (see Figure 2.3) the

Vocabulary building

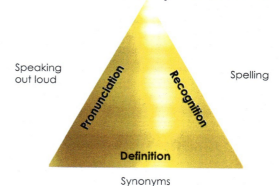

FIGURE 2.3 The 'golden triangle' of vocabulary instruction

likelihood that students will retain new words can be much higher.[20]

As most teachers are now aware, vocabulary can be roughly divided into three 'tiers'. Tier 1 words are those that are common to spoken language and are likely to be well known by students (hat, running, dodgy, slow etc.). Tier 2 words are those that are common to written language but relatively rare in speech (fusillade, substantiate, obsequious, turgid etc.). Tier 3 words are specialised, academic words that describe the concepts of subject disciplines (osmosis, tectonic, algebra, onomatopoeia etc.) These distinctions are important because the way we treat Tier 2 words (topic vocabulary and excellent epithets) should be different to the way we handle Tier 3 words (subject terminology).

When teaching both topic vocabulary and subject terminology, students are asked to go through a familiar process each time they are introduced to a new word. Firstly, students should be asked to self-assess where they rate their understanding using this 4-point scale on their MWBs:

> Please rate how well you know the word **implacable**:
>
> 1. Never seen it before
> 2. Seen it, heard it, unsure what it means
> 3. Understand and can sometimes use
> 4. Confidently understand and can explain

Too often, we choose recognition over understanding. Knowing a word is not the same as

articulate
(verb/adjective)

Say it!
ar-tic-ul-ate

Spell it!
articulate

Pronunciation

Recognition

Definition

Know it! *It's a bit like... speaking clearly*

FIGURE 2.4 'Say It, Spell It, Know It' designed by Tom Pinkstone and David Didau

being able to use it. If students are confident they can explain the word, they should be given the opportunity to do so. Then teachers should go through a process we call Say It, Spell It, Know It (see Figure 2.4). Whenever students are asked to retrieve the word or its definition it's worth asking them to rate their familiarity again. Ideally, over time, all students will become more confident they can explain.

The 'Say It' phase of teaching simply requires the teacher to model the word's pronunciation by segmenting the syllables and then getting the class to repeat it back as a choral response: '1, 2, 3, say after me...' The idea here is that speech is particularly 'cognitively sticky' and that if students have not just heard the word pronounced correctly but also said it themselves, they are much more likely to remember it.[21] **NB**. Students must *not* be taught to write the phonetic pronunciation.*

The 'Spell It' phase of instruction involves the teacher breaking down the word into morphemes, running over how each is spelt and then removing the word from the board and asking students to re-code the sounds into letters. By ensuring students are familiar with both the pronunciation and the spelling, we increase the probability that

they will recognise a word the next time they see or hear it.

Finally, the 'Know It' phase focuses on synonyms rather than definitions. Often, dictionary definitions are unhelpfully opaque and leave students more confused than before. By giving a synonym in everyday language and employing the phrase 'it's a bit like...' we build a bridge between familiar and unfamiliar vocabulary. Most Tier 2 words have straightforward Tier 1 synonyms and so, with a bit of thought, this is easy to do on the fly: *'benevolent' is a bit like 'kind'*. When students ask, as will inevitably happen, 'Why didn't they just say "kind" then?' we can say, 'Because they're not quite the same, benevolent is also a bit like "well-meaning" and is also usually used about someone in authority'.

Also, by teaching students the etymology of words and morphemes we unlock their ability to make connections between *this* word and *that*. If we deliberately teach students that 'plac' means to make calm or to please, but that the prefix 'im-' signals that the root word will take on the opposite meaning, then by adding the adjective suffix '-able' (meaning 'possible') we get an adjective meaning 'impossible to placate'.

As you can see in Figure 2.4, etymology and morphology play an important role in our approach to vocabulary. When students (and their teachers!) learn what the prefixes, roots and suffixes that make up words mean, new insights can be unlocked. One of our favourite examples is the term 'metaphor' – one of those words everyone recognises but often struggles to define. The literal meaning of metaphor – in both ancient and modern Greek – is to transport. There's something rather exquisite about the fact that lorries in modern Greece are still called *metaphores* from *meta* (between or among) and *phoros* (carrying or bearing). When we think about the metaphorical nature of language, metaphorically, meaning is transported from one 'place' to another. This has led us to the agreed definition of metaphor being: *The transfer of meaning from one domain to another, e.g., 'Time is money'.*†

Our work on improving reading fluency, inspired by training from Lexonik,[22] has underscored the

---

* You might think this is too obvious to require stating so explicitly. You'd be wrong.

† Etymonline.com is an invaluable resource in learning about the origins of words (there's also a free app!).

critical importance of morphology in vocabulary instruction. If we think of vocabulary acquisition as, essentially, building knowledge schema, we can begin to see that we can help students to create 'sticky' webs of interconnected meaning. Firstly, we need to understand that many multi-syllabic Tier 2 words can be broken down into their morphemes – in other words, we can decode words by breaking them into prefixes, suffixes and base words. Although this is covered in the primary curriculum, the emphasis there is more usually on spelling, rather than meaning. This is the second step: teaching students the most common meanings for the most common morphemes.

Here's a worked example. If a teacher wants to teach her Year 9 class that Heathcliff in *Wuthering Heights* can be described as 'intractable', she could simply teach them the definition and move on. But as we've seen, that would make confident recall and usage considerably less likely, particularly for those students with the poorest starting vocabularies. Instead, if the teacher spends five minutes breaking the word down: a prefix of 'in' (meaning 'not' in this example), a suffix of 'able' and a base of 'tract'.* Putting this all back together students can then understand that Heathcliff is 'un-pull-able' – a feature of his character that is instantly recognisable and which students can now express in a much more sophisticated way.

Further, once students can confidently recognise and recall 'tract', more useful and academic words can be added to their growing schema, such as abstraction, retraction or subtraction. Morphological knowledge goes far beyond the English classroom and we're beginning to explore how to share these 'coat-hanger' words with our colleagues across the Trust. If we teach a bank of bases that appear in multiple subjects – chrono, audi, tract, pend for example – then we can increase the chances of students being able to decode, understand and use Tier 2 vocabulary fluently.

Subject terminology needs to be dealt with differently. Here, we suggest that students are taught to memorise agreed definitions using the process set out in section 2.6. Often, students will have a vague understanding of words like metaphor, theme or alliteration, but when pressed will often say something like, 'I know what it means but I don't know how to explain it'. By ensuring students (and teachers) have fingertips recall of an agreed definition, they are liberated. They learn exactly what these arcane sounding words mean and, over time, this frees them up to use them with increased clarity and precision.[†]

The other class of vocabulary we specify is what the English department at Ormiston Horizon Academy have called **excellent epithets**. Part of our approach to academic writing is to pre-teach a set of appositives and adjectives for major characters or themes in a text. So, for instance, in the King James Bible module in Year 8, students will learn the following excellent epithets for King David:

David – Appositives: shepherd boy, warrior, King of Israel

- **Audacious** (adj) Willing to take bold risks; audacity (n)
- **Humble** (adj) Having a modest sense of your importance; humility (n)
- **Composed** (adj): Able to keep your feelings under control; calm composedness (n)

The adjectives are chosen to reflect different aspects of a character or theme and (as will become clear in section 2.5) there is a focus on students being able to transform words across word class, particularly from adjective to noun. Very often, if students only learn one form of a word, their writing – and thinking – is held back. If you only know 'patriarchy' and are unfamiliar with 'patriarchal', you end up torturing a sentence to make the version of the word you know fit.

---

* Students in rural parts of the country find 'tract' a very sticky word since it comes from the Latin for 'pull' and the ubiquitous tractors are therefore, quite simply and delightfully, 'pullers'.

† Appendix 1 has a glossary of agreed definitions for all the subject terminology students will encounter in the OAT curriculum.

Epithets are defined as adjectives or phrases which express a quality, or an attribute regarded as characteristic of the person or thing mentioned.

At Ormiston Horizon Academy, we have implemented a strategy we call **excellent epithets** at Key Stage 4 with the aim of improving students' Tier 2 vocabulary, deepening students' understanding of literary characters' personal attributes, improving students' retention of core knowledge and with a view to improving students' independent ability to write academic essays.

Initially, we decided on three ambitious adjectives which we felt most appropriately described the portrayal of each character in the GCSE Literature texts that we teach: *Macbeth*, *A Christmas Carol* and *An Inspector Calls*.

Students use the vocabulary items in Figure 2.5 in all relevant lessons. We discuss what each epithet means and practise saying them aloud, through choral rehearsal, then practise using them correctly in sentences. We then discuss *how* the characters portray these attributes within the texts, using evidence to support these ideas.

Each epithet is specifically chosen to show how the characters develop throughout the course of the novella or play. For example, Eric in *An Inspector Calls* is initially depicted as **juvenile** when through his reckless, volatile behaviour towards Daisy Renton he forces himself upon her in a drunken stupor; however, as the play develops, Priestley later depicts Eric as a **sagacious** individual when he sees the errors of his ways and becomes a **reformed**, philanthropic member of society.

Essentially, the three epithets form a character arc: they enable students to track the development of characterisation and, subsequently, write academic essays to show an in-depth understanding of how each character progresses (or remains static) as the narrative transitions from exposition to denouement.

This strategy has been implemented successfully here at Horizon and has had a significantly positive impact on our GCSE Literature outcomes. As a result, we have now also implemented this strategy into all of our Key Stage 3 schemes of learning.

Sophie Gardner, Director of Communications Faculty, Ormiston Horizon Academy

An Inspector Calls	Birling Sycophantic Obdurate Pompous	Mrs Birling Condescending Haughty Unrepentant	Gerald Croft Manipulative Sanguine Urbane	Eric Privileged Penitent Reckless	Sheila Petulant Perceptive Altruistic	Inspector Omniscient Compelling Vehement	Eva Smith Diligent Victimised Audacious
A Christmas Carol	Scrooge Misanthropic Curmudgeonly Redeemed	Marley Prophetic Tortured Repentant	Ghost of Christmas Past Commanding Ageless Luminous	Ghost of Christmas Present Avuncular Jocund Sincere	Ghost of Christmas Yet to Come Austere Ominous Taciturn	Fred Benevolent Amiable Enthusiastic	Cratchits Impoverished Grateful Estimable
Macbeth	Macbeth Tyrannical Fatalistic Duplicitous	Lady Macbeth Ruthless Domineering Vulnerable	Banquo Loyal Cynical Forthright	Macduff Virtuous Rancorous Suspicious	The Witches Malevolent Duplicitous Oracular	Duncan Naïve Patrician Credulous	Malcolm Pious Patriotic Just

FIGURE 2.5 Excellent epithets at Ormiston Horizon Academy

We can also use excellent epithets to talk about tone. Rather than expecting students to be able to grasp a concept as nebulous as tone independently, we teach specific vocabulary items that allow students to talk about the tones writers employ:

- *Satirical* – mocking, sarcastic
- *Provocative* – designed to cause a strong reaction, often anger
- *Indignant* – showing anger at injustice or unfairness
- *Admonishing* – warning or telling off
- *Nostalgic* – remembering the 'good old days'

- *Melancholic* – expressing sadness or loss
- *Irreverent* – not showing respect, not taking something seriously
- *Assertive* – having confident and forceful opinions
- *Hyperbolic* – exaggeration
- *Celebratory* – expressing pride or happiness
- *Critical* – showing disapproval

These epithets are by no means exhaustive but if students learn and use words in this list to try to describe the tone of a text they will have a much clearer idea of how to talk about the writer's intentions and the effects they attempt to produce.

2.8 COUCH TO 5K WRITING

Our approach to teaching writing should be more like the exercise programme, with easy to achieve goals leading to long-term success.

Writing – the process of making marks to express ideas – is a verb, an action, and as such is not nearly so amenable to study in the way we normally approach it as we would wish.

The only way we can teach children to acquire skill is to try to break the skill in question down into the knowledge it is composed of, teach that, and then get students to practise applying that knowledge in an increasing range of contexts. This being the case, it ought to be obvious that teaching writing can never be a 'once and done' operation. Whilst the required knowledge of how to write could, conceivably, be taught just once, the practice required to acquire any degree of skill is a continuous process. What this suggests is that the teaching of writing might best be served by a 'little and often approach'.

How we tend to go about asking students to write is often counter-productive. Daisy Christodoulou's observation that effective practice tends not to resemble the final performance is well rehearsed; her metaphor of the kind of training required to run a marathon is a useful way to think about writing instruction.[23] But, as most of us never run marathons, maybe it's a more useful analogy to think in terms of getting students to write the equivalent of a five-kilometre run.

As you're probably well aware, the NHS's Couch to 5K (C25K) programme kicks off by interspersing periods of walking with 60 second runs. For anyone unused to running, 60 seconds is a challenge, but – for the most part – an achievable one. We are motivated by our success to believe that running for 90 seconds is also achievable and that, in time and with practice, we'll be able to run for five kilometres if we stick to the programme. Anyone who has used the C25K app will probably remember some of the useful nuggets of running instruction: advice on keeping your head still, or how to use your arms, how to breathe, which anyone can immediately apply and see improvements.

But imagine if the C25K exercise programme took a similar approach to the way we tend to teach writing. Imagine if, on downloading the app, you were expected to run five kilometres straight away. What would you do? The vast majority of us would quit immediately. This is precisely what happens to far too many students faced with the expectation to complete extended writing tasks. And those who do persevere rarely acquire the fluency and freedom that we, their teachers, seem to find so effortless.

The notion of C25k writing is simple: we aim to make students technically proficient, through explicitly teaching how to master a range of written styles and to practise applying this knowledge to the point where it becomes ingrained. To achieve this aim, we start by concentrating on sentence-level mastery. If students can write great sentences, constructing extended pieces of writing is easy. If they can't, then no amount of text-level instruction will have much impact. If students understand how sentences are built and if they practise writing them again and again, then inflexible knowledge is polished into hard-won skill and can be applied to whatever writing opportunities they encounter.

Many secondary teachers mistakenly believe that Year 6 students can write independently at length, when in fact, lots of writing in KS2 is very carefully taught over a number of weeks. C25k writing builds very clearly on this practice and helps to bridge what Jane Considine calls 'the chasm of silent writing'.[24] This chasm, where teachers provide lots of input at the start of the lesson (word lists, mind maps, sentence prompts etc.) and then students are expected to write a complete piece in silence with little direction as to what kind of sentences to write etc., is exactly the kind of gap we want to avoid students falling into.

Along with the focus on **gapless instruction** (section 2.2) and **success before struggle** (section 2.3) the principles of C25k writing are:

1. **Less for longer**: students are routinely rushed into extended writing before they have mastered the sentence. Our approach is focused on sentence-level mastery which we repeat not until students can write well, but until they can no longer write badly.

2. **Practice makes permanent**: what we repeatedly do we get good at. This comes with a downside: if students practise doing the wrong things, they get better at writing badly. Many writing errors are caused not by a lack of knowledge but are due to bad habits. We recommend that students

are held to account for ensuring that all errors are corrected, and feedback is requested where there is uncertainty.

Our C25k writing strategy is divided into two main strands: analytical writing (the deconstructed essay) and transactional/descriptive writing (slow writing).

2.8.1 The deconstructed essay

As with a deconstructed menu item, the idea is to make all the ingredients of an academic essay visible to students.

Our approach to analytical writing is based on a method used at St Martin's Catholic Academy in Leicestershire. This is a school outside OAT which we visited because it achieves a positive progress score of over 1.0 for GCSE English Language and we wanted to find out how. As with all great schools, there are always too many variables to pin down success to any one strategy, but one of the approaches that impressed us was what Head of English, Liz Smart, referred to as 'the deconstructed essay'.

If you were to order, say, a deconstructed burger from a fancy restaurant you'd have the bun, meat, relish etc. all served separately; it is up to the patron to reconstruct the ingredients into a recognisable burger. The deconstructed essay is similar. Each of the elements of an analytical essay has been isolated into a discrete sentence which can be taught and practised to the point of mastery. These sentences have been distributed over the KS3 curriculum so that students are introduced to three analytic sentence types per year.

Year 7

- Sentence 1: Construct personal viewpoints in the form of thesis statements
- Sentence 3: Use the thesis statement to create topic sentences
- Sentence 4: Select and embed relevant textual detail

These sentences should be taught explicitly during Year 7 and practised to the point of mastery.

Sentence 1. Construct personal viewpoints in the form of thesis statements		
Teach	**Model**	**Write**
One sentence to answer the question with two different viewpoints	Think of the surface meaning and then a deeper meaning which is less obvious and more interesting. (*At first glance*)	At first glance [the text] is about _____, but at a deeper level _____.
Begin with a subordinating conjunction: *Whereas, Despite, Although, At first glance, Because, As, Unless* etc.	Acknowledge two or more contrasting interpretations (*Although, Despite, Whereas*)	Although [the text] appears to be about _____, it is also referring to _____.
Use a comma to **pivot** between viewpoints	Acknowledge a causal link between two ideas (*Because*)	Because [first idea], [second idea.]
Use at least three adjectives (and appositives)	Select adjectives + appositives from the **excellent epithets**.	Despite [character + epithet], they can also be seen as [character + epithet].

Sentence 1: Construct personal view points in the form of thesis statements

The thesis statement is the most important part of the deconstructed essay as it not only teaches students to find a way into whatever analysis they're conducting, it also – if written properly – forms the basis for the rest of the essay. As such it forms a crucial part of students' experience of Year 7. The ambition should be for students to practise writing thesis statements so frequently that the process becomes second nature.

We recommend that time and effort is spent drilling students in the definitions of the key grammatical terms: subordinating conjunction (a word that introduces a subordinate clause), subordinate clause (a clause that forms part of and is dependent on a main clause) and main clause (a clause that can form a complete sentence). The idea is that these terms will be used so frequently that eventually students will possess fingertips knowledge of both their definition and application. This will make teaching much more efficient as not only will you be using precise definitions, you will not have to constantly explain meanings as students become more familiar with them.

The purpose of formalising the structure of a thesis statement in this way is that it forces students to write a sentence that contains different perspectives with the comma acting as the pivot or hinge between them. It's important to note that different subordinating conjunctions produce different thesis statements. We start students off by using 'Although', 'Despite' and 'Whereas' before later moving on to 'Because', 'As' and 'Since' (cause and effect) and then 'Once', 'When', 'While', 'After' and 'Before' (relationships). Mastering each of these will provide students with a sophisticated way into any essay question.

'Excellent epithets' become a key part of integrating ambitious vocabulary into essay writing. Teachers are encouraged to introduce their own epithets whenever appropriate, but we have specified a range in each module specifically to be used with thesis statements. The essential teaching point is to show students how to group epithets with similar meanings on the same side of the comma. For instance, if the question students are answering is, '*How is Antony presented in Act 3 scene 1 of Julius Caesar?*' the first step is to consult Antony's epithets:

Mark Antony – Appositives: master orator, friend of Caesar, general, politician

- **Staunch** (adj) very loyal; staunchness (n)
- **Manipulative** (adj) able to control or influence others; manipulativeness (n); manipulate (v)
- **Eloquent** (adv) skilled at speaking; eloquence (n)
- **Ambitious** (adj) having a strong desire and determination to succeed; ambition (n)

'Staunch' and 'eloquent' are both positive adjectives, whereas 'manipulative' is unambiguously negative. 'Ambitious' could fit in either group depending on the context. So, when we come to write our thesis statement, we need to make sure that we use at least one positive epithet and at least one ambiguous or negative epithet. Like so: *Although Antony is **eloquent**, he is also presented as **manipulative**.* Or, even better, we could use more than one epithet on one side of the comma: *Although he is presented as **devious** and **manipulative**, we also see that Antony is a **staunch** supporter of Caesar and an **eloquent** speaker.* Over time, students will be shown how to construct increasingly sophisticated statements. But, once they are confidently using excellent epithets, students are ready to write topic sentences.

Sentence 2 – 'Focus on the effects of the whole text and controlling ideas' – is best taught later on (we have recommended that it be given particular attention in Year 8). However, when students come to reconstruct the notion of controlling ideas, they

should be writing this sentence immediately after their thesis statement. (See page 36.)

Sentence 3. Use the thesis statement to create topic sentences		
Teach	**Model**	**Write**
Each epithet will become the main point of a topic sentence. Adjectives must be transformed into noun phrases, e.g., implacable becomes implacability. Noun phrase must be followed by a verb. The rest of the sentence must link to the question being answered.	Think about the epithets used in the thesis statement to consider how each can be turned into a noun to be explored in a separate topic sentence. Consider how each noun phrase links to the question being answered.	[character, theme, or writer] + [change adjective to noun] + [verb] + [link back to question].

Sentence 3: Use the thesis statement to create topic sentences

A topic sentence depends on a well-constructed thesis statement. The idea is that students should be able to write a topic sentence for every one of the epithets they have used in their thesis statement. If we take our example above, *Although he is presented as **devious** and **manipulative**, we also see that Antony is a **staunch** supporter of Caesar and an **eloquent** speaker*, we can now write linked topic sentences. Our first step is to turn the adjectives in our epithets into nouns:

- Manipulative = manipulation (and deviousness)
- Staunch = staunchness (or loyalty)
- Eloquent = eloquence

This allows us to construct noun phrases that will be the subjects of our topic sentences. For example:

- Antony's manipulation of the crowd
- The staunchness Antony displays in Caesar's defence
- His eloquence as a speaker

To these noun phrases we also have to add a verb and then a connection back to the question, in this case, *How is Antony presented in Act 3 scene 1 of Julius Caesar?*

Noun phrase	Verb	Link to question
Antony's manipulation of the crowd	shows	his skill and ruthlessness at getting what he wants.
The staunchness Antony displays in Caesar's defence	indicates	that Shakespeare wants us to see Antony's virtues as well as his faults.
His eloquence as a speaker	makes	Antony a very attractive and compelling character.

Writing a good topic sentence tends to take more practice than writing thesis statements but, with sufficient repetition, students will master them. And once they're mastered, these two sentence types have the flexibility to be the backbone of all analytical writing.

Sentence 4. Select and embed relevant textual detail		
Teach	**Model**	**Write**
Select evidence that relates to the point being made in topic sentences. Use short, precise parts of the text (not whole lines). Place the quote within a sentence. Place the quote inside single quotation marks. Reference what the quote is suggesting.	Select a part of the text which is interesting and that you'll have something that isn't obvious to say about it. Embed 'quotations' into sentences. Use a comma before beginning a quotation.	The writer refers to _____ as, '_____' and '_____'. The writer compares _____ to, '_____'. When the text states, '_____' it reminds the reader of _____. [Character] says, '_____,' conveying _____. [Writer] repeats, '_____', because _____.

Sentence 4: Select and embed relevant textual detail

The difficulty with Sentence 4 is that it requires students to do two distinct things: 1) to select evidence from the text they have been studying, and 2) to use that evidence to write a sentence which provides support for the topic sentences they have written. Arguably, selection is much harder for students to master than embedding.

The key here is to model finding textual evidence that links to epithets and allow students time to practice this as a discrete skill. Let's take one of our example topic sentences above: *His eloquence as a speaker makes Antony a very attractive and compelling character.* We now have to model finding evidence from Act 3 scene 2 of *Julius Caesar* not just of Antony being eloquent, but also where we like him, where we respond positively to him doing so. For instance, maybe we admire the irony contained within these lines:

> I am no orator, as Brutus is,
> But, as you know me all, a plain blunt man
> That love my friend

But, although this is maybe a clever concealment of his rhetorical skill, it's not really eloquence in the truest sense. So we model discarding this line in favour of another, such as Anthony's first use of the word 'honourable':

> Brutus is an honourable man;
> So are they all, all honourable men

Here we can see him begin to undermine the concept of honour which, through repetition, Anthony will twist to make it seem base and self-serving and so get the crowd ready to mutiny against Brutus and the conspirators.

It is in modelling this process of selection, exploration, rejection and re-selection that students will come to see what they should notice and how they should bring what they have noticed to light.

Year 8

- Sentence 2: Focus on the effects of the whole text and controlling ideas
- Sentence 5: Analyse a writer's use of language, structure and form
- Sentence 6: Evaluate the writer's intent

Each of these sentences should be taught explicitly during Year 8 and practised to the point of mastery. At the same time, Sentences 1, 3 and 4 should be integrated and practised alongside the new essay sentences.

Sentence 2. Focus on the effects of the whole text and controlling ideas		
Teach	**Model**	**Write**
Recall the controlling ideas/themes/intentions explored in the text. Think about how this extract/question addresses these themes and ideas. Consider whether this is consistent throughout the entire text. This sentence comes second in the essay writing sequence. It should be seen as part of the essay's introduction.	What have you been taught about this text? Or, what themes, ideas can you remember? What is it about the extract that makes you think this? How is this similar/different to other texts you've studied, or other parts of *this* text? How do ideas/themes change or develop?	[Text] **explores** the idea/theme of _____. [Extract] exemplifies / reinforces/amplifies the theme of _____. [Writer] challenges/ contradicts ideas about _____.

Sentence 2: Focus on the effects of the whole text and controlling ideas

As stated above, we recommend that the controlling idea sentence – Sentence 2 – is taught out of sequence. When we first started putting the deconstructed essay together, we didn't have a controlling idea sentence. It was only through reading students' work and seeing that some students were writing this kind of thing without having been explicitly taught to do so that we realised we'd left a gap in our instructional sequence.

The reason we leave the teaching of Sentence 2 until Year 8 is because the thesis statement and topic sentence fit so neatly together; once students have got the hang of using excellent epithets, their ability to write topic sentences flows fairly easily. Including this 'big idea' sentence in between seems to muddy the waters unhelpfully. However, students need to be taught that this sentence must come directly after the thesis statement.

Sentence 5. Analyse a writer's use of language, structure and form		
Teach	**Model**	**Write**
Use terminology accurately. Think about *effect* not meaning.	What is the writer trying to achieve in this text? Zoom in: why might the writer have used this specific word or phrase? Is it part of a pattern of similar words? What *effect* does it create? Zoom out: do your ideas make sense *in this context?*	This [literary device] **conveys** a sense of _____. [Writer] uses [device] to **depict/ portray/suggest** _____. Furthermore, the word, '_____' **evokes** an image/ atmosphere/feeling of _____.

Sentence 5: Analyse a writer's use of language, structure and form

By analysing what some students seem able to do implicitly, we were able to work out what we might need to teach explicitly. Essentially, they need to zoom out from the laser focus of the thesis statement to consider the text as a whole: *what are the big ideas the writer wants us to think about?* The thesis statement plus controlling idea make for a very purposeful introduction to an essay.

The big issue with students' analysis is that they can have an unfortunate tendency to reel off potential meanings of words without properly considering the effects a writer might be trying to achieve. Students need to be explicitly taught to zoom in on individual words and phrases to consider their meanings, but also to zoom out to think about whether their ideas fit in *this* specific context. For instance, imagine students are asked to analyse the opening lines of Shakespeare's Sonnet 130:

My mistress' eyes are nothing like the sun;
Coral is far more red than her lips' red

Some students will seize on a word like 'coral', start thinking about tropical fish and write something like, *the word 'coral' implies that the woman is like an exotic tropical fish.* This would obviously be a dangerous misreading of the poem. To mitigate against this tendency, we need to remind students to zoom out, to think again about the big picture they arrived at for their controlling idea, before they commit to a piece of wrong-headed analysis. So, if they remind themselves of the controlling ideas in the whole text – whether it's a poem or a novel – they can then zoom in with much greater focus and clarity.

Sentence 6. Evaluate the writer's intent		
Teach	**Model**	**Write**
Use of adverb opener with a comma to follow. Reference to theme or literary concept. Teach a range of potential literary intents, e.g., *to criticise, to expose, to condemn, to celebrate or to convince.*	Consider why the writer might have written the text. What message might they want the reader to think about?	**Thus**, [writer] is drawing the reader's attention to _____. **Hence**, [writer] is challenging ideas about _____. **Consequently**, [writer] is highlighting _____.

Sentence 6: Evaluate the writer's intent

To ensure the evaluation sentence flows smoothly from the analysis sentence, we ask students to begin with an adverb that shows they are referring to their analysis when trying to work out the writer's intentions. If they have already been through the 'zooming out' process described above, then writing this sentence should be straightforward. We suggest that students refer to one of the themes of the text when making their evaluation. This requires that they understand the difference between theme (the concept that a writer will indirectly explore ideas) and themes (the specific ideas which a writer may have chosen to explore). It's worth reading through section 2.11 to get a sense of how tenor and vehicle can help students understand that theme is a kind of backwards metaphor.

We also suggest teaching a range of generic intentions that a writer might have:

- To evoke pity or sadness
- To create tension and suspense
- To expose the problems in society
- To celebrate something unique
- To explore the problems in human relationships
- To explore a conflict

Once students have learned that all texts are intentional and that these purposes can be applied to pretty much any text, then the actual process of writing evaluatively about a writer's intentions becomes much more straightforward.

Year 9

- Sentence 7: Compare texts in relation to literary concepts, ideas and methods
- Sentence 8: Linking to context
- Sentence 9: Extend: recognising different arguments

Each of these sentences should be taught explicitly during Year 9 and practised to the point of mastery. All other six sentences should continue to be integrated and practised alongside the new deconstructed essay sentences until the whole thing can be reconstructed.

Sentence 7. Compare texts in relation to literary concepts, ideas and methods		
Teach	**Model**	**Write**
Identify a clear similarity or difference between the two poems. Use comparative discourse markers. Use commas after comparative discourse markers (apart from 'whereas'). Reference to theme or literary concept.	Think of interesting similarities and differences in relation to ideas, concepts or methods between the novels studied. *Humour is equally significant in both texts. Nonetheless, in 'Evelina' Burney directs this towards younger men who think too highly of themselves, whereas in 'Pride and Prejudice' Austen directs it to marriage itself, where both men and women are seen to be equally at fault.*	Both texts explore the concept of _____. _____ is equally significant in both texts. In [*Julius Caesar*] it is conveyed through _____, **whereas** in [MLK's speech] it is portrayed as _____. **Conversely**, in [*Julius Caesar*, Shakespeare] presents [focus of the question] as _____. **Similarly**, in [*Paradise Lost*, Milton] _____. **Likewise**, in [text] _____.

Sentence 7: Compare texts in relation to literary concepts, ideas and methods

Comparison is something we seem to be hardwired to do. We judge how good a bottle of wine is by comparing it to other bottles of wine we've drunk. We decide that this TV programme is better or worse than other TV programmes, and we're often prompted to change our assessment of children's

FIGURE 2.6 Comparing a football and a rugby ball

work when we realise the marks we've given it are too high or low compared to the marks we've awarded other essays.

Whenever we teach students to compare texts, we should begin by showing them how easy it is to compare. For instance, what do the two objects in Figure 2.6 have in common?

And what are the differences? Easy, isn't it? Judgements are formed by pointing out similarities and differences.

After this straightforward start, ask for a couple of emotionally robust volunteers and ask the class to compare them. After the nervous giggling and the blindingly obvious are out of the way, their apparently innate ability to compare reveals layers of detail which might easily have gone overlooked when analysing in isolation. When we see things side by side sometimes qualities of which we were previously unaware are illuminated.

Then we move on to carefully selected texts. Poems are a good place to start as they're short and can be easily viewed side by side. We recommend a brace of sonnets as they'll have lots of immediately obvious similarities as well as differences.

Students should find it simple to spot similarities in terms of form, theme and language. This done, looking for differences becomes much more focused and interesting. With a modest amount of modelling and scaffolding, students are well on the way to writing a comparative essay. It certainly pays to explicitly teach students to use a range of discourse markers to signpost their comparisons and contrasts, but what really differentiates between students is how well they know the texts they are comparing and how skilled they are at all the other assessment objectives.

Writing literary essays might be hard, but comparison is easy (or, at least, easier than writing about only a single text).

Sentence 8. Linking to context		
Teach	**Model**	**Write**
Identify a relevant contextual point. Use adverbial time phrases. Use commas after the time phrase. Link to writer/text using 'and' or 'but'. Reference to writer's intent and themes.	Be selective in your use of context: does it add to your overall argument? *At the time, [women were expected to behave according to very strict social rules] and [Burney] shows [the pressure young women were under socially and morally].*	**At the time,** [relevant context] and [writer] depicts [reference to text]. **Contextually,** people were very concerned about [specific social rule], and [writer] employs [technique] to show [writer's intent related to social rule]. **In the mid-18th century,** [relevant context] writers like [named writer] endeavoured to convey [writer's intention].

Sentence 8: Linking to context

The context sentence needs a lot of practice to be done effectively. All too often, students regurgitate rote-learned nuggets of historical or autobiographical knowledge which have little or nothing to do with the argument they have been constructing. Students know they ought to include the contextual knowledge they've learned, but often they do little more than make sweeping and irrelevant assertions. Context (literally, 'with text') must always be deployed in the service of textual knowledge.

Students need to recall the controlling ideas they should have written in Sentence 2 and think carefully what extra-textual information they might have that helps to make this point more clearly.

Sentence 9. Extend: recognising different arguments		
Teach	**Model**	**Write**
Identify an opposing point that you can refute/contradict. Use subordinating conjunctions. Use commas after clauses which start with subordinating conjunctions Reference to theme or literary concept	Be sure to choose an opposing point that you are sure you can argue against. Make your sentence a conversation (They say, I say) *Even though it is possible to argue that [Fielding presents a more polished novel than Richardson], [Pamela] is still [a compelling and persuasive story].*	**Even though it is possible to argue that** [opposing point], it is still the case that [your point]. **Although it may be suggested that...** **Whilst it could be argued that...** While [writer] may seem to saying [opposing idea], an alternative interpretation might be...

Sentence 9: Extend: recognising different arguments

The 'Extend' sentence is the culmination of the arguments that students will have been building towards. It is an opportunity to consider alternative interpretations and demonstrate flexibility of thinking. As such, tentative language is essential.

What students need to be taught is that they can use arguments they either disagree with or are not compelled by to strengthen their own thesis. This is the 'They say / I say' model explored by Gerald Graff and Cathy Birkenstein in their book of the same name (2018), and it helps students to show that their ideas are part of a bigger conversation: in responding to what 'they say' we can more clearly articulate what it is that *we* think.

Students can learn to 'listen' to the writers of the texts they study by viewing texts as conversations. By summarising a writer's point of view, we are more likely to notice the nuance of their arguments. And, by extracting more, we will better develop our own responses and interpretations, both at the level of literature (Shakespeare says / but I say) and at the level of criticism. By 'arguing' with the writers they study, by thinking about what they read and responding with 'yes, but…', students embark on the path to mastery of the discipline of English.

*

Only after students have been taught and practised each of these deconstructed essay sentences should they be assessed on their ability to write an essay. The slow build over three years should allow students time to practise and master the structures as they go, so that by the time they finish KS3 and embark on their KS4 programme of study they should be fluent and assured critical writers.

2.8.2 Slow writing

By explicitly teaching a range of sentence structures and prompting students to use them to create particular effects in short writing tasks we can provide them with the metacognitive tools to be better writers.

The second strand of C25k writing is designed to prepare students to compose transactional and creative writing. The idea stems from a blog post David first published in 2011.

He claims to have first come up with the idea when teaching an intervention class of Year 11

C/D borderline boys in about 2008. He observes, 'Broadly speaking they were willing, but no matter what I tried the writing they produced was leaden, plodding stuff. I gave them all kinds of outlandish and creative prompts which they would dead-bat and produce yet another dreary yawnfest. Needless to say, we were all getting a bit irritated with each other. Out of sheer frustration I decided to give them explicit instructions on how to write a text sentence by sentence'. [25]

Sort of like this:

- Your first sentence must be a question.
- Your second sentence must contain only three words.
- Your third sentence must contain a semi-colon.
- Your fourth sentence will start with an adverb.
- Your fifth sentence will be 22 words exactly.

Much to his surprise not only did they enjoy the process, but the quality of their writing improved immediately and dramatically.

Expert writers think not just about *what* they write, but about *how* they write it. We have the ability to metacognitively engage with our writing and make decisions about what is likely to sound best. Often, we do this at a level beneath consciousness; the questions we ask about our writing are automatic and so well stored in long-term memory that often we're not really aware of what we're doing.

But novice writers don't have this ability. They tend to default to the time-worn narratives they have used before and shape what they know in the simplest most straightforward way they can. As they write they're so busy thinking about what to write that there's little space in working memory to consider how it might be written. Giving pupils sentence prompts frees up working memory so they can shape what they know in a more sophisticated way. These sentence types are constraints which provide pupils with the metacognitive prompts for thinking about what they know and allow them to be creative.

And if we are relentless about asking pupils to practise using a range of sentence structures it eventually becomes permanent. The structures transfer to long-term memory, leaving students' fragile working memories free to think about the content of their writing with greater depth and sophistication.

Although our curriculum specifies a huge amount of sentence-level work, we don't waste any time teaching the difference between simple, compound and complex sentences. This is, for the most part, fairly useless knowledge that will have little or no impact on improving writing. Instead, we have again selected 30 different creative writing sentence structures – some of which are simple, some compound and many complex – and get students to see how they make meaning.

Year 7
1. Comma Sandwich
2. More, More, More / Less, Less, Less Sentence
3. Comparative, More, More
4. Semi-Colon Split
5. Colon Clarification
6. Three Verb Sentence
7. Not, Nor, Nor Sentence
8. Prepositional Push Off
9. Never Did Than
10. The Writer's Aside

Year 8
11. The So, So, Sentence
12. The Big Because
13. But None More Than
14. Past Participle Start
15. Whoever/Whenever/ Whichever
16. Adjective Attack
17. End Loaded Sentence
18. Present Participle Start
19. The As If Pivot
20. The As If Avalanche

Year 9
21. Three Adjective Punch
22. Almost, Almost, When
23. Repeat and Reload
24. Let Loose Sentence
25. Simile Start
26. Or & Or Sentence
27. Without Without
28. Adverb Snap
29. Double Adverb Snap
30. Last Word, First Word

These sentence structures are specified in the curriculum so that ten sentences are taught and practised per year. These are all embedded into modules so that not only are students explicitly taught how to write each sentence type, they are also asked to write about the content they are studying using these sentences.

We've chosen to name each sentence structure in an effort to make them more memorable. Once students have been taught and have practised, say, the Adjective Attack, teachers are able to simply ask them to write another Adjective Attack sentence about whatever it is they are studying.

Each curriculum module specifies which sentences should be taught and which should be practised. For example, here is the slow writing page from the Comedy Teacher Guide:

Slow writing page from the Story of Comedy Teacher Guide

The C25k approach to descriptive/transactional writing is covered in the explicit teaching of the 30 creative sentence types. In this module, the sentence types that need to be explicitly taught are:

17. End Loaded Sentence: After having walked for several hours, getting more and more lost, only losing my way again and again, <u>the choice of paths filled me with dread</u>.

18. Present participle start (–ing): <u>Having</u> no possibility of getting back to where I came from, the way ahead seemed suddenly less daunting.

Students need to practise using these sentence types to the point of mastery. Previously taught sentence types that will need regular recapping and practice are:

1. Comma Sandwich
2. More, More, More Sentence / Less, Less, Less
3. Comparative, More, More Sentence
4. Semi-Colon Split
5. Colon Clarification
6. Three Verb Sentence
7. Not, Nor, Nor Sentence
8. Prepositional Push Off
9. Never Did Than
10. The Writer's Aside
11. The So, So, Sentence
12. The Big Because
13. But None More Than Sentence
14. Past Participle Start (–ed)
15. Whoever/ Whenever/ Whichever
16. Adjective Attack

Students need regular practice of using curriculum content to produce slow writing responses. For example, after students have looked at the scene in *As You Like It* between Phebe and Silvius where she makes it clear she doesn't return his feelings, there is an opportunity for a slow writing exercise which should include the sentences which have been taught. The slow writing prompt could be as follows:

Imagine you are either Phebe or Silvius and write about how you feel after Act 3 scene 5.

1. End Loaded Sentence
2. The Big Because
3. The Writer's Aside
4. Present Participle Start
5. Adjective Attack

Model

After listening to the drivelling idiot drone on about love this, beautiful that, I've had enough of both poetry and men to last a lifetime! Because I'm a woman, I'm supposed to swoon over tripe like that. When he started going on about 'fresh cheeks' and 'invisible wounds' – honestly, where does he get this rubbish? – I thought I'd throw up. Speaking for myself, I like a man who is practical and honest. Simpering and sappy, I just can't stand that milksop Silvius.

See Appendix 2 for examples of how to teach each of these sentence prompts.

*

We recommend the use of MWBs wherever possible during C25k writing for all the reasons discussed in section 2.5.

C25K Writing reflection at Ormiston Victory Academy

Globally, post-pandemic reflection on the loss of learning time within the classroom was something that we were all challenged/confronted with and had time to contemplate as we re-entered the classroom. I recall being asked at the time: *how do we catch students up on what they've missed?* One of the fundamentals for our academy, especially with our Key Stage 3 students, was simple – we needed to get them writing. Writing frequently and writing fluently. Therefore, checklists were soon introduced and the phrase *PEAL paragraph* soon became a frequent one that echoed within our classrooms. Within a week, the mere mention of the phrase was met with a chorus of groans.

However, whenever students were asked to write a PEAL paragraph, the same questions would come up again and again:

- What's the point I need to write down again?
- Can you just give me a quotation to use?
- What am I analysing? The verb?
- What's the question again?
- This is too long
- I'm stuck
- Can we do another model again? (Translation: can we copy yours?)

David Didau and Claire Woozley visited Victory in April 2021 and I was posed with one question: *How did I feel about doing a pilot project around writing?* It was time to get writing right! The metaphor for C25k writing is simple: it's a marathon and not a sprint. Students gradually build up success and resilience, with the long-term goal that students can write well, write independently and have the knowledge and skills to be able to write with confidence and success.

However, to implement it we had to change the ethos for both staff and students. Giving more curriculum time over to writing felt unnatural. How would we fit it all in? Knowledge recall, recap and misconceptions, reading and comprehension, contextual detail covered, planning, then giving ten minutes at the end of the lesson with the success criteria to allow students to reflect and write. On reflection, the likelihood of success here was slim. Writing takes time, good writing practice needs to be embedded; this all meant we needed to give more time in lessons to allow students to write less but write frequently. In short, C25k was, for us, about changing the mindset that students must write lots to be successful.

Students' engagement became clear within days – both staff and students had a common goal, a benchmark to reach: the construction of thesis statements, using a few basic items of knowledge such as using the subordinating conjunctions 'despite', 'although' and 'because' to allow students to reflect on their learning and construct a valid argument based on question prompts. Success was soon harnessed within the classroom, and for the first time in a long time, the sea of hands and bombardment of questions on how to start simply stopped. Silence, reflection and independent good writing practice became part of our daily diet. Of course, lots of modelling and discussion were essential to check for understanding, and the philosophy of 'practice makes permanent' became a helpful classroom mantra. The first cohort of students to experience the C25k approach to writing went on to achieve fantastic GCSE results in 2022.

Following the success of the initial pilot, we have adapted and embraced C25k within our curriculum. Consolidating the academic vocabulary that we wanted students to be using frequently and often has helped them construct their ideas. Teachers explicitly teaching the same terminology and using the same instructional sequence has helped ensure students develop the capacity to write frequently and fluently.

Rikki Cole, Assistant Principal for Key Stage 3 and Literacy, and Director of English, Ormiston Victory Academy

2.8.3 Grammar teaching

As you can probably see from the examples of both the analytical and creative strands of C25k writing, there are lots of opportunities for explicit grammar teaching. However, at no point do we recommend discrete grammar lessons. Our view is that grammar teaching is most effective when it is tied to curriculum content so that grammar knowledge and content knowledge are intertwined. The content of the curriculum must drive grammatical instruction, not the other way around. To put it another way, grammar becomes a tool for making meaning out of curriculum content.[26]

What this means in practice is that students are only taught the grammatical terms they need to make effective choices in writing about the texts they are reading. So, for instance, when exploring whether Odysseus is a good leader, students need to know how to begin a sentence with a subordinating conjunction and how to balance aspects of Odysseus's character between the subordinate and main clauses of the sentence. This *could* be achieved without teaching students the appropriate terminology but, seeing as they will be writing thesis statements for the next five years, it would be very inefficient. If you don't know what things are called, it's almost impossible to think about them.

This means that we specify teaching the grammatical metalanguage that will be most useful to students. Obviously the basic word classes: noun, verb, adjective and adverb, but also conjunction, preposition etc. When it comes to teaching the 30 creative sentence structures, there's a lot of 'stealth' grammar teaching. In our training videos (see appendix 2) we explain the grammatical knowledge teachers need to understand common mistakes and misconceptions and leave it to teachers to decide how much of this knowledge to share with students. You could argue that all grammatical knowledge is potentially useful, but curriculum time is finite. We specify the teaching of terms like 'noun phrase', 'appositive' and 'suffix' not because they are useful (although they are) but because we *use* them throughout our curriculum.

Students' ability to write with intent as well as to peel back the choices made by other writers is only sharpened by having access to labels. And if you're going to teach labels, it makes sense to teach the ones that have the most currency and to use agreed definitions. To repeat what was stated in section 1.6.5, students need enough grammatical knowledge to answer these three questions: 1) What choices are available? 2) Why is one choice preferable to another? and 3) What is the effect of the choice selected?[27]

2.9 READING FOR MEANING

The emphasis of English lessons – especially in KS3 – should be on reading for enjoyment and understanding rather than on analysing texts to death.

As discussed in section 1.10, we recommend that the majority of curriculum time is spent reading and that most of the time students spend reading should emphasise reading for meaning. This means it is essential that teachers do not treat the texts in our curriculum as they would a GCSE set text. **Annotating and analysing texts is a sure-fire way to derail the intentions of the curriculum.**

The texts we've selected are categorically not intended to be objects of analysis – they are the glue which hold curriculum concepts together and provide meaning.

According to a small-scale study conducted by Jo Westbrook and colleagues, 'just reading' can make a significant difference to students' standardised reading comprehension scores. Twenty English teachers were recruited to take part in the study with their normal curriculum replaced by reading two novels back-to-back over 12 weeks. The students were given a standardised reading assessment at the beginning of the trial and again 12 weeks later. Students made an average of 8.5 months' worth of progress, but amazingly, the rate of progress was *doubled* for the most disadvantaged students. What seemed to make the difference was listening to and engaging in cognitively demanding narratives.[28]

Although you may fear that depth is sacrificed by reading more widely, it's more than compensated for by the breadth of literary knowledge students will acquire. By reading that which we find most beautiful, stirring and profound – for its own sake, not (just) because of its cultural capital, not (just) because it expands our knowledge of the world and certainly not (just) because it's in the exam – students might learn to appreciate that, as the sociologist Frank Furedi puts it, 'reading – especially serious reading – is itself a culturally beneficial activity'.[29]

However, huge obstacles get in the way of students reading independently. Too many children will not read independently because they are not fluent decoders. This is through no fault of their own; they simply have not mastered something which teachers (and many students) take for granted. If you can't read fluently, the act of reading can produce an overwhelming cognitive burden. It makes sense why non-fluent readers might try to guess an unfamiliar word – or refuse to read it at all – rather than go to the trouble of trying to sound it out: haltingly sounding out words can be deeply humiliating, especially when everyone else seems to find it easy. If this is your experience of reading, you're likely to avoid it wherever possible.

It's well understood that reading confers all sorts of intellectual advantages.[30] Not only do you encounter more and varied vocabulary, you also learn about different times, places and ideas. All this enlarges our minds: the more you read, the more you will know and the more able you will become to think about an ever-broader range of ideas and contexts. Students who avoid reading will fall further and further behind.

We can overcome some of the disparity between fluent and non-fluent readers by reading aloud. Although this won't address the underlying problem, it will provide non-fluent readers with the cognitive advantages that stem from reading. This is one of the reasons why we recommend the texts in our KS3 curriculum are read rather than studied. Rather than torturing texts by analysing passages every few pages, we want students to enjoy the experience of engaging in great stories.

To this end, we encourage English teachers to spend a significant part of curriculum time reading aloud to their students. Hearing a skilled reader *perform* the words on the page, listening to them use punctuation and syntax to create meaning, getting a sense of the prosody of unfamiliar language, can be wonderful. Students are freed from the shackles of non-fluency and able to step into other times and places, see through other eyes and consider ideas beyond the scope of their experiences.

In her book *Reader, Come Home*, Marilyn Wolf suggests two distinct modes of reading: 'screen literacy' and 'print literacy'. Reading on screens encourages rapid consumption, to skim and scan for information. Print literacy, on the other hand, encourages a communion of minds, deep reflection, critical thinking, the making of analogies and the noticing of detail. How we read, Wolf argues, changes our brain.[31] What we repeatedly do is who we increasingly become. Over the past decade or so, we have all spent far more of our reading lives looking at screens and, on average, far less time curled up with a physical book. The skills of screen literacy have crowded out those of print literacy. For children who rarely if ever pick up books, the likelihood is that they never acquire the tools required for print literacy.

Does this matter? Reading print – particularly fiction – is a unique experience. Nowhere else do we engage so deeply with another mind; there is no other human activity that encourages the same slow, careful exchange of experiences. *Do we value this?* The urgency here is that if we don't use it we'll lose it. Wolf suggests that for adult readers who have fallen out of the habits of print literacy, spending 20 minutes a day over a two-week period can be enough to 're-wire' our brains with the circuitry required for deep reading, an experience we can confirm anecdotally. But what does it take to build this ability from scratch? Even more overwhelmingly, what do we do for the estimated 20% of children who leave primary school every year unable to read fluently enough to access an academic curriculum? How do we get these children to read deeply and independently? Although the process will require specialised and dedicated intervention, it also needs children to be regularly exposed to print.

This is the dilemma English teachers face: if we don't read aloud to students then we will ensure students will struggle to make meaning from the texts we read and that non-fluent readers fall ever further behind. If students *only* listen, they'll never acquire the familiarity with print they need to access exam papers, and the world of words beyond school. If we don't ask students to read print then they will never have the experiences required to develop print literacy. They need to see the patterns of written text, the shape of sentences, the effects of punctuation. For skilled readers this is mainly a question of exposure and determination.

Clearly, we need to both model reading aloud and scaffold students' ability to read independently. Intuitive as it sounds, asking children to 'follow along' as a teacher reads aloud is likely to backfire.[32] Few students read at a pace that will naturally match that of their teacher's read-aloud speed. Some children will want to block out the teacher's voice and read ahead, others will want to put down the book and just listen. Insisting that speeds are matched is likely to result in a split-attention effect where students are focused on what words are coming next rather than on meaning. Although they will give the *appearance* of reading along, they are likely to remember and comprehend less. So, what's the solution?

2.9.1 Echo reading

Whilst teachers reading aloud provides an excellent model of skilled reading it doesn't offer effective scaffolding to help students bridge the gap between non-fluent and fluent reading.

The question of how we can help students to improve at reading aloud is a vexing one. When non-fluent readers are asked to read aloud in class, we may think we are providing them with much-needed practice but in fact we will only be getting them to practise reading badly. As we discussed in the writing section, practising doing something badly only makes us worse. Added to that, there is the problem that a non-fluent reader will actually reduce the comprehension of all other students as they struggle to make sense of mispronunciations and mangled syntax.

All this is at its most frustrating when it comes to teaching drama. We know we need to involve students in performance in order to make a play come to life, but when we assign students roles, we are faced with the choice of only allowing already fluent readers to take part or allowing non-fluent readers to reduce any performance to a stilted, painful mess. The agony English teachers feel is most acute when reading Shakespeare. What we want to be a beautiful, scintillating experiencing of some of the finest writing in the language is destroyed by wooden, stumbling delivery and blank incomprehension. How on earth can we bring the Bard to vivid life?

We first became aware of a potential solution at Wodensborough Ormiston Academy in Wednesbury whilst watching English teacher Rhys Williams reading *The Tempest* with a low prior attaining Year 8 class. He was focusing on the moment in Act 3 scene 1 where Ferdinand and Miranda first begin flirting. What he did was to allocate lines to different members of the class that they would read aloud *after* listening to *him* reading them first, attempting to emulate his tone, emphasis and pronunciation. Although this meant the students were reading aloud with impressive fluency and sophistication, were they following the plot? Did they understand what the characters were expressing? A post-reading discussion made it clear they *did*. Students in the class talked about how much they enjoyed this way of reading the text: it gave them confidence to read aloud *and* helped them understand Shakespeare's meaning.

This approach to reading, called echo reading by Tim Rasinski,[33] isn't going to completely close the chasm between text and meaning, but it's a start. For students who have mastered the phonetic knowledge to decode fluently, this approach really could have the potential to move them from confusion to clarity. Over time, and as students' confidence grows, the space between the teacher's reading and the student's echo can grow; instead of a single line the teacher might read two lines, then three, a whole paragraph and so on. At the same time, students can be encouraged to interpret the text differently and inject their own ideas on emphasis and tone.

With this in mind, echo reading can be used as a highly effective analytical tool. If you want students to engage with a poem, getting them to experiment with different intonations, pacing and emphasis and discussing the impact of changes can heighten their understanding of what a writer is trying to achieve. Here's an example:

Read aloud the first stanza of 'The Charge of the Light Brigade' but do it deliberately badly, reading in a flat monotone and ask students to think about how you could improve your reading:

> Half a league, half a league,
> Half a league onward,
> All in the valley of Death
>   Rode the six hundred.
> 'Forward, the Light Brigade!
> Charge for the guns!' he said.
> Into the valley of Death
>   Rode the six hundred.

If they're struggling to suggest improvements, prompt them by asking which words or phrases should be emphasised,* which lines should be read quicker or more slowly, where volume should be raised or lowered. Intersperse this with explanations of what's going on and the meaning of any unusual vocabulary items. Ask them to think about punctuation, about the connotations of words, about repetition. When students make suggestions, try them out. Model their suggestion and ask if it was better or worse. When a particular version meets with their approval, have them echo it back. If their reading is not quite right, coach them with specific points of improvement and try again. With repeated readings (and a little manipulation) they'll start to hear the rhythm of the horses' hoof beats as the Light Brigade charge to their doom. You can watch some short clips of David Didau teaching Tennyson's poem in this way here: https://english.ormiston academiestrust.co.uk/implementation/reading-for-meaning/

Instead of simply annotating a poem with a teacher's interpretation, prompt them to make notes about how they think the poem should be read and why. By committing time to this trial-and-error

---

* Typically, you first have to teach the meaning of the word *emphasis*.

approach to analysis, students feel their way into a poem (or any other text) and begin to develop a personal response. We recommend that this becomes the standard approach to reading poetry and key scenes from plays.

2.9.2 Fluency lessons

At Cliff Park Academy in Great Yarmouth, Head of English Holly Hammond has made reading fluency a central plank in the department's approach to reading. Watching Holly teach a reading fluency lesson is a humbling experience. In one lesson from the Ancient Origins module, students were given a copy of the first scene from Simon Armitage's brilliant play script of *Homer's Odyssey* and told they would be building up to a whole class performance by the end of the lesson. Holly began by modelling Zeus's first line: 'This is what I say: Odysseus must be punished!' She expertly captured the imperious tone of an angry Greek god. The class duly chorused back the line. They then discussed what Zeus was feeling, what his attitude to Odysseus might be and whether a different tone of voice might work better. Students were asked for suggestions of how to deliver the line and several interpretations were experimented with before they agreed which was most successful. Bit by bit, Holly and the Year 7 class worked through the extract – with some students echoing back lines individually and some being chorused by the whole class – until they had performed the scene with a fair degree of panache. At the end of the lesson, the students were buzzing. When asked what his favourite part of the lesson had been, one boy, with a wild grin on his face, hissed out, 'Everything!'

Predictably, some classes are a harder sell than others. While anyone can get an enthusiastic reaction from a group of Year 7s, it can feel much harder to use this approach with a surly set of Year 9s. That said, it's important for teachers to see the struggle and get a feel for how to make sure every student takes part despite their awkwardness and embarrassment. We recommend always starting with whole class choral response before splitting students into smaller groups, or teams. Maybe one side of the class echoes one line while the other side echoes another. From there, move to smaller groups, then pairs and eventually individuals. At first, some students are overcome with nervous giggles and need to go through their line word by word. Very rarely, students point blank refuse to read and have to be given the choice of following the school's

disciplinary procedure or complying with reasonable instructions. At no point is any individual made to feel humiliated: they're only ever echoing back the teacher's reading of the text in question.

This is as close to foolproof as any approach to teaching English can be. With determination, every class will experience some sort of success. Even groups for whom this approach to reading feels utterly foreign have progressed from halting mutters to a certain degree of confidence. But when it *really* works, students are breathless with excitement and purpose. They feel they've been part of something powerful and are hungry for more. Teachers are often surprised by some of the individuals who shine, with students who are thought of as 'quiet' coming to life. Students who are seen as brash and confident are not always the ones who get the most from fluency lessons: the inclusive group dynamic leads to a sense of accomplishment in which no one is the centre of attention. As with all our core pedagogies, the key to this working is repetition: teachers need to keep modelling and echoing as many times as necessary for reading a line to become fluent. And, of course, the more often students experience fluency lessons, the more culturally normal the experience becomes.

Apart from the fact that students tend to really enjoy fluency lessons, the real point is they experience success at reading fluently. At first, many students listen to the modelled reading and then read as haltingly and erratically as ever. It's when the process is repeated to the point where they are made to be successful that things begin to change. When teachers give instructions such as, 'Listen to what happens when the comma comes up – can you hear the pause? The change in tone? Make yours the same', or, 'Pay attention to the way the pace and volume are picked up here – you need to show you're changing from thoughtful to excited'. This focus on how the detail or a text changes the way we read can transform students' understanding of meaning. As they repeat a line and get it right, they can *hear* what it means. This is especially important for dense, unfamiliar texts like poems or Shakespeare plays, but it can work with pretty much anything.

Fluency lessons work especially well with poetry. With poems as diverse as Edward Thomas's 'Adelstrop', Angelou's 'Woman Work' and 'The Farmer's Bride' by Charlotte Mew, and with classes from Year 7 to Year 13. The way students have to think about the effects of language, punctuation, character and tone really enhances their understanding, building a bridge from text to meaning.

One specialised approach to fluency lessons which we recommend is Readers' Theatre. The idea here is to take a section of text, divide it amongst a class and practise reading it until students have built up to a fluent performance. The EEF recommends a nine-step implementation model[34] which consists of:

1. Adult modelling
2. Echo reading
3. Text allocation
4. Repeated choral reading
5. Close reading (students discuss how lines should be read)
6. Text marking (students annotate their copies of the text)
7. Practising
8. Performance
9. Reflection

We've found that not all of these steps are always necessary. Depending on how impromptu you want the performance to be, steps 5 and 6 can be done as a whole class, and whether or not you feel it's appropriate for students to evaluate their performance will depend on how much lesson time you've committed. On the whole, we tend to skip this final step.

2.9.3 Noticing

The study of English requires that we pay attention in particular, specialised ways and, once we have learned to focus, to be able to experience new insights through seeing that what we are attending to has connections to things we have experienced previously.

By noticing, we mean reading and writing whilst being attuned to the choices and effects of everything that language has to offer: punctuation, sound, diction, syntax, patterns of form, imagery and the way each of these combines to make narratives and arguments. If we read or write without awareness of the effects of language, we are doing so naïvely. If we're not noticing, we're likely to see the writer's choices as merely coincidental and view our own efforts at writing as the product of happy, or unhappy, chance. But if we notice as we read and write then we're alive to possibilities, able to make informed choices and consider multiple interpretations.

Ralph Waldo Emerson called this process 'creative reading':

> When the mind is braced by labor and invention, the page of whatever book we read becomes luminous with manifold allusion. Every sentence is doubly significant, and the sense of our author is as broad as the world.[35]

Echo reading and fluency lessons train students to approach the texts they read in this way.

If we really want to notice what a writer is doing, reading ought to be undertaken with a pen so that students can annotate, underline and make notes. This will help not only to engage with the ideas expressed but to add something of your own; to enter into a conversation with the text. Failing to annotate can have serious consequences. If you don't annotate as you read, 'you will forget what it was you found interesting or funny or sad or perplexing, and you won't be able to find those particularly exciting, enticing, intriguing passages or moments again so easily. You may think you will, but you won't'.[36]

> **NB**. Whilst there's a time and place for close, analytical reading, it should never get in the way of students enjoying the process of reading a text. Our advice is that students should only be prompted to notice, pen in hand, *after* they have read through a text rapidly, focusing first on character and plot.

Teachers, as relative expert readers, can find it difficult to give explicit instructions to novice literary readers on *how* or *what* to notice. Sometimes, the best we can do is to explicitly model the process and articulate why we are paying attention to particular aspects of texts. Helpfully, Bennett and Royle augment this general advice with some suggestions as to what novice students of literature ought to be alert for:

- Striking phrases, arresting metaphors, unusual wordings
- Significant events or changes in the direction of the narrative
- The recurrence of motifs, topics or figures that intrigue
- Moments where a text seems to be referring to itself

- Changes in narrative perspective
- Changes in temporal perspective

2.9.4 Teaching interpretation

Many students will struggle to interpret the meanings of texts and so need to have the process of making interpretations modelled and scaffolded.

The default approach to so much English teaching is to present students with a text and then say some version of, 'What do you think of this?' If you're fortunate enough to work in a selective setting with advantaged students, then this must be a very rewarding way to go about things. The students make their thoughtful suggestions, respectfully challenge each other, and hone their interpretation though the lively cut and thrust of classroom debate.

What tends to happen in schools that are not like this is that a teacher will read a text and ask for opinions. A minority of students suggest ideas. Some of these ideas are discussed and sometimes the teacher will suggest other ideas. Then, eventually, students are assigned a written response. Those students who suggest their own interpretations often write well about their ideas and teachers can be fooled into thinking that this is a successful approach. The fact that lots of other students write badly about their classmates' interpretations is easy to dismiss. After all, what can you do with kids like that? Even in 'top sets' this approach only appears to work because the students sharing their opinions are more likely to have something useful or interesting to say. There, if teachers refuse to give their interpretation of a text, then at least students have the chance to learn what their peers have said.

This default is bound up with the widely held belief that English is 'skills-based'. English teachers, as experts, have automatised the process of pattern matching between the thousands of different literary texts they've read. When we read a new text, we don't notice the near-instantaneous process of comparing it to everything else we've ever read. We just experience the sensation of 'making an interpretation'. Because this is what we *think* happens in our own heads, we believe that if only we can teach students the skill of interpreting, they'll be fine. This, however, is a classic case of expertise-induced blindness. By failing to recognise that our expertise is a product of pattern matching, we neglect to teach

students what they actually need to learn in order to interpret texts a bit more like we do.

In *Making Meaning in English*, David refers to this judicious application of knowledge as 'analogising':

> The more we know – and, in particular, the more we know about language and literature – the better able we are to recognise that this piece of knowledge fits just there, or that the word, image or structural device over which we're currently poised reminds of something we've seen elsewhere. This knowledge is not always literary. When Julia is first introduced in Orwell's *1984*, we're told, 'Winston disliked her from the very first moment of seeing her... He disliked nearly all women, and especially the young and pretty ones'. On reading this, a student who happened to be an aficionado of the 60s rock band The Doors said this reminded her of the line from 'People Are Strange', 'Women seem wicked when you're unwanted'. This is *precisely* how we use analogies to make meaning.
>
> The literary critic and professor of English I.A. Richards once said, 'All thinking from the lowest to the highest – whatever else it may be – is sorting'. Meaning in English is built up by analogies with all we have read and experienced. The broader our literary knowledge, the more attuned we are to intertextual references, the conversations between texts. The more our students know of literary texts and their history and traditions, the greater their facility for comparing what they are studying now with everything else they have read. Developing literary knowledge helps students to hone a sense of connoisseurship with which they can move from naïve responses to the exercise of taste and the stating of educated opinions. Without it, students are limited to the most basic and banal of ideas.[37]

If this is the case, where does that leave our efforts to teach students to interpret texts? All too often, our approach is inadvertently elitist. It privileges those students who already know a lot and leaves those who don't desperately trying to guess what to think. For me, this is an iniquitous approach to education. Those who favour the false dichotomy will say, 'What's the alternative? Just telling students what to think?' Our preferred solution is to hold the 'just telling' and 'just guessing' approaches in creative tension. Students should be explicitly taught competing interpretations and asked to choose which they prefer. Here's how:

1. Read the text. Signpost some of the things you want students to notice by adding emphasis, significant pauses and perhaps even overt eyebrow waggling.
2. Teach students one reading of the text. Show them how the interpretation is backed up by the text itself.
3. Teach students a contradictory reading of the same text, again, using the text itself to support the arguments.
4. Ask the class which interpretations they prefer and why.
5. Explicitly teach that both are made right by being rooted in the text.
6. Maybe model a bad interpretation by suggesting a reading that cannot be supported by the text.
7. Ask students whether any other interpretations can be supported and explicitly encourage students to 'break' each other's suggestions by reference to the text.

NB. None of this precludes discussion. At every stage of the process students should be invited to contribute to the discussion and to interject with alternative propositions.

The goal here – as always – is 'gapless instruction'. Whenever we make assumptions about what students might already know or be able to do, we create gaps. Some students have the wherewithal to fill those gaps themselves (or with the help of their extended networks) but others will fall into the gaps and be unable to progress. Whenever we try to teach a skill without breaking it into component knowledge, we are almost certainly making it more difficult for the least advantaged students to succeed.

There is strong empirical support for the idea that novices (i.e., students) tend to learn more effectively when provided with explicit instruction.[38] Even if we've come to accept the premise of Cognitive Load Theory,[39] English teachers can still feel uncomfortable with teaching students specific interpretations because that would somehow be 'less authentic' or 'less meaningful'. This belief is based on a received notion of what it is to study English literature at degree level and beyond where, increasingly, students are likely to have greater expertise and so

benefit from the 'expertise reversal effect' where an increasing weight of guided discovery approaches becomes desirable.[40] The mistake is to assume that because English is 'done' in one way in universities, this process must be replicated faithfully with school students.

By explicitly teaching contrasting interpretations – by introducing the concept of dialectic – students begin to get an insight into how knowledge is created in literary studies. All students, not just the fortunate few, are given a seat at the table, given the rules of the game and invited to take part in the 'conversation of mankind'. Over time, they should begin to see, especially if prompted, that there are a finite number of ways literary tests tend to be interpreted: hierarchy, injustice, morality, responsibility, love, grief etc. These archetypal interpretations can – and should – also be explicitly taught. Then, when students encounter a new text, you can ask them which of these interpretations fits best. From there you should teach students specific critical lenses: feminism, Marxism, psychoanalysis etc. Over time, it becomes both fair and reasonable to fade out explicit instruction and get students to recall the ideas you've previously taught and apply them to new texts. With patience, students will be genuinely able to make independent interpretations and, as a bonus, be better prepared for further study should they wish to continue with the subject.

As the texts in our KS3 curriculum are not intended to be studied in the same way as set literary texts at GCSE, they appear as essentially unseen to the students other than that they are part of the dystopian genre. Therefore, a post-reading strategy should be used to ensure students can generate as much meaning for the texts they encounter as possible.

The following prompts are designed to train students to think of the bigger picture the writer is trying to create. These questions are also designed to assess students' understanding and address potential misconceptions.

Question prompts to aid comprehension:

- Where does the text take place?
- When does the text take place?
- Who are the characters in the text?
- Who is the main character and what are they like?
- Who is the narrator?
- What happens in the text?
- Is there a change in tone?

- What do you think is the most important event in the text?
- Can you summarise the text in a sentence?

This last prompt requires some explicit instruction. We teach students to be able to answer the prompts: Who/what? (did/will do) what? When? Where? Why? How?

Here's a worked example: What happens in Act 3 scene 2 of *Othello*?

- Who/what: Iago
- (did/will do) what: manipulates Othello into believing Desdemona has been unfaithful
- When: when they are alone together
- Where: in Othello's rooms
- Why: because he is angry at being overlooked for promotion
- How: by hinting at a relationship between Cassio and Desdemona

We then teach them to combine their answers into a single summarising sentence such as this one:

> Because he is angry at being overlooked for promotion, Iago takes his revenge by manipulating Othello, while they are alone together in Othello's rooms, into suspecting Desdemona of having an affair with Cassio.

As summarising is so useful for understanding texts and as a basis for making inferences it should be taught repeatedly to the point of mastery.

2.10 STRUCTURED DISCUSSION

If students are to be academically successful, they need to be fluent in the language of academic success.

Discussion has always been one of the distinctive pillars of English classrooms but seems to be falling into decline. Teachers increasingly report that students are unwilling or unable to take part in classroom debates and that many are silent passengers in lessons. To what extent is this just a 'sign of the times'? Could we, as English teachers, be in part responsible?

As Paul Black and Dylan Wiliam pointed out in 1998, this is nothing new:

> It is common that only a few pupils in a class answer teachers' questions. The rest then leave it to these few, knowing that they cannot respond as quickly and being unwilling to risk making mistakes in public. So, the teacher, by lowering the level of questions and by accepting answers from only a few, can keep the lesson going but is actually out of touch with the understanding of most of the class – the question-answer dialogue becomes a ritual, one in which all connive and thoughtful involvement suffers.[41]

Why does this matter? Well, firstly, there is something particularly cognitively 'sticky' about speech. We are more likely to remember that which we have said than that which we have merely read or heard. The more students speak, the more they are likely to learn.[42] If we allow students to remain silent we may also be allowing them to learn less as a result.

A second problem that teachers regularly encounter is that children who are able to articulate interesting opinions and make useful connections orally will often struggle to record these observations in writing. All too often this is because the way children have expressed themselves is the *only* way they have of expressing themselves.

As literate adults, we have the ability to instantaneously translate between what we say and what we would need to alter in order to write down what we've said. Although they're related, spoken and written language are very different beasts, as anyone who's ever tried to transcribe speech will know. If children are not sufficiently familiar with the academic language code, they will struggle to write down that which they find easy to say out loud.

Quite apart from all the other benefits of students taking part in classroom discussion, intervening with speech is probably the most effective way to intervene in writing. According to Dorothy Latham, 'spoken language forms a constraint, a ceiling not only on the ability to comprehend but also on the ability to write, beyond which literacy cannot progress'.[43] What this means is that our ability to write cannot exceed our ability to speak and our ability to read cannot be better than our ability to listen.

Robin Alexander suggests, 'One of the reasons why talk is undervalued in British education is that there is a tendency to see its function as primarily *social*... but... the function of talk in classrooms is *cognitive* and *cultural* as well as social'.[44] Talk is a particularly powerful lever for cognitive change: if we want to change the way students think (and, after all, isn't this the essence of teaching?) we should first change the way they speak. If we change the way they speak, they will be given the ability to think previously unthinkable thoughts. Once they can say something, they can write it down.

Our solution is something we've called 'structured discussion'. It really isn't anything especially new or exciting, but it does seem different to the way most teachers teach, and therefore it can seem hard to grasp what needs to be done.

Essentially, it works like this: the teacher asks a question about the content being studied and then directs it at a particular student. The student then gives an answer. Instead of either paraphrasing their answer in academic language or just saying, 'great' and moving on, the teacher then asks the student to elevate their response so that they 'speak like an essay'. This can be hard for students to do and so requires the teacher to provide a model for them to repeat or a scaffold to elicit a more academic response. Then, other students should be asked to repeat what the first student has said. If they've said it, they'll be able to write it down. This pattern is then repeated with as many children as possible asked to participate. They can be asked to expand on or reply to other students' answers, but responses must always be mediated by the teacher to make sure children are supported to speak in academic language.

Structured discussion works best when it follows a predictable pattern. The format we recommend is as follows:

1. Retrieval of topic to be discussed

The retrieval phase is fundamentally to prime students on what the content of the discussion will focus on. Ideally, retrieval will focus on the concepts and vocabulary students will need to deploy. As always, the emphasis should be on keeping stakes low and using MWBs to facilitate responses. (See section 2.5 for more detail.)

2. Pose question for discussion

Once students are warmed up, you're ready to pose the question you want the class to discuss. We know that the typical length of time a teacher pauses between posing a question and expecting an answer is less than a second. Then, once students have given an answer, we again respond within about a second. This doesn't give students much time to think and is likely to result in hurried, poorly

thought-out answers. The advice is that we should try to pause for at least four seconds, and preferably ten seconds, between posing a question and expecting an answer.[45] But, as anyone who's tried to wait in silence for three or four seconds in a classroom knows, it can feel like an eternity.

To help create the time required for effective thinking, we recommend using Think-Pair-Share to increase participation and confidence in speaking in class.[46] For anyone unfamiliar, it works like this:

Think: After posing the question for discussion, give students 30 seconds or so to think about their answer in silence. Allowing them to use MWBs to jot down ideas can be really helpful in supporting ideas and reducing anxiety.

Pair: Once students have been assigned a talk partner, ask them to take turns to share their thoughts. Tell them you will be asking them to feed back not what they've just said but what their partner has said. This contributes to a culture where listening is valued as highly as speaking.

Share: Select students to feed back what they've just heard and run through the structured discussion format.

Think-Pair-Share can work especially well if 'blue and green' talk partners are used. At Ormiston Herman Academy, students are divided into 'blues' and 'greens' and paired discussions are run with blue and green talk partners. Teachers will give blues and greens different discussion prompts (e.g., blues to discuss the pros for a proposition, greens to come up with cons) to ensure that each student has something different to contribute to the discussion.

By doing this, teachers should be able to deal with the 'I don't know' gambit. One response might be to say something along the lines of, 'I know you don't *know* – I'm asking what you *think*'.[47] At this point we need to stand firm and make sure that they *do* think. The options at this point are limited. You could hover over them and put them under pressure – which is likely to lead to confrontation – or you could give them some discussion time. Either way, as long as you're clear *why* you're asking the questions and let go of the need for 'right' answers, all should be well.

If, however, the student you've selected to answer your carefully chosen question is in a particularly truculent mood and stubbornly insists that they 'don't know', you need a strategy to deal with this.

Saying, 'I don't know', often means, 'Leave me alone'. If you allow students to decide whether or not they're prepared to participate in answering questions you're already on a slippery downward slope. It's vital to assert that *you* decide whether students answer questions, and to make that work you need to eliminate 'I don't know' as an excuse for not participating.

Ask another pupil the same question. When they answer, return to the student who 'doesn't know' and ask them the question again. Clearly, they will now have an answer as they've just heard one. If the class won't play ball and the second student you ask 'doesn't know' either, you should supply an answer yourself: 'One answer could be…' Then return to the student who doesn't know and ask them the question you've just answered. This makes it clear that 'I don't know' is not an acceptable response and that you will be demanding 100% participation.

It's also important to have a plan for dealing with incorrect answers. One of the most unhelpful axioms in English is that 'there are no wrong answers'. There clearly are. Answers unsupported by evidence from the text being studied should be considered unacceptable. However, where it can get confusing is that there is rarely one unambiguously correct answer either. We want to both signal to students that contributions will be taken seriously and that certain responses are outside the 'field of interpretation'.[48] As shown in Figure 2.7, a simple approach to this is to draw a target on the whiteboard and show students where the answer is in relation to the consensus of what is considered an acceptable interpretation. Instead of branding an answer 'wrong' we can instead say that it is 'outside the field of interpretation'.

3. Target questions at named students

Firstly, and most importantly, teachers need to decide who answers questions and so it's essential to avoid the trap of just getting answers from keen students who shoot up their hands as soon as a question is posed. There are two main problems with this approach. First, teachers only sample the understanding of a few confident students and so are more likely to be misled about the comprehension of quieter class members. Second, and more seriously, the students that speak benefit from answering questions and those who don't are allowed to learn less as a consequence of being allowed to remain silent.

When targeting selected students to respond to questions, it's useful to practise asking the question first before saying who should answer it. This helps to ensure that all students are focusing until the teacher stops speaking as they don't know whether they will be called on to answer until the final moment. As discussed above, the longer we delay before requiring a student to answer, the more students will be involved in thinking. Repeating the question once or twice will help ensure all students are given time to consider a response.

FIGURE 2.7 Validating students' answers

Questioning technique	Who is thinking?
'Sam, why is Macbeth reluctant to kill King Duncan?'	Only Sam.
'Why is Macbeth reluctant to kill King Duncan, Sam?'	The quickest students in the room are thinking up until Sam is named.
'OK, so the question we're discussing is why Macbeth is reluctant to kill Duncan. Why is Macbeth reluctant to kill King Duncan… Sam?'	Everyone in the class is given time to think and formulate a response before Sam is named.

It's also important to monitor which students have contributed as it's very easy to allow some students to fade into the background. Although there are various ways of randomising this, most teachers find there's enough randomness in their classrooms. Fortunately, we can easily keep track of who's answered by ticking off students on a class list or seating plan as they participate.

4. Scaffold academic talk

There are several ways you might want to go about this, but the key is that for students to become fluent in academic language they need to have academic talk both modelled *and* scaffolded. Teachers not only need to consciously narrate how they are using academic language, they also need to provide support to elicit academic answers. A starting point is to repurpose writing frames as speaking frames:

- The writer has used the phrase _____ to imply...
- This might mean... because...
- The writer's intention is to...
- This could also suggest... because...
- The word '____' is effective because...

Although these stems are a good place to begin, students can become reliant on them. We suggest two principles for the effective use of scaffolding.

First, we should never use scaffolding to make easy work easier. We should only ever use it to make the impossible possible. We need to simplify the task sufficiently to allow pupils to attempt it but make it hard enough so that everyone has to do something challenging. Everyone should struggle, no matter their ability.

Second, never erect scaffolding unless you have a plan for taking it down. If we leave it there, students will become dependent on it. They'll never be able to perform without support, and this often ends up stifling their ideas and expression. Clunky straightjackets like PEE (Point Evidence Explain) and its many variants can be useful as a starting point, but as soon as students have mastered using them, they need to be taken away. Taking away the scaffold forces students to struggle. The act of dredging memory for ideas helps the process to become internalised. If students are struggling too much, put the scaffold (or at least some of it) back. And then take it away again. As soon as possible.

This being the case, a useful and simple strategy for scaffolding students' speech is to write down what they say. As soon as they see their words on the board (or under a visualiser) they can immediately see the gaps between spoken and written language.

5. Refinement

Once students' answers are written on the board, we recommend going through a process of asking students to remove redundant elements and to make their answers more concise. *Concision* and *redundancy* are key hallmarks of academic writing.[49]

Imagine a student has said something along the lines of, 'J.B. Priestley is trying to make us see that being a socialist is better than being a capitalist'. Not bad, but it could be refined by making it more concise and removing redundancies. If the teacher asks, 'Is there anything here we can do without? See if you can remove two or three words', students are prompted to think about what is unnecessary. They may also need specific advice about nominalisation (making sentences less verby and more nouny).

To help students shape their answers, we can use the *clarify*, *probe*, *recommend* framework.

If we want pupils to *clarify* their meaning, we might ask something like:

- What did you mean by...?
- Can you explain that differently?
- What other words could you use?

To *probe* answers, we might ask:

- Can you tell me more about...?
- What else do you know about...?
- How else might you use that?

Once they've heard a few different answers, we could ask pupils to make *recommendations* and ask them things like:

- What is better about...?
- Can you explain why you prefer that?
- Why do you agree with...?

With support they will be able to come up with something like this:

> 'Priestley uses events in the play to promote socialism and criticise capitalism'.

6. Repetition

While we're trying to get to this point, we may have concerns that not all students are paying attention when we – the teacher – are speaking. Whilst this is obviously an issue, what we've come to understand is that attention seems to drop off a cliff when other students are speaking. The moment a teacher has selected a student to give a response, all other students seem to believe they have tacit permission to switch off and take a 'cognitive breather'.[50] To prevent this, it's important to build a classroom culture where students are expected to attend to each other's contributions. To this end, it's important to regularly select students to repeat what has just been said. This may sound pointlessly straightforward, but the extent to which students don't listen to each other can be startling when you start looking for it. It's not uncommon to have a classroom interaction where four or five students have been able to successfully repeat a point that's just been made only to find the sixth student, when asked, has no idea of what's been going on.

As with all the other key pedagogies, the key to success here is repetition. Until you have a classroom culture where students know they will be held accountable for their attention, it pays to routinely ask students to repeat what their peers have just said.

However, our aim should be for a lot more than mere repetition. Ultimately, we want students to be able to take part in nuanced debate and discussion. With practice and repetition, students can be supported in using these stems to question each other and in becoming increasingly fluent at debating ideas in the classroom.

Just in case all this has been hard to visualise, here's a rough transcript of a discussion following reading the first part of Simon Armitage's version of the *Odyssey* with a Year 7 class as part of our Ancient Origins module:

Teacher: What impression do we get of the gods and their attitude to mortals? [*pause*] Sarah?

Sarah: They think they're dependent.

Teacher: Good. Can you say that in a full sentence beginning 'The impression readers get of the gods is…'?

Sarah: The impression readers get of the gods is that they think they're dependent?

Teacher: That's better. Ben, what did Sarah just say?

Ben: The impression readers get of the gods is… uh…

Teacher: OK. She said, 'The impression readers get of the gods is that they think mortals are dependent on them'. What did I just say?

Ben: The impression readers get of the gods is that they think mortals are dependent on them.

Teacher: Good. Ahmed, what did Ben just say?

Ahmed: Um. I don't know. I wasn't listening.

Teacher: Ahmed, I really need you to pay attention. Ben, please can you repeat what you said for Ahmed?

Ben The impression readers get of the gods is that they think mortals are dependent on them.

Teacher: Thank you. Ahmed, what did Ben say?

Ahmed: He said, 'The impression readers get of the gods is that they think mortals are too dependent on them'.

Teacher: Good. Maia, how do we know the gods think humans are dependent on them?

Maia: Um, Zeus says… 'It doesn't do to meddle too much. Makes them dependent'.

Teacher: Yes, can you say that so that it sounds more like an essay?

Maia: We know the gods think humans are dependent on them because Zeus says 'It doesn't do to meddle too much. Makes them dependent'.

Teacher: That's a good effort. I'm going to write that on the board… Jake, can you improve on what Maia said without repeating the word dependent? Start by saying, 'The impression readers get of the gods is that…'

Jake: Er… The impression readers get of the gods is that… they are worried humans will get too dependent on them.

Teacher: Yes. Now add 'because' to the end of that sentence.

Jake: The impression readers get of the gods is that humans will get too dependent on them because Zeus says, 'It doesn't do to meddle too much'.

Teacher: Excellent. I'd like everyone to chorus what Jake's said so that we're all more likely to remember it. Jake, I'm going to ask you to repeat what you've just said and then on 3, we'll all say it too.

And so on…

This can be continued for as long as is desired, but our recommendation is to keep it down to no more than ten minutes at first. Speaking in this way requires care and attention and can be exhausting – for you as well as them. As they become more fluent and familiar, their stamina for using academic language will increase, and you can spend longer to ensure topics have been thoroughly explored before a written response is expected.

2.11 TEACHING METAPHOR USING TENOR, VEHICLE AND GROUND

Giving students names for the parts of metaphor can help them to better understand how and why they are effective.

Whilst not a distinct pedagogical approach as such, our approach to teaching metaphor is both important and unusual enough to require some explanation. As we saw in section 1.6.1, the metaphor strand of our Year 7 curriculum is dominated by making sure the concepts of *tenor, vehicle and ground* are embedded. We take this approach because although it's vanishingly rare to encounter a student in secondary school who doesn't know what a metaphor *is*, it's equally rare to find students who are able to provide a precise definition. When pressed, they tend to say things like, 'It's when you say one thing is something else', or 'saying something is something it isn't', or, even more commonly, 'I know what it is, but I don't know how to explain it'.

Does any of this matter? After all, if students can spot a metaphor – and they usually can – why do they need to define one? Our argument is that the inability to define metaphor contributes to students being able to do little more than point them out. As always, the point of noticing a linguistic or structural device is to be able to talk about its *effect*.

Based on the etymology of the word the definition we use is: *metaphor is language that transports meaning from one 'place' to another.*

This brings us to the unwieldy sounding terms tenor, vehicle and ground. Back in 1934, Cambridge professor I.A. Richards saw metaphor as 'a transaction between contexts'.[51] In order to analyse the operations of metaphor he saw the necessity of naming these contexts and proposed the terms 'tenor' and 'vehicle': the tenor is the subject of the metaphor, the vehicle the source of its imagery. Without names for the parts of metaphor, he argued, we run the risk of confusing the relationship between tenor and vehicle for the relationship between the whole metaphor and its meaning.

We can also add the concept of 'ground', the relationship between literal and metaphorical meanings. Considering tenor, vehicle and ground allows us to explain why a metaphor is (or is not) successful.

- Tenor = the subject of the metaphor and its intended meaning

- Vehicle = the language used to describe the tenor
- Ground = the relationship between the tenor and the vehicle

Again, etymology is useful in making sense of these terms. While vehicle and ground are more or less obvious, tenor comes from the Latin verb *tenere*, 'to hold'.* The image in Figure 2.8 is a useful way to explain the relationship between these three components to students. The vehicle 'holds' the tenor and transports it along the ground from one 'place' to another.

The best place to start seeing the relationship between tenors and vehicles is to examine a simile. Here's one from Christina Rosetti's poem of the same name, 'My heart is like a singing bird'.

- Tenor = Rossetti's heart
- Vehicle = 'a singing bird'
- Ground = we think of singing birds as beautiful and peaceful so we're invited to think that Rossetti's heart (here a metaphor for her emotional state) is in a beautiful peaceful place.

Some metaphors are as straightforward as the simile in Wordsworth's poem, 'I wandered lonely as a cloud':

- Tenor = Wordsworth's wanderings
- Vehicle = a cloud
- Ground = Just as clouds are randomly blown by the wind, so Wordsworth's wandering is directionless and without intent.

By examining the ground of a metaphor, we can work out which qualities of the vehicle are being transferred to the tenor. For instance, clouds can be

FIGURE 2.8 A visual representation of the parts of metaphor

---

* In early polyphonic music, it was the tenor's job to 'hold' the melody.

dark and result in rain, but unless otherwise stated we think of them as white and fluffy. This is the quality that is transferred from the vehicle to the tenor in Wordsworth's metaphor.

But many metaphors are less straightforward, and this is where students run into difficulties. All too often, the tenor of a metaphor is unstated. For instance, in Paul Laurence Dunbar's 'I Know Why the Caged Bird Sings' we have to work out what the caged bird represents. This can be tricky without knowing that Dunbar was an African American, writing in 1899. Knowing this we can then infer that he is likely to have regularly encountered overt racial discrimination and that he – and other Black people – are 'caged' in that their potential is held back due to racial prejudice. The vehicle of the caged bird also invites us to consider what sorts of birds are locked in cages. No one would cage a common bird like a pigeon or a sparrow, instead a caged bird is more likely to be rare, beautiful or exotic. So, the ground of this metaphor is that Dunbar sees himself – and by extension all Black people – as both special and constrained by unfair circumstances.

Here's a more complex example: 'I have no spur to prick the sides of my intent, but only vaulting ambition'. The tenor here is Macbeth's ambition to be king and the vehicle is a 'spur'. The ground is that Shakespeare compares Macbeth's desire to be king to riding a horse. There's nothing wrong with ambition *per se*, but just as a spur is a rather cruel way to make a horse run faster, so murder is a reprehensible way of achieving one's desires.

Sometimes metaphors work despite the disharmony of tenor and vehicle. Although metaphors struggle to work where there is little or no point of similarity, sometimes greater tension is produced by the 'unlikeness' than the 'likeness' of tenor and vehicle. Consider this line from *Othello*: 'Steep'd me in poverty to the very lips'.

- Tenor = poverty
- Vehicle = the sea, or a vat of liquid
- Ground = poverty, which should be a state of deprivation, is conceived of as being so much in abundance that Othello is at the point of drowning in it. This disharmony underlines Othello's disturbed state of mind as he frets over Desdemona's supposed infidelity.

We shouldn't be able to drown in the lack of something, but Shakespeare's startling combination of unlikenesses highlights Othello's predicament.

When a metaphor 'works', tenor and vehicle reinforce each other; meanings are transferred in both directions, enriching each other. In Othello's case, the tenor (his poverty) takes on a liquid, clinging viscosity, while the vehicle (a barrel of liquid) becomes an oxymoron that could never quench thirst.

We can also use tenor, vehicle and ground not just to consider figurative language, but to unpick students' understanding of concepts like character and theme. If we think of a character as a vehicle, we're invited to consider the tenor they are intended to represent. We could argue that Inspector Goole is a vehicle for socialism, that Lord Capulet is a vehicle for patriarchy, or that Scrooge is a vehicle for both misanthropy and redemption. On the other hand, themes are tenors in search of a vehicle. If we say that *Jekyll and Hyde* is about duality, the vehicle is the transformation of Dr Jekyll into Mr Hyde. If we say that one of themes of Macbeth is chaos and disorder, its vehicles could be the murder of a king or the intrusion of the supernatural into the 'real' world. Again, the ground is what makes these vehicles successful ways to depict their tenors.

Giving students names for the 'parts' of metaphor is a first step to understanding the metaphorical nature of the constructed world of language and literature. If, on the other hand, all we do is direct students to pick out metaphors from the texts they study, we limit all but the most advantaged to a circumscribed ability to perceive the cracks between the literal and figurative. They may be able to notice the vehicle bobbing on the surface of a text without grasping that there's a tenor lying beneath. Knowing that every vehicle must possess a tenor prompts students to consider what it may be. This, in turn, makes more of the vehicle visible. By introducing the concept of ground, we prompt students to 'show their working out' and make visible the connections they infer between tenor and vehicle. This also helps us to scaffold the movement from concrete to abstract, both specifically for individual metaphors but also more generally in helping to support and improve students' abstract thinking by breaking down the metaphor into parts which can then be discussed and understood in steps and then reassembled, enabling students to make the connection between tenor, vehicle and ground and therefore make meaning. Understanding metaphor is being able to move from concrete to abstract – by using tenor/vehicle/ground, we can plug a gap that is often left unfilled in instructional sequences.

Introducing these terms to students to enhance their ability to analyse metaphor is only useful if you commit. You have to invest curriculum time to repeatedly using the terms and modelling their utility before it begins to pay off.

Also, a word of caution. I.A. Richards himself warned that 'a metaphor may work admirably without our being able… to say how it works or what is the ground of the shift'.[52] Nevertheless, thinking in terms of tenor, vehicle and ground can be a useful way for students to think about the relationship between the components of a metaphor and will help prompt them to move beyond noticing into more analytic analogising.

2.12 MARKING BOOKS

While writing individual comments in students' exercise books is largely a waste of time, teachers must still find a way to hold students to account for the work they do and prevent them from embedding mistakes.

English teachers often feel huge existential guilt about marking. On the one hand, marking students' books is hugely time consuming and the effort-to-reward ratio means that time could be better spent planning responsive lessons. But, on the other hand, if students' work goes unmarked then there is often a catastrophic decline in the quality of work. Marking books may not be an effective way to help students make progress but it can have real motivational impact.

In recent years, many schools have made whole class feedback a cornerstone of their marking policy.[53] This approach depends on teachers reading through students' work, noting down common errors and misconceptions, and then designing a feedback lesson to address these mistakes and give students an opportunity to improve their work.

However, all too often this seems to result in students' books becoming rather unloved and error strewn. We all know what happens when students don't feel their books are being regularly looked at: standards slip, and mistakes become embedded. In practice, much of the writing students do in school actually makes them worse at writing. As we've already discussed, if students are permitted to practise writing in a way that allows them to embed errors, they end up getting better at writing badly. This is in no one's interest.

So, although whole class feedback may score well on the efficiency stakes, there are instances where it can be demotivating for students. In the worst-case scenario, they may end up thinking we just don't care enough to respond to their hard work. The hard reality is that there's some truth in this. There are few things more forlorn than a pile of books with little or no sign of a teacher's oversight and involvement.

The answer is teacher presence. Students' books should *look* like they have been read. Ideally, they should be covered with ticks, underlinings, question marks and other responses to the work students have produced. If students are repeatedly making the same mistakes, teachers need to *know*. Unless we know, the cycle of error will continue indefinitely, and it will be ever harder for students to move on from deeply embedded misconceptions.[54]

So, as you're compiling your notes on what feedback you're going to give to the class, it takes very little additional time to tick and flick as you go. Now, there's no question that kids love teacher comments. The longer the better. But there appears to be an inverse relationship between the length of a comment and the likelihood that a student will read it. And they love ticks (especially double ticks) and stickers almost as much as they like comments![55] By 'marking' we mean reading students' work, ticking, underling and circling while taking notes on what should be fed back in whole class feedback. What used to take two to three hours can be done in 30 minutes or less. Suddenly, marking a set of books a day doesn't feel quite so daunting. Further, ticking, underlining and circling can all be done during live marking or tracking in the classroom, providing students with instant feedback and reducing the amount of time spent doing this outside of lessons.

In addition, the process of reading students' work should hold them to account for their mistakes. If students routinely make careless mistakes, they will automate the process of making mistakes. The solution is to make proofreading your minimum expectation for any written work students complete. If it's not proofread, it's not finished. If it's not finished, then there ought to be some sort of consequence. Building a culture of proofreading is simple but it can take hard work. We recommend giving students a straightforward code like the one in Figure 2.9. Then, all students should *visibly annotate* their work to demonstrate that it has met minimum expectations.

One of the many benefits to this system is that if students identify where they have made mistakes, they are making specific requests for feedback. It

The Proofreading Code
'If it's not excellent, it's not finished!'

Capital letters
Spelling
P – Punctuation
// - Paragraphs
? – doesn't make sense

FIGURE 2.9 The proofreading code

makes sense that when feedback has been solicited, students are far more likely to absorb and act on it.

The deal ought to be that if we feel it's sufficiently important to ask students to spend time writing, the *least* we can do is spare the time to read it. But reading – plus a little light annotation – is also the *most* we should do.

2.13 HOMEWORK

Homework should be as impactful for students and as little effort for teachers to administer as possible.

Of all the vexed issues facing English teachers, homework can feel like one of the most intractable. Faced with pressure from senior leaders and parents, teachers often feel that setting homework is a thankless chore which creates hours of extra marking and admin without having a discernible benefit on those students who need it most.

Our approach to homework is summed up by these two principles:

1. It must help students master curricular expectations.
2. It must not create unnecessary workload for teachers.

Part of our solution to the homework issue is to use Carousel Learning. As discussed in section 2.6, this is an online platform that hosts banks of question-and-answer pairs. Not only can teachers use it as an efficient way to set retrieval quizzes in the classroom, but they can also assign homework tasks to students, monitor their progress and provide in-lesson follow-up if needed. We recommend that English departments agree how often they expect students to access the site and how long they are expected to spend practising and

quizzing. Teachers are able to see how long students are spending and how accurate their answers are, so it becomes relatively straightforward to intervene if students are not meeting expectations.[56]

Obviously, the benefit of this homework practice is dependent on the quality of the items uploaded. We have written a bank of items for each of our curriculum modules which conform to the principles of effective retrieval (questions should be easy to answer, contain useful information and be regularly repeated). We hope that the more rapidly and accurately students can answer these questions, the better their mastery of the subject will be.

We do need to consider the issue of internet access. During COVID-19 lockdowns, schools moved heaven and earth to ensure as many students as possible were able to access remote learning, but where there continue to be issues, these may be resolved by ensuring vulnerable students can complete Carousel homework in school, or by providing them with appropriate devices.

Another recommended homework option is to set Reading Progress assignments using Microsoft Teams. Reading Progress is designed to track students' reading progress. Teachers upload a text into Teams (we recommend texts taken from our Student Anthologies) and students submit a recording of themselves reading this text aloud. There is an option either for teachers to annotate copies of the passage to show where students made fluency errors or – and this is the bit which makes this meet our second principle – corrections can be made automatically, and feedback generated to be shared with both teachers and students. We'd recommend that teachers monitor this process to make sure the feedback is in line with what they would give, but even so, this is a powerful and efficient way to help improve students' reading fluency.

Although traditionally it's hard to check whether students are actually doing it, Reading Progress is a great way of ensuring that reading homeworks are completed. In addition to this, simply telling students and families that there is an expectation that students read for, say, 20–30 minutes a day means that many students who would otherwise not read will do so. The danger, as always, is that this can easily become a gap-widening activity with the students who are most likely to do the reading being the ones who least need to, but teachers can attempt to mitigate against this by setting up homework reading clubs for those students they think need the support. Currently, this is a free product.[57]

Of course, should teachers want to set other homework instead or in addition to Carousel Learning or Reading Progress, then they should feel free to do so.

2.14 USING VISUALISERS

Visualisers are great. They can make a huge difference to English lessons but, all too often, they are left gathering dust in the corner of classrooms. This is, more often than not, due to uncertainty about the value of investing precious time in working out how to get the best out of them.

The main benefit of using visualisers is that they make modelling easy. Of course, it's perfectly possible to model writing on a board but when using a visualiser, the teacher is facing the class which makes it easier to talk through the metacognitive process of writing.

We recommend that teachers have a model exercise book for each of their classes. At the most basic level, this helps ensure the layout and presentation of work is as clear as possible. The teacher writes in the title, date, underlines them and does whatever else seems important and says to students to 'Make yours like mine'. Whilst it's possible to do this on a whiteboard (interactive or otherwise) seeing the layout *on the page* really helps students understand what their books should look like. But this is just the beginning. Beyond presentation, using a visualiser to model work in an exercise book not only helps teachers to arrange the ideas they want students to think about more clearly, but students also find it easier to follow a teacher's thought processes when they are modelled on the page.

The other major benefit of keeping a model exercise book is that you have an easily accessible store of all your previous lessons to hand. If a student has been absent you can show them your work to enable them to catch up on crucial content. And, if you're struggling to work out what a student has written you can cross reference your book with theirs.

There are, however, some practicalities that need careful consideration. A clear workspace is required to give you enough space to place whatever is required under the visualiser. It's not always best to teach from a seated position so, ideally, you might be able to set up a visualiser station on a podium (shoving a handy filing cabinet in place also works) which you could stand behind, allowing you to face the group and interact with the board without moving from the spot. It's sensible to set aside some time after school to work out your optimal visualiser station.

If you're used to displaying PowerPoint slides, using a visualiser can feel a bit messy at first. Like most things, this improves with practice. If you inadvertently move your book around too much it can make it very hard for students to track so it's worth spending some time practising positioning your exercise book underneath the visualiser and writing so that your hand is not obscuring what you're writing. If you display pre-prepared material, sometimes you might want to gradually reveal information as you are ready to talk about it, other times you may just want to cover up extraneous information which may prove a distraction.

Here are a number of activities for which a visualiser can be indispensable:

- I-we-you modelling – this involves the teacher modelling either the 'I' part of the process during the lesson, or collaborating on the 'we' section in response to a model prepared ahead of time.
- Annotation – seeing the process of making notes can really help students to make sense of where their attention should be focused and how to add details which you want them to remember later.
- Connect to Student Anthologies – our anthologies have been designed to be used interactively under the visualiser. If you can point to the part of the page where students should be focusing and draw their attention to key ideas, they will be more engaged with the materials in front of them.
- Displaying student work – if you want to show a class a great (or not so great) example of work, simply pop it under the visualiser to illustrate the point you want to make. Even better, show two pieces of work at once and ask students to work out why one does a better job than the other.
- Live marking – by marking a student's work under the visualiser while you talk through your

thinking, students are likely to get a clearer sense of how they could improve their own work.

As we'll go on to explore in the following sections on Student Anthologies (2.15) and Teacher Guides (2.16), becoming confident with using a visualiser in lessons means there is very little need to spend time creating lesson slides. This can make us much more responsive during lessons as, instead of following the scripted slides, we can make on-the-fly decisions about how and where to direct students' attention.

2.15 STUDENT ANTHOLOGIES

In pursuit of disciplinary equity, all students need the same access to carefully curated reading material designed to be optimally accessible.

In addition to all these approaches to teaching, arguably the most important part to get right when implementing an English curriculum is the provision of the content. Each module comes with a Student Anthology containing the texts we are ambitious for all our students to read. This gets away from teachers having to photocopy lots of different resources which are then stuck into students' exercise books in a more or less haphazard fashion.

We thought long and hard about the approach we should take with these booklets – should they be workbooks with space for students to write, or should they be more like textbooks, which can be reused many times? Whilst there might be many good reasons for the workbook approach, what tipped the balance against it was the unnecessary cost of printing blank spaces for students to write in. We've chosen to design our student booklets as anthologies of reading material which allows schools to choose whether they'll aim to reuse year on year or allow students to annotate.

As you can see from Figure 2.10, the marketing team at OAT have done a fabulous job of producing glossy, colour covers for each anthology which really seems to help students to take pride in and treat them with respect.

The texts in the anthologies are laid out in columns. It's astonishing that almost all resources printed in schools for students are laid out on A4 paper with text spanning the whole page. You're unlikely to find texts laid out like this anywhere else. Professionally produced text laid out on A4 or larger format is *always* in columns. Doing so reduces the cognitive burden on the reader as they only have to keep track of a line of text across a relatively narrow column instead of the greater demands of following across a whole page.[58]

FIGURE 2.10 Student Anthology covers

As you can see in Figure 2.11, text is also numbered every fifth line. We think this strikes the right balance between students being able to quickly locate a particular line and the aesthetic overload of pages being cluttered with numbers for every line.

Where possible, we also use the anthologies to present students with culturally rich visual, as well as literary, art. We don't suggest that each image be examined in depth (or even at all), just that students are exposed to great art. We think of this as cultural capital by stealth.

For the most part, the texts in these anthologies are satellites which orbit the focus text for each module. For instance, when students encounter the Gothic in Year 9, their focus is Emily Brontë's *Wuthering Heights*. The anthology introduces them to a range of other Gothic texts, from *The Castle of Otranto* to *The Tell Tale Heart* to Toni Morrison's *Beloved*. Extracts without a focus text make for an unsatisfying experience with students experiencing literature as just one damned extract after another. Reading a focus text without any supporting extracts makes it difficult for students to see how a single text can be emblematic of a broad literary sweep. Only by combining both can students begin to appreciate the parts and the whole.

One of the main drivers for creating these anthologies was the desire to reduce unnecessary workload. By curating and printing these anthologies we reduce the need for teachers to devote hours to sourcing their own supplementary material and provide a more equitable classroom experience with all students having access to the same breadth of high-quality texts. Of course, teachers still have the freedom to use other texts where and when they feel this will benefit their classes, but the point is that they don't *have* to. Equally, there's nothing to compel a teacher to read every text in an anthology. We provide guidance on the core knowledge to be assessed but this still allows considerable freedom for teachers to determine what they consider to be most appropriate.*

2.16 TEACHER GUIDES

Planning and resources should contribute to teachers developing expertise and knowledge without requiring them to spend hours preparing for lessons.

---

* For instance, one teacher was uncomfortable with the inclusion of Aristophanes' *Lysistrata* (in which the women of Sparta go on sex strike to try to end the Peloponnesian War) in our Year 8 comedy anthology. Our advice was simply to skip it.

In the past, lesson plans existed – if they existed at all – in printed schemes of work. Someone would have gone to the trouble of writing down teaching objectives and a list of more or less sensible activities which were intended to lead to these objectives being fulfilled. When teachers planned lessons, they either made them up or adapted the ideas that featured in the scheme of work. Either way, they had to think about what they wanted to do with their students before the lesson took place.

When the software to create slideshows started to proliferate in schools, teachers would store their slides on a shared drive and other teachers could look at and adapt the slides of others. It felt like a step forward not to always need to make everything from scratch. However, over time it has become increasingly normal for lesson slides to be planned centrally. Teachers have come to expect to be given slides to teach schemes of work with no need for their own input. In the worst cases, this leads to teachers and students seeing these slides for the first time together. Although teachers are almost always told to adapt pre-prepared slides in advance of a lesson, the implicit message is that they're not required to *really* think about what they want students to learn until a lesson is underway.

Typically, sets of lesson slides contain detailed bullet points of exactly what should happen at every stage of a lesson, but in many cases, these instructions are for the benefit of teachers rather than students. The result is that a lot of what students are shown is extraneous, irrelevant or confusing. Sometimes, teachers are given the explicit instruction that lesson slides *must* be adapted for the students in their classes. Of course, the reality is that sometimes this happens and sometimes it doesn't. If you are given the means not to have to plan in advance, it's inevitable that sometimes you won't.

We wanted to shift the focus from lesson planning to intellectual preparation and so, rather than provide teachers with the means of teaching lessons unthinkingly, we wanted a strategy which forced them to engage with the curriculum content before teaching it.

The inspiration for using Teacher Guides as our implementation model came from Ormiston Ilkeston Enterprise Academy in Derbyshire. Kate Spalding and her team explained how they were using Teacher Guides to implement the new ambitious curriculum they'd planned over lockdown. Each Teacher Guide provided annotated versions of the texts in student booklets, instructions on how to teach lessons to deliver the curriculum, and a curated selection of articles and resources designed to ensure each member of the team had access to

The Creation of the World
(Genesis 1-2, KJV)

The Creation of Adam, Michelangelo (1508-1512)

In the beginning God created the heaven and the earth. And the earth was without form, and void; and darkness was upon the face of the deep. And the Spirit of God moved upon the face of the

5 waters.

And God said, "Let there be light." And there was light. And God saw the light, that it was good: and God divided the light from the darkness. And God called the light Day, and the darkness he called

10 Night. And the evening and the morning were the first day.

And God said, "Let there be a firmament in the midst of the waters, and let it divide the waters from the waters." And God made the firmament,

15 and divided the waters which were under the firmament from the waters which were above the firmament: and it was so. And God called the firmament Heaven. And the evening and the morning were the second day.

20 And God said, "Let the waters under the heaven be gathered together unto one place, and let the dry land appear." And it was so. And God called the dry land Earth; and the gathering together of the waters called the Seas: and God saw that it

25 was good. And God said, "Let the earth bring forth grass, the herb yielding seed, and the fruit tree yielding fruit after his kind, whose seed is in itself, upon the earth." And it was so. And the earth brought forth grass, and herb yielding seed after

30 his kind, and the tree yielding fruit, whose seed was in itself, after his kind: and God saw that it was good. And the evening and the morning were the third day.

And God said, "Let there be lights in the

35 firmament of the heaven to divide the day from the night; and let them be for signs, and for seasons, and for days, and years: And let them be for lights in the firmament of the heaven to give light upon the earth:" and it was so. And God

40 made two great lights; the greater light to rule the day, and the lesser light to rule the night: he made the stars also. And God set them in the firmament of the heaven to give light upon the earth. And to rule over the day and over the night, and to divide

45 the light from the darkness: and God saw that it was good. And the evening and the morning were the fourth day. And God said, "Let the waters bring forth abundantly the moving creature that hath life, and fowl that may fly above the earth in

50 the open firmament of heaven." And God created great whales, and every living creature that moveth, which the waters brought forth abundantly, after their kind, and every winged fowl after his kind: and God saw that it was good.

55 And God blessed them, saying, "Be fruitful, and multiply, and fill the waters in the seas, and let fowl multiply in the earth." And the evening and the morning were the fifth day.

And God said, "Let the earth bring forth the living

60 creature after his kind, cattle, and creeping thing, and beast of the earth after his kind:" and it was so. And God made the beast of the earth after his kind, and cattle after their kind, and every thing that creepeth upon the earth after his kind: and

65 God saw that it was good.

And God said, "Let us make man in our image, after our likeness: and let them have dominion

11

FIGURE 2.11 Pages from the King James Bible and Ancient Origins anthologies

105 Dictys, will protect her — and you have far to travel. First you must visit the Grey Sisters and learn from them how to find the Nymphs who dwell at the back of the North Wind: they will lend you all else that you may need, and will tell you how to find the Gorgons, and how to escape
110 from the two who are immortal, when you have slain Medusa."

So Perseus hastened away, his heart beating with excitement at the thought of the high adventure which was his, and the great honour which the
115 Immortals had done him.

He came, as Hermes had instructed him, to the lonely cave in the dark north where the three daughters of the Titan Phorcus lived, the Grey Sisters who had been born old women with grey
120 hair, and who had only one eye and one tooth between them.

Perseus stepped quietly up behind them as they sat near the mouth of their cave; and as they passed the single eye from one to another, he
125 took it from an outstretched hand, and then cried aloud: "Daughters of Phorcus, I have your eye! And I will keep it and leave you for ever in darkness if you do not tell me what I wish to know."

130 The Grey Sisters cried aloud in alarm: "Give us back our eye, and we will swear by Styx to tell you truthfully all you ask. But do not leave us for ever in this terrible darkness!"

So Perseus learnt the way to the magic land at the
135 back of the North Wind and, returning the eye, hastened on his journey.

When he reached the lovely garden of the Northern Nymphs, he was welcomed kindly by them, and he rested for a long time in the
140 paradise where they dwelt for ever young and happy.

But at length he said, "Fair Nymphs, I must hasten away to kill the Gorgon Medusa and carry her head to wicked King Polydectes. Tell me, I beg of
145 you, where the Gorgons live, and how I may kill Medusa."

"We will lend you the Shoes of Swiftness," answered the Nymphs, "so that you may escape from Medusa's terrible sisters. And we lend you
150 this magic wallet in which to carry away the head. There is but one thing wanting, and that is the Cap of Hades, the dog-skin cap which can make its wearer invisible.

Then one of the Nymphs went swiftly down to the
155 Realm of Hades, for she had been Persephone's favourite companion on earth, and could visit the

Queen of the Dead whenever she wished, and returned at will.

She brough back the Cap of Darkness, so that
160 Perseus now had all the things he needed, and was ready for his dreadful task.

He bade farewell to the kind Nymphs, and set out on the way which the Grey Sisters had told him, and he came at last to the stony land of the
165 Gorgons. As he drew near to where they lived, he saw all about in the fields and on the roads, the statues of me and beasts which had been living creatures until turned to stone by the deadly glance of the Gorgons.

170 Wearing the Cap of Darkness, and stepping cautiously, Perseus drew hear, looking only at the reflection in Athena's polished shield. Then he trembled indeed as he saw the terrible face of Medusa pictured on the bright surface; but he did
175 not draw back. Still looking only at the reflection, he drew the adamantine sickle and cut off the terrible head at a single blow. Then, quick as could be, he picked it up and dropped it into the wallet which the Nymphs had given him.

180 But the hissing of the snakes on Medusa's head woke the other two Gorgons, who could not be killed, and they sprang up, eager to avenge their sister.

Perseus and the head of Medusa, Benvenuto Cellini (1545–1554)

FIGURE 2.11 (Continued)

all the specialist knowledge they'd need to teach each aspect of a scheme of work. They referred to these guides as 'CPD in a book' and spent department time showing every member of the team how to turn the information in the guides into lessons. Individual teachers were welcome to put together their own slides should they want to, but the focus was very much on using visualisers to model reading and writing to students.

We took very little convincing that this was how we should go about implementing the OAT curriculum and set about writing Teacher Guides for the schemes of work we were creating. Although these provide suggestions for teaching activities and structures, in the main they focus on specifying, as clearly as we have been able to manage, the content to be communicated to students and the knowledge needed by teachers to make this a success.

To accompany each module, we have made training videos on how to use the Teacher Guides and turn them into lessons. This allows teachers and departments to experiment with teaching the schemes and to foreground what seems most important for their students. Unsurprisingly, this has come as something of a culture shock to teachers raised on being provided with detailed PowerPoints.

2.16.1 Flatpack curriculum

This is not to say that lesson slides are a bad thing *per se*. As a means for displaying visual information they definitely have their merits. We have

---

When I arrived at OIEA in 2020, the English department needed an entirely new curriculum. We needed a vision, we needed challenge and we needed teachers to feel passionate about what they were teaching. The Teacher Guides were born as part of this process.

As a team, our first step was to decide that our mantra would be 'Challenge, Empower, Succeed'. Growing from that, the plans for what we believe is a beautiful and exciting curriculum were laid. At this stage that I realised that I was expecting a very inexperienced team to produce and deliver some very challenging units. Because we did not all have the same level of knowledge and expertise in every area, different team members were asked to lead on and become the experts for different units. Whilst this is one of the things I love about our curriculum – it is truly ours, a team effort where everyone has a role and is an expert in their field – it also raised a challenge. It is one thing to create an ambitious, challenging curriculum but quite another to have teachers with the subject knowledge, confidence and passion to deliver it well.

Enter the Teacher Guide. We realised that, whilst we intended to produce student resource booklets to accompany each unit, there is a lot of detail and information which is either essential or useful to teachers which would simply be unnecessary in the student booklet; things such as the intent of the unit, how it is sequenced, connections to our overall journey,

wider reading, suggested teaching strategies, and of course, the Medium Term Plan itself are all features of our Teacher Guides. We felt it was important for the teacher to have a more in-depth knowledge that went beyond the actual lessons in order to develop their confidence. If, as a teacher, you feel a little rusty on that topic, or have never studied it in your life, the Teacher Guide literally guides you through everything you might need to know as a teacher as well as which parts need to be taught to the students. The Teacher Guides also ensure that staff have one eye on the bigger picture of the curriculum, rather than delivering each unit in isolation.

Further to the subject knowledge and lesson planning support in the Teacher Guides, they are also of practical use. They have evolved to include simple but crucial time-saving details, such as the equivalent page number a text can be found on in the student booklet. The Teacher Guides include the entire student booklet, fully annotated by the unit expert, to guide teachers to the key elements of each extract and are backed up by faculty time spent sharing the best implementation of the unit. In the words of our ECT, it is 'a life saver'. Teachers can now deliver challenging content with confidence, and this allows room for passion and excitement too. Thanks to Teacher Guides, it is not just the person who created it who loves the unit; we all do.

Kate Spalding, Head of English at Ormiston
Ilkeston Enterprise College

no issues with teachers using slides to share pictures, diagrams or moving images with student. The argument here is focused on the widespread practice of using PowerPoint (or any other similar product) as a means of implementing the curriculum.

For some, the notion of having to use the Teacher Guides to plan lessons felt like an unreasonable expectation at first, but most were weaned off using slides with relatively little complaint. Obviously, there have been lots of hiccups along the way, but most of the feedback we've received is that teachers have enjoyed teaching our modules and, through talking to students and looking at the work in their books, we can see the quality of the curriculum shining through.

Planning a curriculum via PowerPoint is suboptimal, even if you produce the best slides possible. We must remember that English covers a huge domain of knowledge. The curriculum samples from that domain, to give students access to powerful and culturally rich knowledge which they will be supported in using to make meaning. If we want students to have a meaningful experience of the curriculum, they need to see how ideas connect and branch beyond the limits of lessons. A lesson selects from a curriculum and seeks to distil complexity into a set of activities and actions that can take place within the confines of 50–60 minutes. There's nothing wrong with the process in itself, as long as teachers understand that it's the *process* of selecting and shaping content that leads to memorable and meaningful experiences. The problem with having lesson slides provided for you is that *someone else* has done that sampling and selecting for you. Unless we engage with as much of the domain – or at least as much of the curriculum – as possible before distilling content into a lesson we won't know much about the content of that lesson ourselves and this can lead to teachers knowing little more than their students.

But what about workload implications? What if you centrally plan 'bulletproof' lesson slides to ensure that early career teachers and non-specialist teachers are fully supported? Wouldn't that be better than asking teachers to spend their precious time planning lessons?

When the DfE conducted their workload survey back in 2015, the biggest complaint teachers made was about *unnecessary* workload.[59] Work that feels worthwhile and meaningful is not something most people tend to object to. But still, no one wants to add to the pressure on teachers unnecessarily. It's important to remember that no one is being asked to plan from scratch. The Teacher Guides contain everything needed to plan lessons and the process tends to take five to ten minutes at most. We try to ensure that teachers are given regular – at least weekly – departmental time to co-plan the week's lessons (see section 2.17) and to talk though potential issues. Our guides are designed to be a 'one-stop shop' containing all the subject knowledge needed to teach the modules and to enable teachers to do the required intellectual preparation to implement the curriculum well. Think of them as being the educational equivalent of flatpack furniture: everything required is in there, but you have to assemble it yourself. This can make a real difference to teachers' expertise and the development of subject knowledge.

The essence of the problem is this: If someone else plans your lessons, you don't learn the curriculum. The best you or your students can hope for is that you learn the contents of the PowerPoint. If you go through the process of turning the information contained in a Teacher Guide into a curated experience for your students to engage with, not only will they learn more, so will you.

2.16.2 Inside a Teacher Guide

Our guides all follow the same basic structure:

- Curriculum intent, knowledge and skills
- Curriculum-related expectations
- Implementation: How to use this guide
- Vocabulary strategy
- Subject terminology
- Topic vocabulary
- Excellent epithets
- Couch to 5k writing
- Slow writing
- Structured discussion
- Overview of sequencing

Each guide also contains a detailed, section-by-section medium-term plan which details the core knowledge to be taught (alongside some suggestions for additional extras which teachers can choose to include if circumstances warrant) as well as questions which students should be able to answer, vocabulary they need to learn and suggestions for

Curriculum intent

To introduce students to the study of rhetoric, the art of persuasion through examples from literature and famous speeches. This is also an opportunity to read Shakespeare's play *Julius Caesar* which provides some great examples of rhetoric. Students will also learn about various rhetorical figures and use them in their own writing. In addition to acquiring the core knowledge specified below, as students progress through the unit, they will:

- take part in a series of structured, teacher-led discussion where the use of academic language is modelled and scaffolded
- learn to write powerful, analytical sentences and comparative statements through the granular 'Couch to 5k' approach to extended writing
- experience regular reading fluency lessons which will focus on mastery and performance of texts.

You can watch the Intro to The Art of Rhetoric video here:
https://www.loom.com/share/320d2fbb78cc43b4bcd31366aa90bb35

Key skill areas
- Construct analytical statements in the form of thesis statements
- Select and embed relevant textual detail
- Make use of appositives and 'excellent epithets' to signal the direction of extended analytical writing
- Use thesis statements to write a series of topic sentences
- Analyse the writer's use of language, structure and form
- Compare texts in relation to literary concepts, ideas and methods

Core knowledge

Content	**The art of rhetoric**
	- Shakespeare - *Julius Caesar*
	- Famous speeches (Paradise Lost, Cicero, Abraham Lincoln, Martin Luther King Jr, Barack Obama,)
Metaphor	- Tenor, vehicle, ground - Flowers of rhetoric - Antithesis, hyperbole, metonymy, synecdoche, transferred epithets
Story	- Genre: tragedy - Drama - Façade/flaw
Argument	- Ethos, logos, pathos - Thesis statements - Arrangement (See JC Act 3 scene 2) - Structuring arguments - Composition
Pattern	- Metrical feet: iambic pentameter - Acts & scenes - Anaphora, alliteration, assonance, isocolon, tricolon
Grammar	- Changing word classes; matching suffixes to word class - Clauses & sentences - Sentences (subjects & verbs; fragments; run-ons)
Context	- Using context to support arguments - Origins of rhetoric (Aristotle & Cicero) - Elizabethan anxieties; attitudes to suicide

FIGURE 2.12 Intent overview from *The Rhetoric Teacher Guide*

C25k writing, structured discussion and reading fluency. (See Figure 2.12.)

Curriculum-related expectations are divided into three sections: terminology students need to be able to **define**, things they should **know** and things they ought to be able to **do** based on the teaching of the module. (See Figure 2.13.)

Then, each section of the guide (see Figure 2.14) includes teaching suggestions, additional reading and annotated versions of the texts in the Student Anthologies. The intention is that if teachers prepare by working through the guide – ideally alongside colleagues – they will have all they need to bring the curriculum to vivid life. For each module we have also produced an 'Introduction to...' video explaining anything tricky or unfamiliar, pointing out key elements of the Teacher Guide and demonstrating how to turn the guide into lessons by establishing the following:

- What needs to be taught, including topic vocabulary and subject terminology
- What to include in retrieval practice (Carousel Learning has all of this ready to go; teachers just need to select quiz items ready for lessons)
- What needs to be read aloud to students and what should be read as part of fluency lessons
- Prompts for structured discussion
- Prompts for deconstructed essay practice
- Prompts for slow writing

These introductory videos can be found on https://english.ormiston academiestrust.co.uk/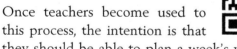
Once teachers become used to this process, the intention is that they should be able to plan a week's worth of lessons in 10–15 minutes.

The guides have evolved based on feedback from teachers about what they have found most useful. Some suggestions have been both obvious and simple to implement such as including a contents page to make the guides easier to navigate. Others have required us to do a fair amount of redesign in order to make them as user friendly as possible.

In addition, most of the modules also come with a slide deck of images and information which a teacher might decide is useful to display to students. Most of these slides are taken directly from the Student Anthology and, where possible, we encourage teachers to display the anthology under a visualiser rather than go to the trouble of creating slides.

2.17 THE IMPORTANCE OF CO-PLANNING

Resources are only part of the solution: teachers need to be supported in sharing expertise, and work cooperatively to do the intellectual preparation required to turn resources into meaningful lessons.

However much of a boon they may be, Student Anthologies and Teacher Guides are not enough. When teachers plan lessons in isolation much can go awry. Essential points may be overlooked or misunderstood; too much time may be spent on one aspect of a module at the expense of other aspects; the content may be covered but students do not always learn what we have taught.

To circumvent some of these pitfalls, we recommend that teachers regularly sit down together to plan their lessons collaboratively. Of course, this requires time. And time is a commodity teachers tend to lack so it's on schools to make sure this time is built into the working week.

If schools want to take curriculum seriously, they must allocate *at least* an hour per week for co-planning. Schools that allocate two hours a week to this endeavour are very much more likely to implement the curriculum well. Some of our schools are fortunate enough to timetable these meetings into the school day, others have dedicated weekly co-planning meetings after work. Either way, this time is critical to making sure the curriculum is implemented well.

Ideally, a weekly co-planning session will involve all teachers bringing along the Teacher Guides for the year groups they're teaching and deciding together what should feature in the coming week's lessons. There is no expectation that teachers read all the background reading in the guides in advance; it is included as a point of reference for those who want or need it. That said, it may be a good idea for a head of department to appoint a module leader for each of the modules being taught so they can read guides in advance and lead the co-planning sessions.

[OAT] KS3 English curriculum War Writing – Teacher Guide

Curriculum-Related Expectations

Students can define the following terms:

Allusion	Blank verse	Caesura
Climax	Characterisation	Irony
Dialogue	Denouement	Dialect
Form	Figurative language	Formalism
Direct address	Foreshadowing	End-stopping
Structure	Realism	Sibilance
Personification	Rhyming couplet	Juxtaposition
Absurdity	Protagonist	Exposition
Caesura	Enjambment	Individualism
Sonnet		

Students know:

- The influence of the First World War on the development of modernism as a literary movement
- *Journey's End* is a modernist play
- What makes a 'well-made' play
- The 3 different types of irony (dramatic, situational & verbal)
- How Aristotle's 5-part plot structure applies to *Journey's End*
- Characters are vehicles which represent particular tenors
- Themes are tenors represented by different vehicles
- Aristotle's dramatic unities and how these apply to *Journey's End*
- How to explain the effects of irony and symbolism
- How characters from different social classes are presented in *Journey's End*
- How heroism, comradeship, class and power are presented in *Journey's End*

Students can

- Use tenor, vehicle and ground to analyse a range of metaphors
- Use excellent epithets to evaluate and analyse characters and themes
- Demonstrate understanding of societal anxiety portrayed through war writing
- Evaluate the processes a writer uses to create characters
- Explain the effects of figures and schemes in poetry
- Develop use of conceptual metaphors to craft own detailed description.
- Use a range of create sentence types in descriptive writing (see Appendix 2)
- Summarise chronological events within Journey's End and the development of tension and conflict.
- Evaluate the roles of Stanhope, Osbourne and Raleigh,and Sherriff's purpose in creating such characters.
- Discuss thematic links between texts

FIGURE 2.13 Curriculum-related expectations from *The War Writing Teacher Guide*

Section 1: How Novels Work

Key questions	Core knowledge	Terminology & vocabulary	Discussion, reading & writing
Big question: Why have novels become the most popular form of literature? **Key questions:** What is a novel? When was the novel invented? How does Dickens use novelistic conventions in *Great Expectations*?	Read Chapters 1-5 of *Great Expectations*: focus on the presentation of Pip as protagonist and narrator. After reading, discuss different definitions of the novel: 1. A fictitious prose narrative of book length, typically representing character and action with some degree of realism 2. A relatively long work of narrative fiction, typically written in prose and published as a book 3. An invented prose narrative of significant length and complexity that deals imaginatively with human experience - What are the key features? Length, prose, content? - **NB.** Read the Eagleton extract below first (not with students!) Ways writers can use symbolism, imagery, and language to develop and convey themes in a story Texts: - Chapters 1-5 of Great Expectations - Lecture on Transportation - Victorian Prisons and Punishments - Dickens Witnesses a Hanging	**Terminology** Exposition Foreshadowing Narrative Perspective Novel Conventions Weather Symbolism **Vocabulary** Innocent Naïve Petrified Vulnerable Convict Ferocious Loyal Fetter	**Structured discussions:** How does Dickens present childhood? Why might Dickens create a feeling of sympathy towards the convict? **Couch to 5k writing:** How is Pip/the convict/Joe Gargery presented in chapters 1 - 5 of *Great Expectations*? **Slow Writing** -The more, the more/the less, the less (2) - The Not, (not), nor, nor sentence (7) -The so, so sentence (11) **Reading fluency:** The exchange between Pip and Magwitch in Chapter 1

Expert knowledge

Pip: As both narrator and protagonist, Pip is naturally the most important character in *Great Expectations*: the novel is his story, told in his words, and his perceptions utterly define the events and characters of the book. As a result, Dickens's most important task as a writer in *Great Expectations* is the creation of Pip's character. Because Pip's is the voice with which he tells his story, Dickens must make his voice believably human while also ensuring that it conveys all the information necessary to the plot. In this first section, Pip is a young child, and Dickens masterfully uses Pip's narration to evoke the feelings and problems of childhood. Pip is horrified by the convict, but despite his horror, he treats him with compassion and kindness. Throughout this section, Pip's self-commentary mostly emphasizes his negative qualities: his dishonesty and his guilt. This is characteristic of Pip as a narrator throughout *Great Expectations*. Despite his many admirable qualities – the strongest of which are compassion, loyalty, and conscience – Pip constantly focuses on his failures and shortcomings. To understand him as a character, it is necessary to look beyond his self-descriptions and consider his actions. In fact, it may be his powerful sense of his own moral shortcomings that motivates Pip to act so morally.

Setting: the "shrouded" marshes of Kent and the oppressive bustle of Mrs. Joe's house – are also important to the novel. Dickens uses setting to create a dramatic atmosphere: the setting of the book always sets the tone for the action and reinforces Pip's perception of his situation. When the weather is dark and stormy, trouble is usually brewing, and when Pip goes alone into the mist-shrouded marsh, danger and ambiguity usually await (Pathetic fallacy). In this section, Pip's story shifts rapidly between dramatic scenes with the convict on the marshes and comical scenes under Mrs. Joe's thumb at home. Despite Mrs. Joe's rough treatment of Pip, which she calls bringing him up "by hand", the comedy that pervades her household in Chapter 2 shows that it is a safe haven for Pip. When Pip ventures out alone onto the marshes, he leaves the sanctuary of home for vague, murky churchyards and the danger of a different world. This sense of

FIGURE 2.14 Section overview from *The Story of the Novel Teacher Guide*

Co-planning sessions create a forum for teachers to interrogate and understand the curriculum. Working together allows teachers to develop shared approaches to the curriculum and to form strong foundations for their own knowledge. At Cowes Enterprise College, this has been vital as we've developed our own knowledge of a range of new texts and new pedagogical approaches to support the effective delivery of the OAT curriculum. Working together in this way has allowed us to come together in a fear-free, supportive environment, and to discuss how to teach the core elements of the curriculum. This has enabled us to develop new skills, as well as to build on our existing expertise.

One of the most effective strategies we've begun to embed this year, and one that has been essential in building teacher knowledge and confidence, has been the implementation of pre-unit briefings to ensure that the core concepts of the unit are clearly understood, and that any potential misconceptions can be addressed before we start to teach. These are attended by all staff whether or not they are teaching the year group in question. This ensures knowledge and expertise are developed across the department, and also that the sequencing of the curriculum is explicitly shared with everyone.

To make the briefings as effective as possible, one member of the team becomes the 'expert', or the module leader, in the unit, and then presents the core concepts and knowledge to the department, allowing time for questions, debate and discussion to ensure staff have confidence in their understanding of the specifics of the unit. Each teacher in the department has both a teacher and student guide, as well as a copy of the end of unit assessment, so that as a department, a coherent approach to covering the unit is clearly developed, potential misconceptions are addressed and, perhaps most importantly, an opportunity for questions and exploration is provided to ensure that the core concepts and knowledge are at the forefront of the smaller group planning sessions within the weekly timetable.

Because of the size of our department – we currently have 16 members of the team working, many of whom are part time – we divide into teams focusing on specific year groups. Planning

in isolation can lead to misunderstandings or inconsistent coverage; co-planning is really helpful in mitigating this, allowing the team to share key information for the week ahead, resource materials and assessment information with the rest of the department.

One of the fundamental benefits of co-planning is ensuring all students can access the same core knowledge, giving time and consideration to adaptive teaching strategies. Scaffolding strategies can be built into the planning, thus helping to ensure that every student has access to the same high-quality learning and knowledge. Take, for example, metaphor, one of the curriculum's underpinning concepts. The way it is taught, through naming the constituent parts of metaphor (tenor, vehicle and ground) has been new to staff and students, so not only have we had to develop our own subject knowledge, we've also had to really focus this year on how to ensure that the specified knowledge becomes 'sticky' for all students. Exploring together how to scaffold the lessons so each student is able to learn and retain this key knowledge has been invaluable. Co-planning has provided us with time and space to consider how we can best adapt the teaching of core concepts to ensure that every student is able to access and acquire the core knowledge and achieve success.

Our co-planning sessions have allowed time to explore how we can structure our lessons to ensure that the five core pedagogies form the bedrock of learning. Each lesson across our department now starts with a 'five-a-day' retrieval practice, built on the core knowledge which students need to know. Department co-planning has allowed us to really focus on getting this aspect right and we've been able to develop a consistent approach which is now securely embedded across all lessons in our curriculum. Similarly, we've built vocabulary instruction into lessons, adapting core vocabulary to suit the needs of our context and learners as we've progressed through the year; we now ensure that a range of word classes are taught alongside the key word to enable students to have greater flexibility and control in their vocabulary use. Co-planning then ensures that definitions are consistent for all students and that our approach aligns with the curriculum.

We've also been able to use the time to explore how to move away from PowerPoint lessons, which have been such a staple part of our planning and delivery for so long. While we still use slides, having a forum to focus on how using a visualiser can support the delivery of the curriculum, or to think about how we can use mini-whiteboards effectively, has meant that staff have felt empowered to try these approaches in their classrooms and to see the benefits. While this is definitely a work in progress for us, it has been joyful to see staff and students embracing these approaches.

An ideal co-planning meeting might run as follows:

- Teachers review previous learning and use the specified core knowledge and concepts to inform the forthcoming week's planning
- Teacher and student guides form the basis for planning, with Teacher Guides essentially becoming the planning document
- Teachers have time to discuss and explore core concepts and to develop their own subject knowledge in order to ensure they are fluent and flexible in order to aid delivery
- Teachers use the suggested teaching strategies and see where/how these might work best in conjunction with the guides
- Retrieval questions are developed to ensure students have a successful start to the lesson
- Core vocabulary is identified and added to where necessary
- Teachers have time to scaffold the learning to ensure all students can access the learning

- Teachers might work together to focus on an extract for echo reading, or collaboratively create worked examples of sentence types to support teaching of thesis statements, for example
- Misconceptions that have arisen / might appear can also be discussed, foregrounded and resolved for both staff and students
- Opportunities for re-teaching are identified

Co-planning has allowed for ongoing adaptation and reflection and has been instrumental in developing staff confidence. It's also been hugely valuable CPD for teachers, challenging staff to think about teaching and learning from a different perspective. Of course, the implementation of any curriculum is going to create bumps along the road, and it would be disingenuous to suggest that our implementation of this has been perfect, but the time provided by our co-planning sessions means we can address issues in a timely and supportive fashion. Perhaps the most significant benefit, though, is the clear sense of collegiality and co-operation which is firmly embedded within our department; we are just as likely to be discussing teaching strategies over our lunch in our shared workspace as we are in our designated co-planning or after school meetings. It is this culture of support which both leads to, and is a result of, effective co-planning and shared department time.

Kate Moloney, Lead Practitioner (South) and Teacher of English, Cowes Enterprise College

2.18 SCALING ACROSS MULTIPLE SCHOOLS

When working with teachers across multiple schools, curriculum support needs to be high quality and easy to access.

It's hard enough to implement a curriculum within a single school; attempting to ensure faithful implementation across multiple schools is a near-insurmountable challenge. One possible solution is to be completely prescriptive about lesson planning but, as we've already discussed, this is antithetical to the approach we've taken. Instead, we've decided it's better to take

a hit on fidelity to allow teachers to enact the curriculum in ways that best suit their contexts.

We're very clear that everything in our Teacher Guides is suggested rather than required. If there's a text you don't like, don't read it. If there's an activity that doesn't make sense, don't do it. We make it clear that teachers should feel free to take what they want and leave what they don't. But we've also been careful to signpost what we think is 'core' knowledge. As already mentioned, (and as is discussed in detail in section 3.6) we make clear what we believe to be reasonable curriculum-related expectations (CREs). These CREs form the basis of both our curriculum assessments as well as the homework and retrieval practice questions made available through Carousel Learning. If a department decides to depart from our CREs they will need to find alternatives to assess whether students are learning what they have been taught.

Another way we have attempted faithful implementation is through blatant bribery. Printing class sets of our Student Anthologies is expensive and, as a Trust, we have covered this expense. So much time and effort has gone into creating beautifully produced and curated resources that once teachers – and students – have access to the materials they tend to be enthusiastic about using them in the classroom.

But, as we've seen, enthusiasm and some shiny booklets aren't enough. It's also important to provide high-quality training on implementation. Each member of the English Lead Practitioner team spends time working with English departments, modelling lessons, working alongside teachers, and taking part in co-planning sessions. We also run regular network events both virtually and face to face to pass on and discuss aspects of the curriculum.

As necessary as this is – and as awesome as we are – there just aren't enough of us to meet every demand and so we have also recorded training videos of us detailing how to approach the trickier, least familiar aspects of the curriculum. These are hosted on a platform inaccessible to teachers outside OAT but, to give readers a sense of what's needed, you can view a sample of some of our training videos on https://english.ormistonacademies trust.co.uk/training-resources/.

Lessons learned from implementation at Ormiston Cliff Park Academy

Whilst we wouldn't have chosen many of the challenges that we faced at Cliff Park during our first year of teaching the OAT curriculum, it was certainly a rigorous and effective way to quality-assure our KS3 curriculum. For context, Cliff Park serves a coastal community with double the national average of unemployment and only 10% of the local population educated to degree level; historically student behaviour has been very challenging, and the school has been through some difficult times. However, there are also growing local opportunities in the offshore energy sector and in both local hospital and local authority management and administration and we had an enthusiastic and experienced team of practitioners in the department.

Here are some of our key takeaways:

1. Prepare and consider possible hiccups and obstacles before implementation begins. As we know, when we try something new in a school – especially something as large as curriculum change in an entire key stage – there is often a dip in performance at first, before we see improvements.[60] By preparing the team, discussing possible solutions ahead of time and being frank with senior leaders, we were better able to navigate the inevitable bumps in the road.

2. Commit to the basics. The core pedagogies discussed in the book are central to the delivery of the curriculum, and without them, successful implementation becomes less likely. This means changing the way teachers do things, such as no longer analysing KS3 texts in minute detail. Before the curriculum is implemented, as much time as possible should be spent ensuring staff are confident in using the core pedagogies in the classroom, as well as regularly revisiting and sharing good practice throughout the school year.

3. Before teaching, staff need time to read, prepare and discuss the curriculum content and concepts. It is essential to focus more on intellectual preparation and subject knowledge development and less on planning individual lessons. Co-planning redundant as a team is integral. There is a wealth of resources and signposts for teachers to explore and this needs some guidance. Whilst a lot of new content is daunting to begin with, it can also be a great source of professional development.

4. Reading texts together is one of the best uses of time in the classroom. This may seem obvious, but it's important to reiterate it, and then empower staff to focus more on class reading. Our introduction of weekly fluency lessons further supported this shift in our thinking, as did strategies such as Reader's Theatre.[61] Hearing *The Odyssey* being chanted and enjoyed in classrooms up and

down the English corridor has been one of the proudest moments of my career.

5. KS2 knowledge is deliberately interwoven within the OAT KS3 curriculum. Having pre-teaching knowledge checks built into our Year 7 units provided an excellent way of gauging students' prior learning, as well as liaising with our local primary feeders. Students in Year 7 particularly enjoyed making connections with topics they'd studied in Years 5 or 6 (even when that learning had been disrupted by COVID). Staff were surprised by how much their students knew which helped to raise the level of challenge and teacher expectations.

6. The modules focused on drama texts work brilliantly for piloting. We received very positive responses to *The Odyssey*, *Journey's End* and *Oedipus Tyrannus* in particular, both informally in staff meetings and conversations, but also in student panels and surveys. If you're considering piloting a module, our experience would suggest starting with Ancient Origins in Year 7, Comedy in Year 8 and War Writing or Tragedy in Year 9.

7. It's absolutely worth the effort. Implementing an entirely new KS3 curriculum all at once was a gargantuan task which required a lot of work from everyone involved. But the results speak for themselves. There has been pleasing external validation in the form of Trust reviews and an Ofsted inspection, but more importantly, external assessments such as GL tests and participating in Improving Secondary Writing indicate that students are improving across the key stage in reading, writing and oracy. The most satisfying feedback of all, of course, has been from staff and students with a renewed buzz in the department and, as one of the team told me, 'We're enjoying teaching English again'.

Claire Woozley, English Regional Lead Practitioner, East

IMPLEMENTATION: KEY POINTS

1. **The aim of implementation should be to achieve *gapless instruction*.**

   If we accept that students – particularly the most disadvantaged students – struggle because we have left gaps in our teaching, then we should commit to identifying and eliminating gaps. Wherever students struggle there is a need for greater clarity or skills to be further broken down into teachable chunks of knowledge which can then be practised and mastered.

2. **Teachers need training and support in the five core pedagogies.**

   We cannot take for granted that teachers know how to implement the five core pedagogies we have identified. Our approaches to retrieving knowledge, learning vocabulary, practising reading, writing and discussion all need training and support if teachers, and therefore students, are to be successful.

3. **Curriculum-related reading material should be curated into booklets/anthologies.**

   A great English curriculum must be centred around great material. It's not enough to provide teachers with an anchor text and expect them to supplement it with high-quality supporting texts themselves. Not only is this hugely time consuming, it leads, inevitably, to an asymmetry of access where some students get a less rich diet than others. Centrally curating resources also means being able to guarantee minimum standards of presentation and design which can help students to access reading material more easily.

4. **Teacher Guides offer flexibility and support the development of teachers' expertise.**

   Expecting teachers to plan great lessons from scratch is unreasonable but it's equally unacceptable to simply hand out pre-written resources that teachers don't have to engage with prior to teaching. If we care about implementing a meaningful curriculum experience for students, then Teacher Guides offer a 'flat-packed' version of the curriculum in which all the resourcing and thought has been done in advance but self-assembly is required to turn this into lessons.

5. **Co-planning is essential for successful curriculum implementation.**

   It's not enough to provide teachers with high-quality, pre-written curriculum materials and expect students to get a brilliant experience of English. If we care about the implementation of the curriculum, we must make sure teachers have a *minimum* of an hour a week to work collaboratively, using their Student Anthologies and Teacher Guides, to plan great lessons.

Impact

Assessing the curriculum

3.1 WHAT WE MEAN BY 'IMPACT'

The impact of the curriculum lies in the effect it has on students and whether they have been able to master the concepts and processes they have been taught.

Quite simply, the curriculum is having an impact if students know, remember and can do what has been specified. To this end, we need mechanisms to discover whether students know what we *think* they know, and a clear plan for what should be done when, inevitably, we discover some students can't do what we think they should be able to do. We can only know whether students have learnt what we want them to learn through assessment. This might sound obvious enough but what's less clear is what such assessments should look like and what we ought to do with the information they generate.

Ofsted have told us that because no one can be confident in the reliability or validity of schools' assessment processes, 'inspectors will not look at school's internal progress and attainment data'.[1] On one hand, we might breathe a sigh of relief that there is no external pressure on schools to produce spreadsheets, flightpaths or any of the byzantine number systems which have proliferated in recent years, but on the other we have to wonder why 'data' has become such a dirty word.[2]

Although we should be liberated by not being required to provide data for inspectors, it is easy for us to be so concerned with proving the impact of our curriculum that we start doing silly things. In the worst cases, this results in schools obsessed with filling children's exercise books with 'proof' of their progress. Such attempts are not only misguided (written work can only ever offer cursory glimpses of students'

ephemeral performance and never their learning[3]); they will lead inexorably to drudgery and misery for both teachers and students. Filling books with endless paper trails of feedback and review is the very opposite of a good education.

What *does* matter is whether teachers are able to say, 'Most students have learnt what I've taught them because they were able to recall and apply it independently weeks or months after we last discussed it in class'. One sure way to check that students are learning what you hope is to provide them with regular opportunities for retrieval practice; if they – and you – can see that their fluency and mastery are incrementally improving then you can be fairly sure of the impact you're having.

As discussed in section 2.4, we define learning as the retention and transfer of knowledge to new contexts. Retention is a marker of the durability of learning; transfer is indicative of its flexibility. Although this sounds straightforward enough, the difficulty comes in *how* we know whether students are learning what we intend. This means that in order for our curriculum to show the impact we desire, students need to remember the important conceptual information they are taught throughout their time studying English, and to be able to apply it to a range of different texts and question types both in the classroom and, ultimately, in the examination hall. This means that the way we assess must focus on the core conceptual knowledge we have specified – the knowledge contained within the six organising concepts discussed in Part 1 – and not the hinterland knowledge that will have enlivened and illustrated these concepts. In order for us to have confidence that students are retaining and able to apply conceptual knowledge, this regimen

DOI: 10.4324/9781003455622-3

of assessment will need to include both informal, formative quizzes and well as more formal, summative tests.

All too often, English teachers attempt to make judgements about the impact of the curriculum by using vaguely worded proxies based on the language of exam board mark schemes. While these *may* be appropriate for making a judgement of students' performance at the end of a course, they are, we believe, a poor way to gain information about how effective a curriculum is and how well it's being taught. This belief leads to two connected principles:

1. Assessments should lead to judgments being primarily of the curriculum and its implementation, not of students' ability.
2. Students should only be assessed on whether they know and can do the things they have been taught; if we haven't taught something, we consider it both unfair and unhelpful to assess it.

From these principles, all else in Part 3 of this book follows.

3.2 USING THE CURRICULUM AS A PROGRESSION MODEL

If students know and can do what has been covered in the curriculum, then they have made progress.

Historically, we have tended to view students' progression in English as meeting a series of generic skills descriptors. As Michael Fordham has pointed out, 'By focusing on broad, generic statements about the nature of the discipline we find ourselves unable to say what is distinct about what we do'.[4]

Instead, we conceive of progression in English as being inescapably linked to students learning and practising the knowledge contained within the curriculum. Getting better at English means mastering specifics such as the ability to define and deploy subject terminology; to interpret specific texts with increasing fluency and confidence and to convey these interpretations using a range of analytic structures; to understand the different parts of metaphor, demonstrate an appreciation of how they have been used by other writers and to use them in one's own writing; to learn the different patterns writers use to bring coherence and meaning to their work, to notice the effects of these patterns and to use them to structure their own writing, and so on. In short,

the disciplinary and substantive knowledge set out in Part 1 of this book.

As we saw in section 1.5, the curriculum fails to be an effective progression model if it is not specific enough and is not coherently sequenced to allow students to make progress. In both cases, some students – usually the more advantaged – will be successful despite curriculum weaknesses. They come to school with enough background knowledge to make sense of our vague explanations and assumptions and have enough support outside school to cope with any deficits. The students who suffer will be the most disadvantaged, who possess neither the required background knowledge we've failed to teach, nor the external support to recover from our failures. If these students are getting good outcomes in English, we can be reasonably sure it's because we've done a good job.

Using the curriculum as a progression model simply means that we make judgements of progress based on how much of the curriculum a child has learned. The more carefully we have specified what we intend to teach, the more easily we can assess whether they've learned it. Unlike an age-related expectation (which is just something an average child of a particular age is assumed to be able to do, regardless of what they've been taught), having curriculum-related expectations (see section 3.6) helps us to specify, teach and assess the knowledge we expect children to acquire. It becomes reasonable to expect children to have met these expectations because they are – or should be – directly connected to what has been taught.

If many students have failed to meet our expectations, we should assume that the fault is with either the curriculum or its teaching. If a few students have failed to meet some of our expectations, we can assume that they might need extra support and begin the process of establishing what knowledge they are missing.

This is the essence of what it means to use the curriculum as a progression model. If you're using age-related expectations or flightpaths, this is inimical to using *the curriculum* as your progression model.

3.3 THE MADNESS OF FLIGHTPATHS

Predicting the path an individual student will take from Year 7 to Year 11 is both impossible and actively harmful to students.

Schools are, on the whole, determined to find ways to predict students' progress from year to year and between key stages. Seemingly, the most common approach to solving this problem is to produce some sort of 'flightpath'. Predicting an individual student's progress is an impossibility. At the level of a nationally representative population sample, we can estimate the likelihood of someone measured as performing at one level at point *a* attaining another level at point *b*, but this is meaningless at the level of individuals. It should therefore be obvious that using flightpaths to inform assessment or guide teaching compounds an error. So, why do some schools continue to use them?

The answer is threefold. First, many school leaders still believe someone somewhere requires them to do this. Second, some actually believe it's possible or desirable to make a meaningful statement about an individual student's chances of achieving a prediction. Third, there's a belief that reports to families, governors, inspectors or some other shadowy party must be based on numbers.

First and foremost, school leaders need to understand that there is no requirement for schools to predict students' grades. Ofsted explain why inspectors ignore pointless data:

> Data should not be king. Too often, vast amounts of teachers' and leaders' time is absorbed into recording, collecting and analysing excessive progress and attainment data within schools. And that diverts their time away from what they entered the profession to do, which is to be educators. And, in fact, with much of that progress and attainment data, they and we can't be confident that it's valid and reliable information… **inspectors will not look at school's internal progress and attainment data.**[5]

Secondly, we need to understand that it is neither possible nor desirable to make meaningful statements about an individual student's chances of achieving a predicted grade. As Mike Treadaway has demonstrated, measuring pupil progress involves more than taking a straight line. As you can see from Figure 3.1, children

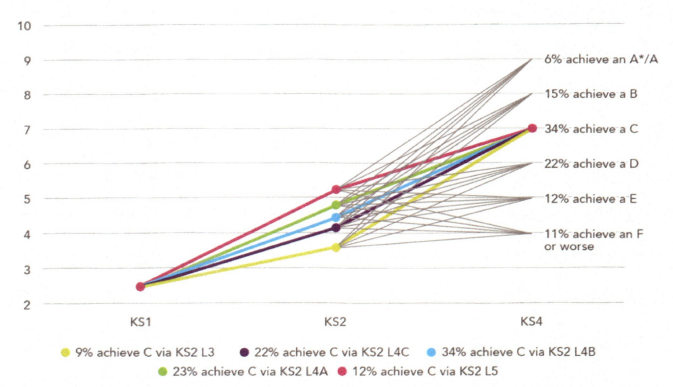

FIGURE 3.1 Linear progress of pupils from their Key Stage 1 assessment forms the basis of targets. Note: Average attainment, grouped by Key Stage 1 sub-level, for children aged 16 between 2008 and 2010 Key Stage 1 = average English and maths levels; Key Stage 2 and Key Stage 3 = average English and maths test fine grades; Key Stage 4 = average English and maths GCSE grades (A* = 10; G = 3)

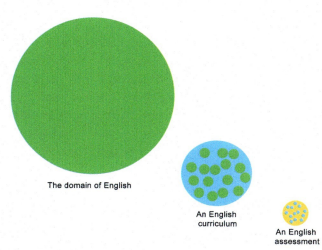

The domain of English

An English curriculum

An English assessment

FIGURE 3.2 Assessments sample from the curriculum which samples from the domain. A curriculum – or an exam board specification – takes some (but not all) aspects of a domain and then an assessment samples some (but not all) aspects of the curriculum. Ostensibly, this is to test whether students have mastered the domain, whereas in fact it can only ever provide a tiny snapshot of the knowledge contained within the domain.

cases, a spurious combination of bias, coin tosses and post-hoc rationalisation.

When predictions are made about individual students' performance, these predictions can become self-fulfilling. If students (or teachers) believe that they can't do better than a Grade 4, many will stop trying. Why would we ever want to convince anyone that children are less capable than they might be? As the graph in Figure 3.1 shows, prior attainment does allow us to make meaningful predictions about very large groups of pupils, but these predictions are probabilistic. They are not fate. Additionally, focusing only on GCSE predictions also increases workload and skews the curriculum towards what is sampled by exam boards, rather than mastery of the domain as is shown in Figure 3.2.

Finally, whilst schools have a statutory obligation to report to families on students' progress, there is no requirement for these reports to be based on internally collected progress or attainment data. For the same reason that inspectors ignore such reports, there is no external requirement that families or governors must receive reports based on made-up numbers. Reporting and assessment are not the same. When it comes to knowing how their children are getting on in schools, families have the right to receive an annual report but the form this report takes is for schools to determine. We'll explore some recommendations for reporting to families in section 3.15.

attaining identical scores in KS1 go on to achieve widely varying results at the end of KS2, and by the time they're 16, the best we can say is that *66% of them will achieve a grade other than the one they were predicted to get*. And of those 34% who do hit their prediction, 'More children get to the "right" place in the "wrong" way, than get to the "right" place in the "right" way'.[6]

These predictions are based on data derived from standardised national examinations. As such, we can make empirical statements about their reliability and the validity of our inferences. Reliability varies from subject to subject but for more subjectively assessed subject areas (English, history etc.) reliability might be as low as 0.6.[7] Essentially, what this means is that 40% of papers would have received a different mark if marked by a different examiner. And there are also issues about whether a student would receive the same mark if they sat the paper on a different day. This might sound alarming but it's infinitely better than the vast majority of internal assessments conducted by schools where no one even attempts to collect data about reliability, never mind the host of other variables that might be out of kilter. What this boils down to is that internal progress and attainment data is, in most

3.4 SHOULD WE GRADE STUDENTS?

Grades have an inevitable and often negative effect on how students view themselves and how they are viewed by teachers.

The routine use of a tool changes us; when society incorporates a tool, society is changed. If we view grades as a tool we should consider the function they accomplish. Maybe the routine use of grades in education has changed us in ways we haven't really considered.

Jared Horvath argues:

Because grading is simply a tool, we learn little by asking questions like 'Will students learn better if we employ more nuanced grades?' or 'How can we organize assessment in a way that will improve student outcomes?' The more instructive question to ask is 'What world view do grades espouse?' In other words, what does the tool of grading itself suggest about the world, how it functions, and how it should be approached?[8]

Grades alter reality by forcing us to reify, quantify and rank. To reify is to turn an abstract concept into something more concrete. This happens a lot in education. For instance, 'learning' is an abstraction. Although we all think we know what it is, we can't perceive it with our senses. When we say, 'I can see lots of learning going on in that class', we have reified learning in order that we can speak about it as if it's a thing, but – regardless of how we use language – it remains an imperceptible abstraction. Then, once we've reified something we can quantify it. It's a short step from the claim you can 'see learning' to believing that you can see how *well* students are learning. This has led to inspectors judging learning on a four-point scale. Then once a thing can be quantified, it can be ranked. If you can 'see' that *this* teacher's students are learning more or better than *that* teacher's students then we can rank teachers as better and worse. In turn this invites us to ask questions like, who is the best teacher? The point, of course, is that this is a nonsense. Learning remains an abstraction and all you ever see are proxies.

This is exactly what happens with grades. Examination boards attempt to precisely reify the abstraction of academic performance within the domains of English Language and Literature; they produce examinations which quantify students' performance and then each individual student's performance is ranked, and they are awarded a grade. We *know* grades can have a toxic and distorting effect, which is precisely why Ofsted (and most schools) stopped grading teachers. However, we still appear to think that grading schools – and students – is a good idea.

Let's think about what grading students does to the system. Students' identities become increasingly dependent upon external validation. If we want students to be driven by more than an external sense of their self-worth, maybe

we should reflect on the thought that what we do in education is a major part of the problem. How much of our day-to-day effort is invested in increasing our students' rankings? The inescapable, grinding focus of raising students' rank has a seriously warping effect on the curriculum. We don't just teach the syllabus; we drill students in test performance in order to ensure they get the best possible results. Essentially, grading is only beneficial for someone else. GCSE grades help post-16 providers sort students into academic or vocational pathways; A level grades are useful for universities; university classifications are (somewhat) useful to employers. But why should it be the job of schools to make it easier for universities to recruit the students they'd prefer to recruit?

Whilst most of this is out of the hands of school leaders and English teachers, we do have considerable freedom about how we use grades within school. If we're going to use grades we should be clear on what the costs and benefits might be. As we'll see, there are three main reasons why we continue to grade students internally.

Families want to know how their children are getting on in school and the only way the information their teachers provide becomes meaningful is when they are given some sense of their performance relative to that of others. One of the reasons schools report students' progress using GCSE grades is because families have a sense of what they mean. Of course, the information these grades supply is, in part, illusory because schools are unable to grade accurately, but, in broad terms a child who is reported as achieving a grade 7 in English is clearly doing a lot better than a child given a grade 3. Parents and families want to know how their children compare. But why? Is it just to vicariously validate their own self-worth?

Schools also reify, quantify and report students' rank in effort. By comparing effort grades with attainment grades, parents and families have a sense of how hard children are working. If they're working hard but performing poorly, families would intervene differently than if they're not working hard. If students are trying hard and doing well, families can feel content that nothing more is expected.

Exam grades are a quick and easy way to hold schools to account. After all, if there were no grades, some schools or some teachers might slacken off and not bother teaching the parts of their subjects either they or their students found hard. How would we know which schools, which teachers were doing a good job? This kind of blunt accountability measure is likely to produce perverse incentives. English teachers feel huge pressure to scour examination reports for hints and tricks, pay examiners to provide training and replace a broad curriculum with one focused on maximising test performance. No one – teachers, students or families – really wants this.

Can we assess without grading? Getting rid of grades certainly doesn't mean getting rid of assessment. Assessment is the life breath of teaching; without out it we'd be working entirely in the dark. As we'll see, our approach to assessing the impact of the English curriculum is to check whether students are meeting clearly defined curricular expectations.

we are left with are vague statements which only make it harder for teachers and leaders to make sound decisions.

Second, an ARE provides little sense of *why* an expectation is or isn't being met. Teachers assess students' work in an effort to fit what they have produced to the levels or descriptors they're working with. It's perfectly possible for a school to decide that a child is 'working towards' a particular expectation without anyone being any the wiser about what, specifically, the child needs to do in order to meet the expectations of what some similarly aged children are able to do. There's often just a general sense that some children are 'less able' than others.

The broader point to make is that AREs are simply another form of grade used to reify curriculum concepts and quantify and rank students' performance. The fact that verbal descriptions are used instead of numbers doesn't change how they are perceived by teachers, students or families. If we shouldn't use grades then neither should we use AREs as our progression model.

3.5 THE PROBLEM WITH AGE-RELATED EXPECTATIONS

The notion that students will be able to work at a particular level because of their age is inimical to using the curriculum as a progression model.

There are several reasons why the concept of age-related expectations (AREs) is every bit as unhelpful as flightpaths. The first reason is that they are guesswork. We look at what *some* children can do at a particular age and then label this as an expectation for what *all* children of that age should achieve. These expectations are then given levels or descriptors. Children are then described as 'working towards', 'working at', or 'working above' these standards. Alternatively, they might be given labels such as 'emerging', 'meeting' or 'mastering'. This might be a convenient way to compare children – it is easy to see that some appear to be making more progress than others – but it's a poor way to understand what progress an individual student is making in learning a specified body of knowledge.

Data is information that allows us to improve our decision making. Without meaningful data, all

3.6 CURRICULUM-RELATED EXPECTATIONS

If we have designed clear expectations of what students should know and can do we can assess against these expectations to ensure the curriculum is our progression model.

If we want to use the curriculum as the progression model, one of the key things to get right is to clearly specify our curriculum-related expectations (CREs). And getting this right will disproportionately benefit the most disadvantaged students we teach. This requires us to state what *specifically* we want students to know and be able to do.

Here's an example of a bad CRE: *Students will learn how to write an analytic essay.*

It's unclear how students will learn to achieve the curricular expectation and, consequently, it's very easy to miss out important steps and make unwarranted assumptions about what is required to be successful. Then, at some point down the line students are assessed on their ability to do something they haven't been taught how to do.

Here's an example of a curricular expectation that's a bit better: *Students will learn how to scaffold an analytic essay using PEE [or one of its many variants].*

This is more precise and the likelihood that teachers will spend lessons showing students how to craft points, select evidence and explain their choices is greatly increased. However, there are still likely to be lots of gaps between what is assumed, what gets taught and what is learned.

If we are genuinely determined that all students can be successful, we need to do better. Here's an example of a CRE that is more likely to have the required effect:

Stage 1: Students will learn how to write a thesis statement (a single sentence answer to an essay question showing two opposing points of view) beginning with a subordinating conjunction and using pre-taught adjectives to frame the arguments they will develop.

This curricular expectation makes it clear that teachers must teach students what a subordinating conjunction is and how to use it, as well as necessitating the teaching of the link between adjectives used in a thesis statement and what then gets written in the rest of the essay. It's probably still far from perfect but it's getting a lot closer to the kind of specificity needed for the curriculum to be used as an effective progression model.

When specifying CREs, remember these must be *reasonable* expectations of what students should learn. This means we need to have thought carefully about order of precedence: is there anything students need to know first? Could the CRE be usefully broken down into smaller, hierarchical 'chunks' As always, the more specific we are, the more likely we are to teach and assess what has been specified.

Potential benefits of such an approach might include:

- The lack of emphasis on raising students' rank means that the curriculum is less likely to be warped by proxies
- Less need to reify and quantify aspects of the curriculum

- Clearer sense of what has been taught effectively
- More precise knowledge of what each student has and has not learned
- Clearer sense of what needs to be re-taught
- Greater clarity of which students require intervention in which areas
- No need to assign global grades of competence to individual students
- Less risk that students who have not met a CRE are likely to view this as an inherent quality
- Less risk of students seeking the external validation of a grade

Each of our modules includes a clear set of curriculum-related expectations which are broken down into terms which students need to be able to **define**, information we want them to **know** and things we want them to be able to **do**. Figure 3.3 provides an example of how these are laid out.

As you can see, this just an overview and the level of specification is very vague. The Teacher Guides for each module (see section 2.16) provide detailed suggestions for how each of these CREs should be taught.

Once we have specified our curriculum-related expectations, we should be in a position to start using it as a progression model. But how will we know if students are meeting our curriculum-related expectations? The obvious answer is assessment.

By assessing what students know, remember and can do we can adapt not only our instruction but also our curriculum. It's important to remember that in most schools, assessments will take two different forms: in-class formative assessment and more formal summative assessments.

In-class assessment is accomplished by simply checking whether students know, remember and can do the things you have been teaching them *and then acting on the outcomes of this assessment.* Too often, this second stage is missed out. For instance, a teacher might start a lesson with a retrieval quiz which demonstrates that students do not know essential curriculum content but then not adjust future lessons in response.

Curriculum related expectations

Students can define the following terms:

Allegory	Bildungsroman	Characterisation
Epistolary novel	Exposition	First person narrative
Foreshadowing	Irony	Motif
Omniscient narrative	Protagonist	Satire
Third person	Subjective narrative	Theme

Students know

- Novels developed how writers can explore characters' internal lives
- The different ways writers can develop a character (description, action, dialogue, internal monologue)
- Novels have a range of purposes: to entertain, to criticise, to satirise, to highlight social issues, to argue the strength of weakness of ideas etc.
- Charles Dickens' novels were often a form of social commentary about the plight of the poor and dispossessed
- Early novels were usually given the appearance of a 'found narrative' to give them verisimilitude
- The conventions of Bildungsroman novels

Students can

- Use tenor, vehicle and ground to analyse language
- Use excellent epithets to evaluate and analyse characters and themes
- Write thesis statements using excellent epithets
- Use thesis statements to write topic sentences
- Expand thesis statements by exploring the themes and ideas in a novel
- Select and embed relevant textual detail
- Analyse the writer's use of language, structure, perspective and form
- Evaluate the writer's intent
- Use creative sentence types to craft descriptive passages.

6

FIGURE 3.3 Curriculum-related expectations for The Story of the Novel

3.7 WHAT IS ASSESSMENT *FOR?*

While English teachers regularly assess students we do not always consider the purpose of the assessment nor how it should change depending on the purpose.

Professor Rob Coe argues that for assessment data to be useful it must meet five criteria. Assessments must be:

1. Informative – they must tell you something you don't already know and have the potential to surprise.

2. Accurate – we must be able to weigh the trustworthiness and precision of data.
3. Independent – if there is an expectation that students should achieve at a particular level this will distort any data produced.
4. Generalisable – we should be able to make useful inferences about what students are likely to achieve in other circumstances.
5. Replicable – if data would be different at a different time or place then it tells us little of any use.

If any of these criteria cannot be applied to the data produced by an assessment then, Coe argues, it was not actually an assessment.[9]

Assessment comes from the Latin for 'sitting alongside' (the same root as assistant). This suggests that assessment should assist us in our teaching. This is very much the approach that we take in thinking about how assessment sits alongside our curriculum: how can it be used to help us to make better decisions which impact on our teaching and students' learning?

Assessment is best thought of as a process of collecting evidence – sampling students' retention and application of the things we have taught – and using it to make inferences about what students know and can do. We then make use of this evidence to make judgements and provide guidance for the next steps in learning. Responsive teaching must, by definition, be driven by data (information) about students' learning.

If we are using the curriculum as our progression model all we need to know is how well students have learned *this* aspect of the curriculum. As we'll discuss in section 3.8, if the curriculum is perfectly specified and taught, all students would get close to 100%. Realistically, we'll never come near this state of perfection, but we need to be determined that performance should be as high as possible and that where there are gaps in student performance there will almost certainly be gaps in instruction.

Over the long term, if students fail to meet a threshold of confidence the default assumption should be that there is a problem either with the design of the curriculum or in its teaching. In the short term, if a minority of students fail to reach the threshold we have set we are left with this problem: how can we scale the time and resources required for all students to be successful?[10]

The best we're currently able to suggest is that we need to have specified and sequenced our English curriculum to focus heavily on the most crucial concepts within the subject discipline and to ensure these, at least, are mastered. If our guiding assumption was that any test score below a specified threshold (say, 90%) highlighted some fault in specification or instruction, this could transform the educational experiences of our most disadvantaged students.

Any assessments we conduct will produce raw scores which can then be turned into percentages which data managers can use to populate spreadsheets. And herein lies the danger: numbers are seductive. They are derived from inherently unreliable proxies which then take on the appearance of objective reality. As we'll consider in section 3.12, there *is* a role for numbers, but it should be a limited one.

TABLE 3.1 Purpose and types of assessment used to understand the impact of the English curriculum

Purpose of assessment	Types of assessment
Impact on learning	Formative, in-lesson assessment, hinge point questions, retrieval quizzes
Support school decision making	Standardised, discriminatory assessment: GL Assessment's English Progress Test, No More Marking's Improving Secondary Writing
Inform classroom teaching	Mastery assessment: KS3 end of module tests

Assessment, to be useful, should also conform to three basic purposes. It should:

1. impact on learning
2. support school decision making
3. inform classroom teaching.[11]

As we'll go on to discuss, there are different sources of assessment data which we use to understand the impact of our curriculum, each of which help us to achieve these purposes in different ways. These purposes and types of assessment are set out in Table 3.1.

Each of these purposes will be explored in the following sections.

3.8 MASTERY ASSESSMENT

Whereas traditional assessment models are of assessment of students' ability, mastery assessment is primarily useful as an assessment of the curriculum and its implementation.

As there are no external audiences interested in schools' internal data, if we're going to go to the trouble of getting students to sit formal assessments, we should be very clear about the purpose both of the assessments and the data they produce.

For the most part, the purpose of assessment data appears to be discriminatory. The purpose of GCSEs, SATs, A levels and other national exams is to discriminate between students – to determine each individual's performance into a normally distributed rank order and then assign grades at different cut-off points – so that we know who is 'good' and 'bad' at different subjects. Whatever you think of this as a system of summative assessment (and there are some reasonable arguments in support of it), there's absolutely no necessity for schools to replicate the process internally.

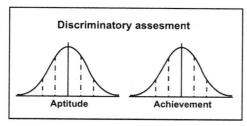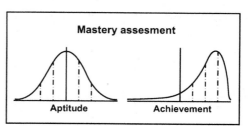

FIGURE 3.4 Mastery assessment vs discriminatory assessment

The purpose of formal internal assessments should be twofold. First, they should seek to provide periodic statements of competence, that students have mastered curriculum content sufficiently well to progress onwards, and second, as a mechanism for assuring the quality of the curriculum and how well it's taught.

As Figure 3.4 shows, this approach to assessment – mastery assessment – would be expected to provide a very different 'shape' to traditional, discriminatory assessment.

When assessment is designed to discriminate between students it will, given a normal distribution of students' aptitude, produce a normally distributed bell curve, but an assessment designed to allow students to demonstrate mastery of the curriculum should produce something that looks a bit more like a slope.

A discriminatory assessment is designed to produce winners and losers; to celebrate some students as 'able' and some as 'less able'. While we might tell ourselves that the purpose of such an assessment is to find out who needs additional support, in most cases this should be clear to teachers well in advance of formal assessments. We might also believe that discriminatory assessments may be motivating. It's certainly true that those who find themselves near the top of the distribution may well enjoy competing against each other (and it's equally true that there might be fierce competition to avoid being at the bottom), but most students will, by necessity, learn that they are distinctly average. Doing poorly in this style of assessment is likely to create a self-fulfilling prophecy in which students learn early on that they're 'rubbish' at English. What's motivating about that?

With mastery-style assessment, if students fail to meet a minimum threshold, our default assumption should be that there is a fault either with the design of the curriculum or in its teaching. The fault should be acknowledged as ours, rather than something to be blamed on students. If our guiding assumption

was that any test score below, say, 80% highlighted some fault in the curriculum or instruction, this could transform the educational experiences of our most disadvantaged students. Instead of seeing tests as demoralising pass/fail cliff-edges, they might come to see that they provide useful benchmarks of progress to strive towards.

To move towards mastery-style assessment, we need to be clear on the following principles:

- Never assess students on something that hasn't been explicitly taught.
- Any areas of the curriculum that can be described as 'skills' must be broken down into teachable components of knowledge which can be learned and practised.
- Until the curriculum has fully sequenced the teaching of these skills, test items should be as granular as possible to allow all students to be successful.
- If students struggle to answer test items, we should assume the fault is with the curriculum (students across multiple classes struggle) or with instruction (students in a particular class struggle).
- Not only do we need teaching to be responsive to students' needs, but we also need to think in terms of responsive curriculum.[12]

Mastery assessment is primarily important for quality-assuring the curriculum and its implementation.

3.9 PROBLEMS WITH ASSESSING ENGLISH

The traditional model of assessing students' progress in English is not only discriminatory, it also focuses on attempting to assess students on things they haven't been explicitly taught to do.

The de facto approach to assessing English at KS3 has been to use extended writing. After all, this is what students will be faced with in their GCSEs so it seems to make sense that this was what we should get them used to as early as possible. To take this approach, we need a mark scheme. Most mark schemes attempt to identify the different skills areas students should be demonstrating and then award marks based on how well these skills are demonstrated. The main weakness of using mark schemes – or rubrics, if you prefer – is that it comes down to an individual marker's judgement to determine how well a student has demonstrated a skill. The trouble is human beings just aren't very good at doing this. If that were the only problem, we might be able to overcome it by using comparative judgement (see section 3.13) but, unfortunately, it's not.

It's also important to remember that English at GCSE is very different to the subject at KS3. The texts studied at KS3 must be vehicles for important curricular concepts that will continue to matter in KS4; the texts themselves cannot meaningfully be assessed in the way they are at KS4. Because of this, marking KS3 assessments in a similar way to GCSE assessments is not only unnecessary, but also actively harmful.

The bigger issue with the essay approach to assessment is that it inevitably ends up assessing students on things they haven't yet been taught to do. This is unfair and will significantly disadvantage those students who are already most disadvantaged. It's also unhelpful in trying to identify with any precision what students know and can do.

If we want to use assessment to assess how well students are mastering the curriculum, we need to think carefully about the constructs. Constructs here mean the hypothetical concepts that a test is meant to measure. Once we know what these are, we then consider what we want students to learn and how best we can ascertain whether they have been mastered.

To do this we need to be sure that we're actually testing what we think we're testing. And to do that, we need to be sure about the constructs (big ideas) that make up skilled performance in English. So, what are these? When we attempt to measure something as broad as 'reading' or 'writing', it's very difficult to see what aspects of the construct might be causing an issue.[13] Exam boards break constructs down into Assessment Objectives such as, 'Use a range of vocabulary and sentence structures for clarity, purpose and effect, with accurate spelling and punctuation', or 'Compare writers' ideas and perspectives, as well as how these are conveyed, across two or more texts'. These are still almost impossibly unwieldy.

If the aims of assessment are to impact on learning, support school decision making and inform classroom teaching, then we must do a lot better at breaking constructs down in order to see the precursors and successors that make up skilled performance. Figure 3.5 shows how this relates to the construct of 'reading fluency'.

So, when students are asked to read and respond to an unseen extract, such as the beginning of a novel by Graham Joyce in which a young married couple are on a skiing holiday in the French Pyrenean mountains,[14] what are we actually assessing? We may *think* we're assessing their ability to 'identify and interpret explicit and implicit information and ideas, select and synthesise evidence from different texts, explain, comment on and analyse how writers use language and structure to achieve effects and influence readers, using relevant subject terminology to support their views, and evaluate texts critically and support this with appropriate textual references'.* In actual fact, we're as likely to

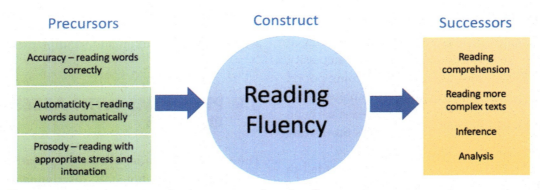

FIGURE 3.5 The precursors and successors for the construct of reading fluency

---

* You probably recognise these as reading AOs taken from AQA's scheme of assessment for GCSE English Language.

be assessing students' general knowledge of skiing holidays and conditions in the Pyrenees.[15]

Consider the construct validity in each of these examples:

- Year 7 essay: 'How does Charles Dickens represent Oliver's progression as a character in the novel?'
- Year 8 multiple-choice quiz that students have seen before, and the teacher has explicitly taught throughout the term.
- Year 9 knowledge organiser quiz that tests some but not all of the items on the knowledge organiser.

What is being tested? How much of the domain of English is being sampled? What might be missing? What inferences will we be able to draw from students' performance on each of these assessments?

If, as is so often the case with assessment in English, the construct isn't clear then we are inevitably creating gaps in our instruction – gaps which disadvantaged and SEND students fall into and struggle to climb out of by themselves.

Let's take the first example – a Year 7 essay on Oliver's progression as a character. The problem here is that the assessment has a very broad construct including but not limited to: knowledge of the text, knowledge of Oliver's character, knowledge of character tropes, knowledge of the Bildungsroman genre, knowledge of writing an essay. As a direct result of this overly broad construct,

if students then don't do well, it will be extremely difficult to pinpoint why they haven't done well. Instead, we're advocating for a much sharper focus on specific knowledge, where we are crystal clear on the construct being assessed, which in turn should mean we are clear on the next steps for that student, class or indeed in our teaching of the curriculum.

The main point of our assessments is to find out how successful we have been at specifying the constructs we think are important, and how well individual teachers are implementing the curriculum. Our starting assumption should be that if students cannot demonstrate mastery of a concept, then either the curriculum or its implementation is at fault. Teachers know that these are the expectations students need to meet, and that if students can't meet them, then that's on us.*

Once we are clear on the CREs students should be able to meet, we can design an assessment that tests whether students can meet these specific expectations. Then, assessments need to test when students *actually* know and can do these things. To make it clear precisely what students do and don't know and what they can and can't do, we've designed our assessments to only assess those things that students have been taught and been given multiple opportunities to practise. It should go without saying that these CREs *must* also be the subject of regular and frequent formative assessment.

We can see what this might look like by examining the following example from our War Writing unit.

Question	Task	Marks
1	**Read the following extract:** **Raleigh**: The Germans are really quite decent, aren't they? I mean, outside the newspapers? **Osborne**: Yes. [*Pause*] I remember up at Wipers we had a man shot when he was out on patrol. Just at dawn. We couldn't get him in that night. He lay out there groaning all day. Next night three of our men crawled out to get him in. It was so near the German trenches that they could have shot our fellows one by one. But, when our men began dragging the wounded man back over the rough ground, a big German officer stood up in their trenches and called out: 'Carry him!' – and our fellows stood up and carried the man back, and the German officer fired some lights for them to see by. **Raleigh**: How topping! **Osborne**: Next day we blew each other's trenches to blazes. **Raleigh**: It all seems rather – silly, doesn't it? **Osborne**: It does, rather. Answer these questions about the extract: a) Who is in the extract? b) What did they do? c) When did these events take place? d) Where did these events take place? e) Why did the characters act as they did? Now use these answers to write a sentence summarising what happens in the extract.	(Summarising) 2 marks (Sentence combining) 2 marks

---

* Obviously, this will not always be strictly true: students might have been absent or otherwise have chosen not to engage with the curriculum.

Question	Task	Marks
2	Suggest **three epithets** could you choose to describe both Osborne and Raleigh.	(Recall) 2 marks
3	How does Sherriff suggest that war is **absurd**? a) Write a **thesis statement** that answers this question. b) Give two **examples** that support your answer. Choose an example from the extract and one from your knowledge of the play as a whole.	1 mark for thesis statement + 2 marks for each item of evidence 3 marks
4	What advice would you give to the actors playing Osborne and Raleigh about how they should perform their roles?	2 marks for 2 points about each character. Up to 4 marks
5	'Well, if you want to get the best pace out of an earwig, dip it in whiskey – makes 'em go like hell!' Use **tenor, vehicle** and **ground** to explain what the earwigs symbolise.	1 mark each for referring to tenor, vehicle and ground 3 marks
6	How do you think an audience should react to Raleigh in this scene? a) Write a **thesis statement** that answers this question. b) Explain how this links to a theme from the play. c) Use your thesis statement to write **two** linked **topic sentences**. For each topic sentence: d) Select a quotation that illustrates your point. e) Analyse what you notice about these examples. f) Evaluate why Sherriff might have made these choices.	1 mark for each correctly written sentence Up to 10 marks
7	Give definitions for the following terms: a) Realism b) Dialogue c) Denouement d) Absurdity e) Juxtaposition f) Protagonist g) Characterisation h) Irony	1 mark each, up to 8 marks (recall)
8	Suggest **two reasons** why *Journey's End* might be described as 'modernist'.	1 mark for each (recall)
9	Explain how Stanhope can be viewed as a tragic hero.	2 marks (recall + application)
10	Suggest **two examples** of symbolism from *Journey's End*.	1 mark for each (recall)
11	What poetic form is Wilfred Owen's poem 'Futility'?	1 mark (recall)
12	What are Aristotle's unities? How does *Journey's End* conform to them?	3 marks (recall + application)
13	Write the correct definition for each of the words below: a. What does **patriotism** mean? b. What does **ambivalent** mean? c. What does **fatuous** mean? d. What does **incompetent** mean? e. What does **futility** mean?	1 mark each, up to 5 marks (recall)
14	Write a paragraph describing life in a First World War trench Make sure you include the following sentence types: - More, More, More - Three Verb Sentence - Past Participle Start - Simile Start - Let Loose Sentence	2 marks each for each correctly written sentence type, up to 10 marks **NB**. Marks should not be awarded for 'creativity' as this is not something explicitly taught in the curriculum.

As you can see, this assessment not only focuses on assessing the CREs covered in the War Writing scheme, but there is also clarity about what constructs are being assessed in each item on the assessment. This provides two advantages. Firstly, and most importantly, it allows teachers to see clearly where students have struggled. If students have struggled to recall a definition, then the assumption should be that either the teaching of this term was unclear or that students were not given sufficient opportunities to practise recalling it.

If students have been unable to complete either the analytical or creative writing tasks, then the assumption should be that there's either a gap in the instructional sequence which they've fallen into, or that – once again – there has been insufficient practice. If there are gaps at an individual student level then it may be appropriate to determine what specific support individuals might need, but if there are gaps at a class level then it should be much clearer that either the implementation or the intent of the curriculum is at fault. Taking responsibility for students' struggles can completely transform assessment culture where missed marks are viewed as a deficit in the curriculum rather than a deficit in students.*

The second advantage is that this style of assessment is much less time consuming to mark. In fact, because there's no need to rely on a subjective mark scheme and because of the different way in which mistakes are viewed, students can even mark each other's tests with minimal teacher oversight.

It's worth restating that our ambition is for *all* students to be successful at *every* question. For this to be possible, we recommend that departments adapt their assessments to ensure that they reflect the CREs they have explicitly taught and that teachers take responsibility for their students' ability to answer the questions as fluently as possible.

It is equally important to note that students should be given as long as necessary to complete the assessment. Some students or classes may be easily able to complete this in a single lesson but for other students it might be beneficial to chunk the assessment up into 10–15 minute segments and complete over a series of lessons.

Sample assessments for all our curriculum modules can be found on the OAT English website: english. ormistonacademiestrust.co.uk

3.10 FORMATIVE ASSESSMENT AND IDENTIFYING GAPS

Every lesson is an opportunity to establish whether students are mastering the content of the curriculum and then responding to what is established.

Teaching and assessment are – or should be – inextricably linked. Unless sequences of instruction include regular checking for retention, understanding and application, they are unlikely to be effective. Or, more properly, we'll have no way of establishing whether they are effective.

The flowchart in Figure 3.6 is an attempt to illustrate what might happen in response to students' performance on in-class assessment. This is simple enough to be applied to any in-lesson formative assessment but is particularly applicable to hinge questions.

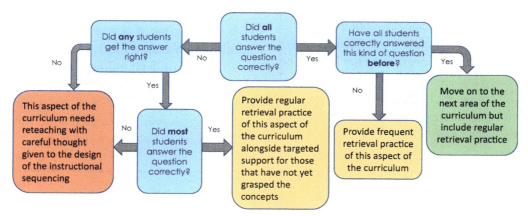

FIGURE 3.6 A flow chart demonstrating responses to students' assessment

---

* We should also consider the behaviour culture in a school. If teachers are struggling to implement the curriculum due to poor behaviour, this of course must be addressed.

The starting point whenever students have been asked a question or set a task is to ask whether all of them performed as expected. If the answer is no, we then need to ask whether *any* students managed to perform as expected. If most students are unable to meet our expectations, then we ought to assume the fault is with either our teaching or the curriculum. It's become popular to state that we should 'obtain a high success rate', but what does this mean? According to Rosenshine's Principles of Instruction, 'it was found that 82 percent of students' answers were correct in the classrooms of the most successful teachers, but the least successful teachers had a success rate of only 73 percent'.[16] This is a bit of a concern. If only 80% of students are successful, that means 1 in 5 students are failing. Maybe instead we should take this to mean that *all* students achieve a success rate of 80%? According to Barak Rosenshine, 'A success rate of 80 percent shows that students are learning the material, and it also shows that the students are challenged'.[17]

However, we need to think seriously about what we mean by challenge. Should we deliberately ask questions we think most – or some – students will be unable to answer? The principles of 'success before struggle' and 'gapless instruction' would suggest not. We suggest that teachers should aim for a success rate of close to 100%. If students are unable to answer crucial hinge point questions (see section 3.11) it should be assumed that something has gone wrong, either with our specification of the curriculum or in our implementation. If more than one or two students are struggling it makes sense to go back to the drawing board, think carefully about whether any gaps have been left in the instructional sequence and reteach with new explanations and examples. Everyone – even those students who have already been successful – will benefit from additional practice.

If all students are successful, we next need to ask whether this is the first time. If it is, we should be cautiously pleased but assume that lots of additional practice will be necessary. If it isn't, we should move on but remain mindful that students will inevitably forget over time and plan to return to this area in the not-too-distant future.

Wherever possible, it's important to have subject-level discussions with colleagues teaching the same curriculum to see if they are experiencing similar difficulties or have useful advice to offer. If it's a curriculum you haven't planned yourself, it's probably worth speaking to whoever designed it to get a sense of whether their expectations match yours.

3.11 USING HINGE POINT QUESTIONS

In order to teach responsively, we need to be able to quickly identify misconceptions and check students' understanding.

A hinge point question is a diagnostic tool deployed at a point in a lesson – the hinge – where teachers need to know whether students are ready to move on or require further instruction. Students' responses should provide teachers with information about what actions they should take next. A well-designed hinge question should reveal potential misconceptions which can then be addressed.

Students need to be able to answer the hinge question quickly – ideally in less than two minutes – and teachers should be able to read and interpret answers in about 30 seconds. For this to be possible, students will need to complete answers on MWBs and questions must be asked in a multiple-choice format.

Writing effective multiple-choice questions (MCQs) takes practice. The aim should be to eliminate guessing: students who know the answer should get it right; students who don't know the answer should be distracted by one of the distractors. An MCQ should have an unambiguously correct answer and at least two distractors.

Consider this example:

What is a volta?

a) Where the tone of a poem becomes negative
b) The halfway point of a poem
c) A change in mood or thought or both

One of the keys of writing distractors is that they should be plausible and expose potential errors in students' understanding. Poorly written MCQs often contain implausible, or even absurd, potential answers which make it easier for students to guess the correct answer. We're used to seeing these kinds of MCQs on TV phone-in quizzes:

Who wrote *Romeo and Juliet*?

a) William Shakespeare
b) Mickey Mouse
c) Ant and Dec

Ideally, distractors should contain true information which does not accurately answer the question. They should also be tempting. Students should have to think through why they're wrong. If all distractors are not equally plausible, questions can end up being simply true or false, which students then have a fifty-fifty chance of guessing correctly.

With the example given above, 'What is a volta?' c) is unambiguously correct, the other two answers are, hopefully, plausible and based on common misconceptions. Students often come to think that a volta must be negative (it may be sometimes but by no means always) or that it will come at the halfway point (again, it might, especially in a Petrarchan sonnet, but it doesn't have to). If students are tempted by either of these options, the teacher will know they have to either review curriculum materials to make sure the definition is more clearly stated or finesse their teaching to ensure the definition doesn't go missing.[18]

Imagine that students have just read Wilfred Owen's 'Dulce Et Decorum Est'. If they are not clear on the meaning of the poem, they will struggle to meaningfully analyse it. This is a clear hinge point in a lesson: can you move on to analysing linguistic techniques or does the poem require further explanation and discussion? Instead of checking with the one or two students with their hands up, an MCQ will provide a snapshot of all students:

> Why did Wilfred Owen write 'Dulce Et Decorum Est'? Which 2 of the following statements are most accurate?
>
> a) To celebrate the bravery of the soldiers
> **b) To criticise the horrors of war**
> **c) To expose the trauma experienced by soldiers**
> d) To reveal the lack of comforts soldiers experienced

The first distractor (a) should be completely *implausible* except for the fact that students, if they haven't been paying attention, may assume that this is what all war poems are doing. The final distractor (d) is true but not does fulfil the criteria of being 'most accurate' when compared with (b) and (c) which are equally true and are therefore both acceptable as answers. The fact that there are two correct answers now opens up the possibility of a structured discussion around which of these statements students feel is the best fit.

Hinge questions can – and should – also be used to check that students have understood the big ideas which underpin a text. Here's an MCQ on another Wilfred Owen poem:

> Which sentence most accurately describes the poem 'Exposure'?
>
> a) Owen describes the soldiers' exposure to harsh weather conditions such as 'merciless iced east winds that knive us'
> b) Owen illustrates the soldiers' exposure to enemy fire such as when 'bullets streak the silence'
> **c) Owen depicts the suffering caused by exposure to conditions in the trenches**

Here, the two distractors are both correct answers made more plausible by their length (often used by students as a proxy for accuracy) and the fact that they contain quotes from the poem. In this case, (c) is the most accurate answer because it doesn't limit the notion of 'exposure' to either weather or enemy fire but encapsulates both in 'conditions in the trenches'.

> What is Mrs Birling's function in the play? Pick two answers:
>
> **a) To highlight the vulnerability of the lower classes**
> b) To demonstrate how horrible some members of the middle classes could be
> **c) To convey the lack of empathy in society towards the lower classes**
> d) To look down on the Inspector and show her contempt for those in power

In this example, students are being asked to show their understanding that characters are constructs used to represent a writer's intentions. If they have fully understood this they ought to choose (a) and (c) but if they haven't they may be tempted by b) because it's difficult for some students to get past how unsympathetic they think Mrs Birling is or (d) because this accurately describes her behaviour towards the Inspector. Again, after the question has been reviewed, there's an opportunity for low-stakes discussion about why some answers are better than others.

We recommend using two or at most three distractors. Although including more distractors results in making it statistically harder for students to get the correct answer through guessing, this benefit is outweighed by the cost of the time and effort it takes to come up with plausible distractors that help reveal students' misconceptions. And remember, a well-designed hinge question should attempt to eliminate guessing.

3.12 THE ROLE OF NUMBERS

Although numbers can play a useful part in overseeing whether students know more, remember more and can do more of the curriculum, they can also obscure the actions students and teachers need to take.

Think about this statement: *A student's performance in an assessment is 64%.* Is this good or bad?

At this stage we don't have enough information to know. What about if we also knew that the average performance in the class was 57% and that the average performance in the year group was 79%? Now we have a clearer sense of how well an individual student is progressing through the curriculum: information becomes more meaningful if it is comparable. **But** a system that just communicates numerical aggregates doesn't answer the most important questions: Where am I? Where am I going? How am I going to get there?

What we **can't** do is compare the percentage a student gets in Term 1 with one achieved in Term 6 and attempt to draw a line between them indicating progress. This would assume that the second test was objectively more difficult and that if the numbers go up, then progress is being made. We may believe this to be true but it's very rare to find schools that have put the effort into calculating the difficulty of test questions required to make this a defensible claim.

Rebecca Allen has made the following point:

> When we use… tests to measure relative *progress*, we often look to see whether a student has moved up (good) or down (bad) the bell curve. On the face of it this looks like they've made good progress and learnt more than similar students over the course of the year. However [the test] is a noisy measure of what they knew at the start [and] the end of the year. Neither test is reliable enough to say if this individual pupil's progress is actually better or worse than should be expected, given their starting point.[19]

Tests are very useful for assessing how well students are learning particular curriculum content but cannot be used to measure the rate at which students are progressing towards better future test performance.

Just because a student has learned a lot about, say, *The Merchant of Venice* or using subordinating conjunctions, we cannot claim that they will perform equally well (or better) on a test of *King Lear* or the subjunctive mood. And if they do less well on a subsequent test, we cannot claim that students are making negative progress. What we can – and should – recognise is that they don't know some aspects of the curriculum as well as others and intervene accordingly.

It is helpful to think about lateral and longitudinal comparisons. Lateral comparisons make it possible to compare how different students performed on the same test. This not only possible but desirable. If students in Class 1 perform much worse than students in Class 2 on the same assessment, we could infer either that students in Class 2 class are, on average, cleverer than those in Class 1, or that the teacher of Class 2 has taught the curriculum better. While the first inference may be true, it is not useful. 'Top sets' are routinely filled with students from more affluent backgrounds who are often successful *despite* rather than *because* of the choices we make. Rather than worrying about ability, we might do better to track indices of social disadvantage: if our more disadvantaged students are doing well, we can be reasonably sure this is due to how well we've specified and taught the curriculum. It might be useful to *only* use these pupils when analysing test data.

Longitudinal comparson seeks to compare how the same students perform on different tests and measure the progress they are making. Even if we don't make the lamentably common mistake of assessing students' ability to do things we haven't actually taught them, the test students sit will only sample from the domain of what they were taught. How students perform in that test gives us *some* sense of how well an individual student has learned the curriculum relative to their peers but it's only by establishing a scalogram of student performance vs item difficulty (see Figure 3.7) that we will get a sense of what individual test scores might mean.

Typically, we just see a test as a mechanism for measuring students' ability, or level of development, and fail to understand that getting 50% in a harder test might actually be better than getting 70% in an easier test. But we should also understand that if one student gets 70% and another gets 35% on the same test, that does not mean the first student has

Averages vs Individuals

Students	Items								Ability	n/N%
	c	a	b	d	f	h	e	g		
E	1	1	1	1	1	1	1	1	7	100
F	1	1	1	1	1	0	1	0	6	86
B	1	1	0	1	1	1	0	0	5	71
D	1	1	0	0	1	0	1	0	4	57
A	1	1	1	0	0	1	0	0	4	57
G	1	1	1	1	0	0	0	0	3	43
C	1	0	1	0	0	0	0	0	2	29
Difficulty	7	5	5	4	4	3	3	1		
n/N%	100	71	71	57	57	43	43	14		

FIGURE 3.7 Scalogram showing students' performance against item difficulty

done twice as well as the second student. Getting less than 35% is far easier than getting more than 35% and, in a discriminatory assessment, items will get progressively more difficult and thus better measure individual students' performance.

Figure 3.7 shows a scalogram that compares students' performance against item difficulty.

Item difficulty is established by working out which questions students answer correctly; the more students answer an item correctly, the easier that item is, and the fewer students answer an item, the harder it is. So, we can see that although students A and D both acheived the same test score, Student D was able to answer more difficult questions than Students A and G. One explanation could be that Student D had not been present in class when some of the content most students found easy to answer was taught. Or, similarly, it could be that Student G missed some of the later curriculum content. Either way, the test score tells us relatively little about these students' ability to make future progress but quite a lot about what they have learned to date. It ought to be clear that we should not intervene with these three students in the same ways. It ought to be equally obvious why drawing a line between performance in two different tests is likely to tell us little of any use about students' progress.

But remember, if we're using a mastery assessment test scores will tell us less as the assessment will have been designed so that all students can pass. In this case, rather than looking at over all percentages, it's much more useful to look at which questions – and therefore which constructs – students have struggled with.

The key to using numbers sensibly is to only compare scores across space (laterally) and not across time (longitudinally). While it might make perfect sense to compare how different students, classes or cohorts have performed *on the same assessment*, it is never meaningful to compare the results of *different* assessments.

3.13 SUMMATIVE ASSESSMENT AND COMPARATIVE JUDGEMENT

Limited use of discriminatory assessment is essential: if our students perform poorly on a nationally representative test then we know the curriculum is ineffective.

Human beings are exceptionally poor at judging the quality of a thing on its own. Although we generally know whether we like something, we struggle to accurately evaluate just how good or bad a thing is. It's much easier for us to compare two things and weigh up the similarities and differences. This means we are often unaware of what a 'correct' judgement might be and are easily influenced by extraneous suggestions. This is compounded by the fact that we aren't usually even aware we've been influenced.

Some assessments are easy to evaluate; the answer is simply right or wrong. As discussed in section 3.11, there can be great advantage to designing multiple-choice questions which allow us to make good inferences about what students know, as well as giving us a good idea of their ability to reason and think critically. But however well designed, this type of question struggles to assess students' ability to synthesise ideas, consider evidence and pursue an analytical line of reasoning at any length. Consequently, English departments opt to assess these things – at least in part – through extended written answers. Evaluating the quality of an essay or a piece of creative writing is a difficult job and so we produce rubrics – mark schemes – to indicate how a student might be expected to respond at different mark boundaries. Teachers then read through the essay and attempt, as best they can, to match the content to that indicated in the mark scheme.

The problem is that we are very bad at doing this. The psychologist Donald Laming says, 'There is no absolute judgement. All judgements are comparisons of one thing with another… comparisons are little better than ordinal'.[20] What this means is that we can reliably put things into a rank order, but that's about it. Mark schemes give the appearance of objectivity but in actual fact, when teachers mark a set of essays, they often find that halfway through they come across an essay that is much better or worse than all the ones they'd marked to that point. This results in going back to change the marks to allow for the new essay to be ranked according to its merits.

Understanding students' performance depends on huge amounts of tacit knowledge. Because it's tacit it's very hard to articulate – even (maybe especially) for experts.[21] In our attempts to break down what experts do we pick out superficial features of their performance and make these proxies for quality. For instance, it may well be that a good writer is able to use fronted adverbials and embedded relative clauses, but they would never set out with this as their goal. By looking for these proxies we run the risk of limiting both our own understanding and students' ability.

A solution is to do away with mark schemes and use instead a system of comparative judgement. Judging is

different to marking in that it taps into our fast, intuitive modes of thinking. Marking, on the other hand, requires slow and error-prone analytical thinking.

Comparative judgement requires a judge to look at two essays at once and make an intuitive decision on which is better. These judgements are then aggregated (the formula for reliable judgements is five times the number of scripts) to form a highly reliable rank order of students' work. The advantages for teachers are that the process is not only significantly quicker than traditional marking (judgements should be made in about 30 seconds) it's much more reliable and allows us to make better inferences about students' ability.

There are, however, some common misconceptions to consider. First, there are concerns about accuracy. It's understandable why we might feel sceptical that a fast, intuitive judgement can tell us as much as slow, analytical marking. Surely spending ten minutes poring over a piece of writing, cross-referencing against a rubric, has to be better than making a cursory judgement in a few seconds? On one level this may be true. Reading something in detail will obviously provide a lot more information than skim reading it. There are, however, two points to consider. Firstly, is the extra time spent marking worth the extra information gained? This of course depends. What are you planning to do as a result of reading the work? What else could you do with the time? Secondly, contrary to our intuitions, the reliability of aggregated judgements is much greater than that achieved by expert markers in national exams. The reliability of GCSE and A level marking for English examinations is about 0.6. This indicates that there's a 40% probability that a different marker would award a different mark.[22] Hence why so many papers have their marks challenged every year. But if we aggregate a sufficient number of judgements (5 × n) then we can end up with reliability above 0.9. Although any individual judgement may be wildly inaccurate, *on average* they will produce much more accurate marks than an expert examiner.

All assessments provide us with a proxy; the point is whether or not it's a *good* proxy. Comparative judgement allows us to make better inferences about learning as an abstract thing because it's so focused on the concrete. The absence of rubrics means we are one step nearer to the thing itself. Additionally, not having a rubric also means we are likely to get a more valid sample of students' ability within a domain. Because a rubric depends on attempting to describe indicative content it warps both teaching and assessment; teachers use mark schemes to define the curriculum and examiners search for indicative content and ignore aspects of great work that didn't make it into the rubric. (Look again at Figure 3.2 on page 77 for a visual representation of this issue.)

Another concern is that the presence of a systematic bias might reduce the accuracy of the process (after all, a measure can be reliable but still be invalid). However, teacher assessments are more likely to judge the child rather than their work, as investigations into the 'Halo effect' have consistently shown. We are all inadvertently prone to biases, which end up privileging students based on their socio-economic background, race and gender.[23] Whilst concerns that the seemingly irrelevant aspects of students' work – such as the quality of handwriting – affect comparative judgement are fair, these biases also affect every other form of marking. If anything, comparative judgement is less unfair than marking.

In an ideal world, maybe teachers would put the same effort into reading students' work as they put into creating it. Sadly, this thinking has led to the steady rise in teachers' workload and mounting feelings of guilt and anxiety. No teacher, no matter how good they are, will ever be able to sustain this kind of marking for long. But maybe we've been asking the wrong question. Maybe instead we should ask, *If students have put all this effort into their work, is it fair that we assess it unfairly and unreliably?*

It's worth noting that the 30-second intuitive judgement is only desirable during the judging process. When a rank order has been obtained, teachers can use the time gained to explore much more interesting and personal aspects of the writing, especially where judges make different judgements of the same piece of work.

In essence, comparative judgement is a way of making quick and reliable summative assessments. In order to provide meaningful formative feedback, of course you actually have to spend time reading the work too.

As a Trust, we subscribe to No More Marking's Improving Secondary Writing project for students in Years 7–9. Twice a year, students complete a short, written task in response to prompts like 'Should computer games be banned for teenagers?' or 'Write a review of a film or book you have recently read or watched'. This is a standardised assessment which gives us a snapshot of students' progress over the year which we can compare to national averages. If our students are improving at the same rate as the national average, then we can be content that our curriculum and its implementation are effective. If our students make more progress than the average, we have cautious cause for celebration. However, if our students make less progress than average, if they fail to make progress, or, in the worst cases, if they regress over the course of the year, we will have clear, unambiguous evidence that something needs to change.

Using comparative judgement to validate your writing curriculum

Sequencing the curriculum

Over the last few years, a number of Trusts, schools and teachers have started to focus on the importance of the curriculum, and the importance of using well-designed and well-structured curriculums.

But what is the right way to sequence curriculum content? For some subjects, like early reading, a great deal of external research exists already, and schools can choose from a range of research-backed reading programmes that take students from their first steps in

decoding to being able to read independently and fluently. For many other subjects, particularly at secondary, these research-backed curriculum sequences simply don't exist. Schools have to do their best with the research that does exist, and then make sure that they are assessing and checking how their students are doing to see if their model is working.

When it comes to teaching and assessing secondary English, comparative judgement can play a crucial role in validating the success of a particular curriculum. It offers two particular benefits: first, it provides reliable and robust standardised assessment for writing, which is hard to achieve with other assessment methods. It's also flexible and not tied to a specific rubric.

Reliable assessment of writing

Writing is one of the key skills we want to teach in English, but it's also one of the hardest to assess. Traditional methods of rubric-based assessment are time-consuming and not as reliable as we might like, even when carried out by exam boards with significant resources. Comparative judgement is a more reliable way of assessing open tasks like writing. It is based on the psychological principle that humans are not very good at making absolute judgements, but that we are much better at making comparative judgements. So instead of looking at one piece of writing at a time and trying to place it on an absolute scale, we should look at two and decide which is the better piece of writing.

Of course, one judgement like this would not be enough. In the big national assessment projects we run, thousands of teachers will take part, each making dozens of judgements. We combine together these judgements to create a national measurement scale for writing from Years 1–9. As well as providing schools with robust and externally standardised real-time data, this also allows them to see how their students are progressing over time. Over the last five years, we've assessed a million pieces of writing in this way and have been able to chart some of the unexpected shocks in student attainment due to the pandemic.

Assessing open tasks flexibly

Comparative judgement allows for a more flexible assessment of writing that is not tied to the specifics of any one particular rubric. When teachers make a judgement about two pieces of writing, they have just one criterion to consider: which is the better piece of writing. Although this may feel very subjective, it actually provides more reliable and consistent scores than a specific rubric. It may seem surprising, but teachers in different contexts, different phases and even different countries do tend to agree on what makes good writing. So comparative judgement will provide you with a national standard but won't tie you to a specific rubric.

Learning more about what makes good writing

Of course, whilst comparative judgement won't tie you to a specific rubric, what we hope is that over time it will help us to identify the key features that make good writing, and also show which types of curriculum are best at getting students to write well. We have done some other work to help schools with this approach – for example, sharing exemplars of good writing, developing lessons and CPD on the features of good writing, and creating quizzes on our new Automark website – which provide schools with precise feedback on sentence structure. In this way, we hope that the Improving Primary and Secondary Writing projects will not only measure writing, they will help improve it too.

Daisy Christodoulou, Director of Education,
No More Marking

3.14 THE NEED FOR STANDARDISED ASSESSMENT

Unless we get external validation from students' performance on standardised tests, we could fool ourselves into believing students are making progress when they are not.

Despite arguing that internal assessments should be mastery assessments, there is still a need for students to sit some standardised, discriminatory assessments. At OAT, as well as using No More Marking's Improving Secondary Writing assessment, we also use GL Assessment's English Progress Test, both of which allow us to compare our students against national averages.

While we're pretty sure that our English curriculum is great, we also know that because of all the time and effort we've invested in it we are prone to be fooled into thinking we see progress where none exists. In order to use the curriculum as a progression model, we need internally designed mastery assessments but we also need to be sure that students are performing well on standardised tests. If they're not, we will have unambiguous proof that either the curriculum or the way it's being implemented isn't working as intended.

Standardised tests do two things: they place individual students in a rank order and they allow us to compare our schools' performance curves against the normal distribution of national average performance. While it may be interesting to see rank orders, we need to be careful about what we do with this information. If you decide to share it with students or families, there's a risk that you will undermine your efforts to make the curriculum your progression model and inadvertently demotivate students. What's much more important is the ability to see whether the progress of the whole cohort is at least in line with national averages.

Why use the Progress Test in English

1. Evaluation

The beauty of using a standardised assessment like GL Assessment's Progress Test in English is that you have immediate validation that what you have taught has 'stuck' and can be applied in a different context.

Having an external, standardised test that sits alongside your curriculum allows you to evaluate how individual students, key groups, year groups and schools have performed against a national sample, arming you with information to make evidence-based decisions for timetabling, CPD, curriculum planning and more. It also allows you to evaluate your curriculum and check it is meeting the needs of your students. You can therefore use the data to support an 'assess, do, review' cycle.

These tests are not intended to be taught *to*; you do not need to worry about preparing students for the assessment.

2. Accuracy

The Progress Test in English is a standardised test, which means that all students sitting the test answer the same questions and are scored in a consistent manner. It was developed with a wide sample of UK schools and 37,000 students in all, ensuring a robust and nationally representative dataset.

The test provides you with a Standardised Age Score – a student's raw score converted into a standard score that considers the student's exact age and is benchmarked to a national sample. It also provides a national percentile and group rank, indicator scores for Key Stage 2 SATs Reading and GCSE English Language, and a breakdown of English skills and comprehension.

3. Information

The Progress Test in English provides a wealth of information. Where schools find it particularly useful is when they can sit as a team and identify gaps in their students' knowledge. The conversations that spring from this information can be invaluable – not only do they save marking time, but also any interventions can be more accurately and effectively targeted.

The evidence teachers gain from question-level analysis highlights how much of what they teach has been effective, and those insights can be used to make teaching much more responsive. Some results may be expected, but it is the unexpected that can be especially valuable. For example, if you have spent weeks teaching figurative language but the assessment shows a knowledge gap, any misconceptions can then be addressed and quickly corrected, allowing the class to move on.

The assessments also include 'teaching and learning implications' with strategies to use in lesson and at home. They are designed to work alongside your knowledge of the student so that their needs can be fully met. Some of the things that would take teachers weeks to discover can be uncovered in just over an hour.

Georgina Cook, Assessment Specialist, GL Assessment

3.15 REPORTING TO DIFFERENT AUDIENCES

The need to report on students' progress is in large part responsible for many of the poor decisions made around assessment.

So, your students have sat an assessment. What now? The first thing is to head off any attempt to steer us back to filling in APP* grids where teachers tick off lists of curriculum-related expectations. Not only is this burdensome, it leads us away from using the curriculum itself as the progression model and instead reifies curricular objectives. That is to say, what starts as a breakdown of what should be taught – only ever a proxy for the experience itself – becomes a measure against which students and teachers are judged with the inevitable result that objectives take on an independent life of their own.

This tendency to want to use CREs as an assessment tick list is contained within what we've called the specificity problem: if CREs are too specific we risk generating endless tick box checklists. If they're too broad, they risk becoming meaninglessly bland. Essentially, the way out of this thicket is thinking carefully about what levels of specificity are needed by different audiences. CREs need to be both very specific *and* very broad **depending on the audience.**

3.15.1 Students

Students need to know where they are now, where they are going and how they are going to get there. The first question is answered by students being aware of their performance in assessments. How well do they know what they have been taught? How fluently can they perform the procedures on which this knowledge depends? The second question is the province of the curriculum; where they are going should have been carefully and coherently sequenced so that they can build on prior knowledge. The third question concerns instruction. It is contained both in the feedback teachers take from students' performances and in the feedback students are given on what they need to do to improve.

This feedback should be explicitly linked to the CREs students are being taught to meet. This should be fairly straightforward. If a student has failed to recall the agreed definition for, say, symbolism, they will need to practise recalling it. If, they are unable to use one of the specified creative sentence structures, they will need to practise using it in different contexts. If it's not clear what a student needs to do to improve, this is likely to down to one of two reasons. First, it might be because the assessment is too vague to work out why a student has lost marks. If this is the case, the assessment needs to be rewritten so that we can see which constructs students have not mastered if they have not answered a question. If the assessment question *is* clear, then the problem is likely to be that the CRE in question has either not been taught clearly enough or that students have not been given sufficient practice at applying it.

3.15.2 Teachers

Teachers need to know what gaps they need to fill, both at the level of individual students and the class. Teachers need to know what to teach next in order that all progress through the curriculum. And because the process of assessing students' curricular knowledge will reveal inadequacies both in instruction and the curriculum, teachers need to be prepared and able to be responsive both at a curricular as well as instructional level. To be responsive at an instructional level, we need to think about pedagogy (e.g., are we checking all students' understanding? Are our MWB routines consistent and clear?). To be responsive at a curricular level we need to think about improving the specificity and sequencing of curriculum content.

For instance, in the process of designing our C25k writing programme, we noticed that some students – without being asked to do so – were expanding on thesis statements to link to themes. Obviously enough, most weren't because no one had taught them to do so. It became clear that this was a gap we had left in our instructional sequence. By examining what some students were doing successfully and what others were struggling with, we were able to fill the gap with Sentence 2: Link to controlling ideas.

Our aim should be gapless instruction. If students have struggled to answer particular questions we need to reflect on why. For instance, when we look

---

* Assessing Pupils' Progress (if you don't know, don't ask!).

at test performances, are there identifiable patterns? If many students have failed to answer a question, there's a good chance we've made an assumption or left a gap into which they've fallen. We may need to rethink how we have taught this aspect of the curriculum or whether additional practice is required for students to achieve mastery. Remember: students shouldn't practise until they're successful, they should continue practising until they can no longer be unsuccessful.

If teachers are unclear on how to help their students make progress, they will need the support and guidance of their curriculum leader.

3.15.3 Curriculum leaders

When Heads of English look at the performance data deriving from summative assessments, their needs are different. They will need to be alert for teacher gaps and for this they need to be able to compare the performance of different teaching groups so they can investigate causes and resolve issues.

Remember, the ambition of mastery assessment is that *all* children will be successful. If students in some classes are not successful this should not be interpreted as a failing in the students but as a problem with either the assessment itself (questions could be confusingly worded), the curriculum or its implementation. If there are teacher gaps (where one teacher's classes have performed worse than other classes) then the initial assumption should be that something has gone wrong in that particular classroom. This could be due to teacher absence – in which case the curriculum leader should consider how cover is spread across the department to minimise disruption for students – or maybe a poor grasp of how the curriculum should be implemented. In the best cases, curriculum leaders will use the gaps revealed by assessment data to provide training and development for team members. For instance, if students across an entire cohort are all struggling to write about metaphor, it would be worth reading section 1.6 to consider whether the concepts are being taught effectively. If teachers are confused then we shouldn't be surprised if students are too. Very often, the most egregious of these gaps can be closed through good co-planning (see section 2.17) but sometimes they may require extensive coaching and support.

Heads of English also need to use assessment data to work out how well the department as a whole is teaching particular aspects of the curriculum. Have students in all, or most, classes struggled to analyse metaphors or write thesis statements? If so, this suggests a training need for all teachers. This might be addressed through a department meeting in which teachers share ideas about how they are currently teaching these aspects of the curriculum. As a Lead Practitioner team, we are always on hand to provide support, either in person or through the training videos we share. Either way, assessment data is revealing where students and teachers are struggling and helps to pinpoint where support is needed to close gaps.

It's probably not useful for curriculum leaders to make summative statements of progress. There's very little benefit to claiming that students have achieved an arbitrary benchmark when they are part-way through their curricular journey. Instead, they need to know how much of the curriculum has been learned, what to do if students are *not* learning it and to constantly monitor whether the curriculum requires greater levels of specificity or alterations in its sequencing.

To that end they need to be able to conduct question-level analysis of students' performance in tests. In all probability, this task will be made easier if students' performance is converted into numbers. The key question when collecting data should always be, how will this information be *used*?

When Cliff Park began using our assessments to judge the impact of the curriculum, some of the teachers felt that the assessments were 'too hard' for their students and pointed to the fact that their students were performing poorly. Thankfully, Holly, the Head of English, had assigned herself classes made up of the lowest prior attaining students in each year group and was able to argue that if her students could be successful, then so should students in other classes. This became essential leverage for showing teachers that if 'kids like these' could be successful, then so could all students!

If curriculum leaders are unclear on how to support their teachers in helping their students make progress, they will need the support and guidance of senior leaders.

3.15.4 SLT/Governors

At the level of Senior Leadership or Governance, the level of detail needed is much less. At this point what is needed are summaries. Leaders and governors need to know which teachers need development and whether the cohort is on track. Again, when it comes to summaries of cohorts being on track, numbers can help to make comparisons and spot trends. Whilst it's vital to remember that grades are holistic and can **only** be applied summatively after a course is complete, average percentages have far less narrative power to deceive us and still allow for comparison and pattern spotting, as long as leaders remain mindful that while lateral comparisons can usefully be made, longitudinal comparisons cannot (see section 3.12).

If senior leaders are unclear on how to support curriculum leaders in helping their department to make progress, they may be looking at the wrong things. If senior leaders are in the habit of looking only at data overviews without understanding, for instance, the dangers of longitudinal comparison they may need support. Difficulties are also caused when senior leaders don't have sufficient knowledge of the English curriculum and how it is assessed. Addressing these issues in a large MAT like OAT, this is relatively easy to arrange. As Lead Practitioners, it is a crucial part of our role to help non-specialist senior leaders to understand how best to line manage English departments. However, if you're leading a stand-alone school or a school in a small Trust, not only might you find it harder to get support, you might also find it harder to recognise you need it.

3.15.5 Parents and families

Reporting to families is where a lot of otherwise good practice combusts. Far too many school leaders mistakenly believe they need to report how likely students are to get particular GCSE grades and this then warps everything else they do. Whilst there's a statutory obligation to regularly report students' progress to families what form this takes is up to us. Parents may think they want to know GCSE predictions but, in large part, that's because they have been trained to expect them. In actual fact, parents generally want to know three things:

1. How is my child performing (relative to other members of the group)?
2. Are they working hard? (What, *specifically*, do they need to improve?)
3. Are they happy?

None of these questions can be adequately answered by grades or numbers and they should obviously

never be based on the hocus pocus of attempting to forecast students' future performance.

Instead, we recommend that families are told which of the CREs for the modules students are studying have been met and which have not. This provides clarity about where students will need further support and is a better basis for a conversation than a number.

If families are unclear on how to support their children in making progress, that's on us. The good news is that if we have designed a carefully specified and coherently sequenced curriculum, been systematic, been rigorous in our implementation, and designed meaningful assessments that support using the curriculum as a progression model, this won't happen.

IMPACT: KEY POINTS

1. **In order for the curriculum to be used as a progression model we must avoid distractions like target grades and age-related expectations.**
   If the curriculum is your progression model, students are making progress if they are mastering the material taught in the curriculum. Grades, level descriptors or age-related expectations are their own progression models and only act to make it more difficult to see if the curriculum is having the impact we intend it to have.

2. **Specifying clear curriculum-related expectations allows assessment to focus on supporting students in mastering the curriculum.**
   If our expectations of what students should be able to do are clearly linked to the curriculum we teach it becomes straightforward to work out whether our curriculum is having the impact we intend. By chunking the curriculum into CREs which are specified in detail in teaching materials, we provide a clear guide for students on where they are, where they are going and how they will get there.

3. **Summative tests should ensure that students are not assessed on skills which have not been explicitly specified, taught and practised. Instead, they should concentrate on clear curriculum constructs so teachers can see exactly what students have and have not mastered.**
   If we design assessment questions to explicitly test whether students have mastered curriculum constructs (and if these constructs are explicitly

linked to the CREs we are teaching) then assessment can be used effectively to provide assurance that our curriculum and its implementation are having the impact we intend.

4. **Although internal assessment should emphasise quality assuring the curriculum and its implementation rather than on discriminating between students, standardised tests should be used to ensure that mastering the curriculum also results in students performing in line with national expectations.**

Carefully designed internal assessments linked to our curriculum content are essential in using the curriculum as a progression model, but we still need to be sure that our curriculum is an *effective* progression model. To be confident about this we need the reassurance that our students are performing at least in line with national averages on externally provided standardised tests.

5. **Reporting to parents (and other audiences) should not be based on the impossibility of trying to apply grades part-way through a course. Parents should be told whether students are meeting curriculum-related expectations.**

Parents (and other audiences) may think they understand what progress means when it's communicated with a grade, but not only is this guesswork, it conceals the crucial information we need about where students may be struggling and where they need support. By communicating which CREs have been met and which have not, we provide a much clearer picture for parents about how they might support their children.

The curriculum in detail

Our KS3 curriculum is loosely based on the model outlined by David in *Making Meaning for English* but has been adapted to respond to the input of OAT's English Lead Practitioner team. The KS4 curriculum has been formulated in partnership with our academies and is based around the most popular choices for study at GCSE. Between us, we have written and resourced all of the resources discussed below.

How to allocate time to the modules that comprise the KS3 curriculum needs some consideration. Covering everything in the Teacher Guides and Student Anthologies would be impossible in a year, because we've built choice and flexibility into our modules than can be expanded or contracted (usually the latter) to ensure the curriculum-related expectations can be taught and practised in the time available. There are 39 teaching weeks in the school year and, if we assume that there are four hours of English timetabled per week, you should be able to adapt the timings we suggest to best suit your circumstances.

4.1 YEAR 7: THE ORIGINS OF ENGLISH

The guiding idea behind the Year 7 curriculum is to provide students with a foundational knowledge of where literature – and especially English literature – came from and has developed over time. We introduce concepts that will be returned to on multiple occasions as the curriculum unfolds with the intention that students will be able to make meaningful links and connections. In addition, a great deal of effort is spent on laying the groundwork for the deconstructed essay and on using tenor, vehicle and ground to think about metaphor.

4.1.1 Ancient Origins

The first module of our curriculum is centred around Simon Armitage's radio play based on

Content	- *Epic of Gilgamesh*, the *Iliad* - Creation myths - Greek mythology (heroes) - **Homer's Odyssey**, Simon Armitage - "Medusa" by Carol Ann Duffy & "Siren Song" by Margaret Atwood		
Metaphor	- Definition of metaphor - Tenor, vehicle, ground - Homeric epithets	Pattern	- Beginnings, changes and endings: in medias res - Morphology
Story	- Sense making - Mythology - Plot: five act structure - Heroes; the epic	Grammar	- Syntax: subject verb agreement - Fragments & phrases - Nouns & adjectives - Complex sentences - Subordinating conjunctions - Commas as pivots
Argument	- Debate: Is Odysseus admirable? - Thesis statements - Summarising	Context	- Literary timeline - Aristotle's poetics - Development of writing (cuneiform) & literature (Gilgamesh)

DOI: 10.4324/9781003455622-4

Homer's *Odyssey*. It's an earthy, accessible and often very funny version of the epic which provides students with lots of opportunity for reading fluency practice as they perform various set pieces. Teachers need to be aware that there are two 'f-bombs' in the play and that care needs to be taken, particularly with the scene in which Odysseus confronts the witch Circe after she has failed to turn him into a pig.

Students will also explore the concept of mythology in terms of the origin of stories. They will read a range of creation myths from around the world as well as exploring what it is to be a hero by comparing various stories from Greek myth as well as extracts from the *Iliad* dealing with the story of Achilles and the Sumerian *Epic of Gilgamesh*, the oldest piece of literature of which we are aware. Gilgamesh, Achilles and Odysseus present a complex counterpoint to some of the simpler, more sanitised versions of the hero found in some of the other stories and students are asked to think about whether and to what extent these characters fulfil the role of hero, and how the concept of hero has changed over time.

Students will also read texts inspired by the *Odyssey* by Tennyson, Margaret Atwood and Carol Ann Duffy and think particularly about the presentation of female characters in the *Odyssey*.

The resources for this module can be downloaded here: https://english.ormistonacademiestrust.co.uk/year-7/ancient-origins/

4.1.2 Links to Legends

This module builds on the ideas presented in Ancient Origins and shifts the story of English to some of the earliest works of literature in English. Students will experience *Beowulf*, the oldest existing piece of English literature, alongside some of the texts it has inspired. Students will read extracts from both Seamus Heaney's and Maria Headley's translations as well as a brief foray into Old English. From there, students will jump to Arthurian legend through the lens of Simon Armitage's version of *Sir Gawain and the Green Knight* as well as extracts from Mallory's *Le Morte d'Arthur*. Finally, students will read some of the foundational legends from China (*Journey to the West*, Wu Cheng'en) and the Middle East (*A Thousand and One Nights*).

Whilst all of our units can be taught independently, we have also carefully interlinked the units to build on concepts and ideas incrementally. The Legends unit, for example, deliberately builds on students' understanding of classical heroes – making connections between Beowulf and Achilles in their physical prowess, but also highlighting how medieval writers reimagined heroes through a Christian lens.

The resources for this module can be downloaded here: https://english.ormistonacademiestrust.co.uk/year-7/links-to-legend/

Content	- *Beowulf* (Heaney & Headley) - *Journey to the West* - Arthurian legend (Mallory) - **Sir Gawain and the Green Knight** (Armitage)		
Metaphor	- Tenor, vehicle, ground - Abstract to concrete - Metaphors in words - Kennings	**Pattern**	- Phonemes - Schemes: Alliteration - Caesura
Story	- Epic - Heroes - Plot: five act structure - Characterisation	**Grammar**	- Morphology – roots & fixes (spelling & decoding) - Changing word classes; matching suffixes to word class - Noun phrases - Clauses & sentences
Argument	- Debate: What makes a good ruler? - Thesis statements - Topic sentences - Summarising	**Context**	- Identifying relevant context - Old English - Christianity

4.1.3 The Art of Rhetoric

This introduction to rhetoric revolves around Shakespeare's play, *Julius Caesar*. Not only is this an unapologetic opportunity for students to have their first meaningful encounter with the Bard, but because of its setting in ancient Rome (and the fact that Cicero is a character in the play) it also fits nicely into the story of the development of rhetoric and oratory. In addition, the module takes extracts from Mark Forsyth's *The Elements of Eloquence*, Sam Leith's *You Talkin' To Me?* and Jay Heinrichs's *Thank You for Arguing*.

The module is divided into five sections, each focusing on one of the five acts of *Julius Caesar* and also on one of the five parts of rhetoric: invention, arrangement, style, memory and delivery. In each section, students are introduced to a range of great speeches from literature and history including Satan's monologue after being cast out of Heaven from Book 1 of *Paradise Lost*, Cicero's condemnation of Cataline in the Senate, Mark Anthony's funeral oration for Julius Caesar, Abraham Lincoln's Gettysburg Address, Martin Luther King Jr's 'I have a dream' speech and Barack Obama's 'Audacity of hope' speech.

The module has two main aims: that students should read, perform and enjoy *Julius Caesar*, and that they should be introduced to and experiment with different rhetorical forms. We recommend that the play is not studied in any depth and that the only scene to be analysed in detail should be Act 3 scene 2 which contains both Brutus and Anthony's funeral speeches.

The resources for this module can be downloaded here: https://english.ormistonacademiestrust.co.uk/year-7/the-art-of-rhetoric/

4.1.4 Romance

The final module of Year 7 explores the genre of Romance from its origins to its transformation into Romanticism. Students begin by reading Nevil Coghill's verse translation of Chaucer's 'The Knight's Tale' as well as experiencing some of Patience Agbabi's modern 'grime' remix of the *Canterbury Tales*. This is the first of three of Chaucer's Tales students get to read and some time is taken to establish the context in which Chaucer lived and wrote.

To help students embed the conventions and concepts of Romance, students will read extracts from two Shakespeare plays: *A Midsummer Night's Dream* (focusing on Oberon and Titania, but also making explicit links to 'The Knight's Tale') and *Romeo and Juliet* (centred on Mercutio's Queen Mab speech). From there, students get a glimpse into the world of Spenser's *Faerie Queen*.

Students also read a range of poetry: Keats' 'La Belle Dame Sans Merci', Rosetti's 'Goblin Market', Tennyson's 'The Lady of Shallot' and Yeats' 'The Second Coming'. All are examples of how medieval romance has been repurposed and reimagined by later writers. Then, finally, students consider how Romance has become the modern fantasy genre by looking at Tolkien and N.K. Jemisin.

Alongside an introduction to the genre of Romance, students will also follow a thread through all the texts from Chaucer to Jemisin around the presentation of women. Since the unit is arranged chronologically, students can track the development from the silent and silenced Emily in 'The Knight's Tale', via the vociferous and argumentative young women in Shakespeare's plays, to Jemisin's

Content	- Shakespeare – **Julius Caesar** - Famous speeches (*Paradise Lost*, Lincoln, MLK Jr, Obama) - Cicero & Aristotle - Extracts from Forsyth, Heinrichs & Leith		
Metaphor	- Tenor, vehicle, ground - Flowers of rhetoric (antithesis, hyperbole, metonymy, transferred epithets)	**Pattern**	- Metrical feet: iambic pentameter - Acts & scenes - Schemes (anaphora, alliteration, assonance, isocolon, tricolon)
Story	- Genre: tragedy - Drama - Character & plot – façade/flaw	**Grammar**	- Changing word classes; matching suffixes to word - Complex sentences - Subordinating conjunctions - Commas as pivots
Argument	- Ethos, logos, pathos - Thesis statements - Topic sentences - Selecting evidence - Arrangement (Act 3 scene 2)	**Context**	- Using context to support arguments - Origins of rhetoric - Elizabethan anxieties

Content	- Chaucer, **'The Knight's Tale'** - Patience Agbadi, *Telling Tales* - Shakespeare, *Romeo & Juliet* and *A Midsummer Night's Dream* - Keats, 'La Belle Dame Sans Merci' - Tennyson, 'The Lady of Shalott' - J.R.R. Tolkien and N.K. Jemisin		
Metaphor	- Tenor, vehicle, ground - Symbolism - Characters as vehicle - Theme as tenor	**Pattern**	- Rhyme, alliteration, metre - Binding time: theme & motif - Lines, stanzas - Form
Story	- The romance; quests - Tragedy & comedy - Poetry	**Grammar**	- Changing word classes; matching suffixes to word - Sentence types & complexity - Semantics & pragmatics
Argument	- Summarising - Thesis statements - Topic sentences - Selecting and embedding evidence - Tentative phrasing	**Context**	- Find connections between contexts - Middle English - Courtly love

first-person narrative of Yeine Darr who challenges and ultimately upends the ruling order.

The resources for this module can be downloaded here: https://english.ormistonacademiestrust.co.uk/year-7/the-story-of-romance/

4.2 YEAR 8: THE DEVELOPMENT OF FORM

Although this year is intended to revolve around the idea of form, we've also taken the opportunity to shoehorn in the King James Bible both as a literary text in its own right and as possibly the most influential text on the rest of English literature. The year kicks off with a module on the study of the sonnet form over time and is a beautiful sequence of sonnets from Petrarch to Shakespeare to Wordsworth to the modern explosion of the form.

The Bible module celebrates William Tyndale as one of the most important unsung heroes of English as well as presenting some of the most enduringly popular Bible stories as well as a smattering of some of the literature influenced by the King James Bible.

Our Comedy through Time module takes students from the ancient origins of the genre, spotlighting Aristophanes' *Lysistrata*, through Chaucer's 'The Miller's Tale', via one of Shakespeare's less-studied comedies, *As You Like It*, through the Restoration and into the modern era.

The year then ends with our take on the story of the novel, beginning with Aphra Behn's *Oroonoko*

and then sweeping through the eighteenth and nineteenth centuries and being anchored around Dickens' *Great Expectations*.

4.2.1 The Sonnet Form

The sonnet, one of the oldest, strictest, and most enduring poetic forms, comes from the Italian word *sonetto*, meaning 'little song'. In this unit, students trace its origins to the 13th century, to the Italian court. Although Giacomo de Lentini is credited with its invention, the jumping-off point for our exploration is though Francesco Petrarca (Petrarch), who was its most famous early practitioner. We then move on to see how the form was adopted and enthusiastically embraced by the English in the Elizabethan period, most notably by Shakespeare, who gave it the structure we commonly think of today: 14 lines of rhymed iambic pentameter.

From here, students then track the history of the sonnet through key literary periods into modern times, where experimental poets have pushed, and are still pushing, the boundaries of what the form is and means. In this module, students will not only become experts in poetic form, but also have the opportunity to see how concepts and themes have been influenced by societal shifts and seismic literary movements across the canon.

The resources for this module can be downloaded here: https://english.ormistonacademiestrust.co.uk/year-8/the-sonnet/

Content	- Petrarch to Shakespeare to Donne to Wordsworth to Duffy and Dharker		
Metaphor	- Tenor, vehicle, ground - Systematised metaphor - Irony	**Pattern**	- The sonnet form - Rhyme schemes - Metre (iambs & trochees)
Story	- Can sonnets tell stories, or are they arguments? - Theme	**Grammar**	- Adverbs & adverbials - Sentence combining - Sentences (subjects & verbs; fragments; run-ons)
Argument	- Volta as crux of argument - Analysing writers' use of language, structure & form - Comparative statements - Summarising - Focus on the effects of the whole text & controlling ideas	**Context**	- Conventions of Petrarchan & Shakespearean sonnets - History of the sonnet - Elizabethan; Romanticism

4.2.2 The Bible as Literature

The central concerns of this module are to introduce students to the importance of Bible knowledge in the study of English literature and to celebrate the work of William Tyndale, translator of most of the King James Bible and probably the most influential individual on the development of the English language. Studying the Bible both *as* literature and its influence *on* literature and language should be seen as entirely separate from studying the Bible as a religious and spiritual text. Whatever else people believe it to be, the Bible has a unique place in the study of the subject of *English*. Students are asked to think about why translating the Bible into English was so important to people like Tyndale and the influence his prose has had on generations of readers.

We are also keen to make sure students are aware of a range of Bible references. They read the creation story from Genesis (and compare it to some of the creations myths they read about in Year 7), Adam and Eve, Cain and Abel, Noah and the flood (which they compare to the flood in the Epic of Gilgamesh), Samson and Delilah, the judgement of Solomon, and Daniel and the lions' den. They also look at a selection of Biblical poetry as well as the gospels and the story of Paul's conversion on the road to Damascus. Alongside this they read a medieval mystery play based on the story of Noah, extracts from *The Pilgrim's Progress* and *Paradise Lost* as well as poetry inspired by the King James Bible from William Blake and Emily Dickinson as well as song lyrics from Bob Marley.

The resources for this module can be downloaded here: https://english. ormistonacademiestrust.co.uk/ year-8/the-king-james-bible/

Content	- Medieval mystery plays (Noah) - Tyndale and the King James Bible - Extracts from *Paradise Lost, The Pilgrim's Progress* - Poetry: Blake, Dickinson & Marley		
Metaphor	- Biblical imagery - Allegory - Symbolism	**Pattern**	- Tyndale's style - Diachronic change - Iambic pentameter; rhyming couplets
Story	- Mythical bases for stories - Narrative perspective - Characterisation	**Grammar**	- Uses and effects of conjunctions - Embedding and moving clauses - Varying subordinating conjunctions for effect
Argument	- Controlling ideas - Analysing writers' use of language, structure & form - Evaluating writers' intentions - Summarising	**Context**	- The influence of King James Bible on English - Lyric poetry - William Tyndale

4.2.3 Comedy through Time

One of the difficulties for students studying comedy is that they don't always find the texts they read funny. The idea that comedy is synonymous with amusing is tackled early on and we offer the definition that comedy is a plot structure which moves from chaos to order. That said, we also hope to show students that the texts we've selected are also laugh out loud funny. Students get to see this concept played out across history, first in Aristophanes' play *Lysistrata* in which the women of Sparta organise a sex strike to try to end the Peloponnesian War. Students also get to think about the satire of the Roman writers, Juvenal and Horace.

From there we move to Chaucer's 'The Miller's Tale'. Students will already have experienced Chaucer's 'The Knight's Tale' in Year 7 and here we continue to use Nevill Coghill's excellent verse translation. The tale of the relationship triangle of John, Alisoun and Nicholas is both farcical and extremely scatological: perfect for a Year 8 audience!

The anchor text for this module is Shakespeare's forest romp, *As You Like It*, in which the cross-dressing Rosalind, one of his finest female characters, outwits everyone before everything is resolved happily and conventionally. As always, the idea is that students should read the anchor text in its entirety but not to study it in depth. It is there both to be enjoyed and as a vehicle for understanding the key concepts of comedy.

From there we travel to William Wycherley's scandalous Restoration comedy, *The Country Wife*, take in Swift's 'A Modest Proposal', look at some comic extracts from Dickens and Oscar Wilde before finishing with the comic verse of Edward Lear, Lewis Carol, Spike Milligan, Pam Ayres and Wendy Cope.

The resources for this module can be downloaded here: https://english.ormistonacademiestrust.co.uk/year-8/the-story-of-comedy/

4.2.4 The Story of the Novel

Exactly where the story of the novel begins is an entire academic debate, but for our purposes we begin with Aphra Behn's 'proto novel' *Oroonoko* and Daniel Defoe's enduring classic, *Robinson Crusoe*. From there we sweep through the 18th century taking in extracts from Richardson's *Pamela*, Fielding's *Tom Jones*, *Evelina* by Frances Burney and *Pride and Prejudice* by Jane Austen. We then consider Dickens, George Eliot, J.D. Salinger and, finally, Chimamanda Ngozi Adichie's *Purple Hibiscus*.

The anchor text for the module is *Great Expectations* and students will follow the story of Pip alongside that of the novel form. As you'll be aware, this is a very long text and whilst we want students to read it in its entirety, there's no time for any analysis. We also recommend that several chapters are glossed so students can enjoy the more exciting parts.

Content	- Aristophanes, *Lysistrata* - Chaucer, 'The Miller's Tale' - **As You Like It** - Restoration comedy - Oscar Wilde		
Metaphor	- Analysing metaphors - Motif	**Pattern**	- Epigrams - Comic structure - Form - Caesura & enjambment
Story	- Genre - Comic plot: disorder to order - Comic archetypes - Dialogue - Theme	**Grammar**	- Planning & drafting essays; writing purposes - Morphology - Using pronouns; sentence combining - Varying subordinating conjunctions for effect
Argument	- Analysing writers' use of language, structure & form - Evaluating writers' intentions - Summarising	**Context**	- Embedding context - Literary: How comedy has evolved - Satire - Conventions of comedy over time

Content	- Dickens, ***Great Expectations*** - Extracts from *Oroonoko, Robinson Crusoe, Gulliver's Travels, Pamela, Pride and Prejudice, Catcher in the Rye, Purple Hibiscus*		
Metaphor	- Extended metaphors - Motif - Irony	**Pattern**	- Serialisation; chapters - Form - Beginnings, changes & endings - How prose 'binds time'
Story	- Narrative voice - Narrative structure (frames, cyclical structures etc.) - Characterisation; dialogue - Epistolary writing ('found' narratives)	**Grammar**	- Semantics & pragmatics - Paragraphing - Serial sentences - Understanding the effects/uses (disinterest/avoiding responsibility etc.)
Argument	- How does the novel try to persuade us? - Controlling ideas - Analysing writers' use of language, structure & form - Evaluating writers' intentions - Summarising	**Context**	- Caxton & mass literacy; letter writing - Serialisation - Historical: 18th century - Feminism

Along the way we take in some Victorian non-fiction writing on crime, the effects of serialisation, the concept of the Bildungsroman as well as enjoying William Hogarth's series of etchings, *The Rake's Progress*.

The resources for this module can be downloaded here: https://english.ormistonacademiestrust.co.uk/year-8/the-story-of-the-novel/

4.3 YEAR 9: INTO THE WORLD

The purpose of Year 9's selections is to give students a sense of where and how English has changed, travelled and evolved. The year begins with an exploration of the Gothic genre, centred around Emily Brontë's classic *Wuthering Heights*, moves swiftly into the 20th century with our War Writing module, anchored around R.C. Sherriff's play *Journey's End*, before returning once again to ancient Greece with the story of tragedy. This story shows students how the genre has developed from Oedipus to Othello to Okonkwo (the tragic hero of Chinua Achebe's novel *Things Fall Apart*). Depending on the depth with which the previous modules have been studied, there is the option to study our Freedom module which, as well as looking more widely at the Harlem Renaissance writers, is anchored around Zora Neale Hurston's stunning novel *Their Eyes Were Watching God*.* And

then, finally, KS3 ends with a synoptic review of everything studied throughout the three years with the Women in Literature module. Female writers are already deeply embedded throughout the curriculum, but this module, which leads students from Sappho onwards and is focused on Charlotte Perkins Gilman's *The Yellow Wallpaper*, attempts to consider why women have been marginalised but also celebrates the achievements of some of the greatest writers in English.

4.3.1 The Gothic Tradition

The primary focus of the Gothic is to welcome students into a world of wild and remote landscapes, vulnerable heroines, supernatural happenings and uncanny events. Gothic fiction has intrigued and unsettled readers for more than two centuries and, as a result, the Gothic has become a staple of the academic study of literature: the very question of humanity and the human condition, as well as suffering and romance, are all key themes brought up and reflected in this dark and mysterious fiction.

It is crucial that rather than just studying a range of authors considered 'Gothic', time is dedicated to the development of the genre itself, moving from the introduction of the Gothic, Romanticism and the Sublime, to the Victorian and American Gothic and the transformation into modern day Gothic symbolism. Students will gain an understanding of the critical literary movements and how different writers exploited the fears of the time, focusing on *Wuthering Heights* as the primary novel but using a range of other texts and authors such as the Brontës,

---

* For those who really want to give more time to all the modules, there is the option of studying the Freedom module in Year 10 (see section 4.4).

Content	- Gothic anthology (*The Castle of Otranto, Vathek, The Monk, The Italian, Northanger Abbey*) - *Dracula, Frankenstein* - Emily Brontë – **Wuthering Heights** - Angela Carter, *The Werewolf*		
Metaphor	- Conceptual metaphors, systematised metaphors, motifs and symbols	**Pattern**	- Periodic sentences - Beginnings, changes & endings - Binding time
Story	- Characterisation, narrative perspective, narrative structure, narratology, theme, setting)	**Grammar**	- Summarising; explaining; discussing; describing
Argument	- Comparing texts in relation to literary concepts, ideas and methods - Debate/thesis statements/structuring arguments: Dialectic (they say / I say) analysis of language - Focus on the effects of the whole text & controlling ideas	**Context**	- Romanticism - Gothic conventions - Victorian social anxieties (science, religion, the supernatural, women, race), psychoanalytic theory

Content	- A selection of war poetry (including Owen & Sassoon) - R.C. Sherriff, **Journey's End**		
Metaphor	- Irony - Symbolism - Language analysis	**Pattern**	- Noticing poetic patterns (figures and schemes) - Scenes and acts
Story	- Thought - Perspective - Theme: concrete (object in text) to abstract (idea external to text)	**Grammar**	- Thesis statements & controlling idea - Introductions & conclusions
Argument	- Debate/thesis statements/structuring arguments: War as argument - Types of argument - Focus on the effects of the whole text & controlling ideas	**Context**	- 20th century drama (the 'well-made' play) - 'The Great War' - Realism; modernism; Aristotle's unities

Toni Morrison, Mary Shelley and Edgar Allan Poe to present the development of Gothic literature through the centuries.

The resources for this module can be downloaded here: https:// english.ormistonacademiestrust. co.uk/year-9/the-gothic/

4.3.2 War Writing

The second Year 9 module is based around R.C. Sherriff's play *Journey's End*. Not only is this an excellent introduction to structure and language of later 20th century drama such as J.B. Priestley's *An Inspector Calls*, it's an excellent narrative in its own right. Students are gripped as tension builds throughout the play and are often aghast at Osbourne's untimely death in the trenches.

Alongside this, students will also be exposed to a range of First World War poetry, especially the poets Wilfred Owen and Siegfried Sassoon, as well as extracts from novels including Sebastian Faulk's *Birdsong*, Pat Barker's *Regeneration* and Erich Maria Remarque's *All Quiet on the Western Front*. As well as all this there are various pieces of non-fiction.

It would be a huge opportunity missed not to spend some time looking at Richard Curtis and Ben Elton's *Blackadder Goes Forth*, particularly the clear parallels between Mason and Baldrick. Finally, students will experience the now practically forgotten one act play *Mine Eyes Have Seen* by African-American writer Alice Dunbar-Nelson.

The resources for this module can be downloaded here: https:// english.ormistonacademiestrust. co.uk/year-9/war-writing/

4.3.3 Tragedy through Time

Tragedies are an inherent part of human culture and literature. They are centred around sadness and death – misfortune and the descent of heroic characters. Ultimately, tragedies were designed to be, and still are – over two and a half millennia after they were created – cathartic. Catharsis allows us to release emotions, not just in traditional ways but as a group audience. Tragedies, though they show purposefully depressing subject matter, bring us together – we identify with the main character because we have gone through the same things they are experiencing on stage. This is the great mirror which allows tragedy to resonate so deeply with us.

This unit looks to cover the key periods of tragedy. We begin with it its formation by the Greeks, before going on to look at how the conventions of Greek Tragedy were then adapted in the medieval period and later into the Renaissance era. We then finish by looking at modern tragedy and its development from the classical tragedy earlier in the unit.

The resources for this module can be downloaded here: https://english.ormistonacademiestrust.co.uk/year-9/the-story-of-tragedy/

4.3.4 Freedom

Whether you decide to include this module in Year 9 or as part of the Year 10 curriculum will depend on the time taken on the previous three modules. The anchor text is Zora Neale Hurston's novel, *Their Eyes Were Watching God*. Some of the themes are mature – the

Content	- *Oedipus the King* (Sophocles) - 'The Monk's Tale' (Chaucer) - *The White Devil* (Webster) - **Othello** (Shakespeare) - *A View from the Bridge* (Miller) - *Things Fall Apart* (Achebe)		
Metaphor	- Symbolism & motif: definition, identification and effect	**Pattern**	- Noticing patterns in plays/novels: structural patterns (acts, scenes, chapters – rising action, climax, denouement); motifs; theme; character arcs
Story	- Themes: Fate, morality, reputation, justice - Characteristics of the tragic hero - Structure: prologue, parodos, stasima, exodus	**Grammar**	- Semantics and pragmatics: Direct meaning vs intentions - Complexity: The deconstructed essay/ structuring arguments
Argument	- Debate/thesis statements/structuring arguments: How should we live? Pity or fear? What is our fascination with human suffering? Victim or hero? Private vs public justice? - Linking to context - Extend: recognising different arguments	**Context**	- Venice/Ottoman Empire; attitudes to race in Renaissance era; patriarchal hierarchy; religious conflict - Conventions of Greek tragedy/Aristotelian unities; conventions of medieval period, Renaissance/revenge tragedy & modern tragedy (modest & ordinary)

Content	- Olaudah Equiano - Civil rights – biographies & speeches - Extracts from Baldwin, Angelou (Ch 19, *I Know Why...*) Morrison, Milk & Coates - Zora Neale Hurston, **Their Eyes Were Watching God**		
Metaphor	- Metonymy - Symbolism & motif - Language analysis	**Pattern**	- Noticing patterns in novels - Beginnings, changes & endings
Story	- Identity - Theme: understanding the difference between theme & motif - Dialogue (punctuating speech; varying speech verbs; using speech to reveal character)	**Grammar**	- Using discourse markers; linking paragraphs
Argument	- Debate/thesis statements/structuring arguments: Arguments for justice - Ethos, pathos, logos - Focus on the effects of the whole text & controlling ideas - Comparing texts in relation to literary concepts, ideas and methods - Linking to context - Extend: recognising different arguments	**Context**	- Slavery & colonialism; the canon - The Harlem Renaissance - Marxist literary theory - Embedding into essays

text deals frankly with domestic violence as well sex and relationships – and some teachers may be hesitant about reading a text which is written mainly in African American vernacular. It is, however, well worth the effort. One of the motivations for including this text in our curriculum is the fact that many of our schools were teaching Steinbeck's *Of Mice and Men* in Year 9. While this continues to be a fine novel, it can be difficult for some students (and some teachers) to read about the isolation and abuse experienced by women and Black people in a novel written by a white man. The fact that Hurston's novel is not only an exceptional work of fiction but is both about the experience *of* a Black woman and written *by* a Black woman make it a compelling candidate to include in the English curriculum.

Alongside this, students will read the work of other important figures of the Harlem Renaissance such as Langston Hughes, Claude McKay and Paul Laurence Dunbar as well as other writers who have used English either to argue for or as an expression of freedom. There are extracts from writers as diverse as Ta-Nehisi Coates, WEB Du Bois, Maya Angelou and Alice Walker.

The resources for this module can be downloaded here: https://english.ormistonacademiestrust.co.uk/year-9/freedom/

4.3.5 Women in Literature

The main purpose of the topic of Women in Literature is to allow students to explore a category of writing that has often been criticised and judged but also commended and celebrated due to the powerful battle for identity that it represents within society dating back as far as the Ancient Greeks.

Women in Literature is often defined as a category of writing done by women. However, this definition is so limited and restrictive, symbolic of how women in society and female writers have felt for centuries. It is instead an area of study of powerful figures, marginalised by history, who told their lives through literature while occupying a unique socio-political space within culture for centuries.

Although this module is rooted within societal movements and developments which affected everyone, it focuses on women in literature; female writers, female narrators, iconic female protagonists that reflect a feminist movement in society. Beginning with the introduction of the greats such as Sappho and Aphra Behn, to the Brontës, and Charlotte Mew's modernist poetry, to the transformation into modern-day literature such as the dystopian *The Handmaid's Tale* and *Purple Hibiscus* as they battle for freedom and hope for the future. Through this topic, students should gain an understanding of the critical literary movements and how different writers exploited fears, hopes and a battle for identity as women struggled in society, focusing on *The Yellow Wallpaper* as the primary novel but using a range of other texts to present the development of feminist literature through the centuries.

The resources for this module can be downloaded here: https://english.ormistonacademiestrust.co.uk/year-9/women-in-literature/

*

Content	A feminist 'retelling' of the story of English - Sappho; Chaucer, 'The Wife of Bath's Tale' & Zadie Smith, *The Wife of Willesden* - Aphra Behn, *Oroonoko*, Mary Wollstonecraft, Virginia Woolf, The Brontës - Charlotte Perkins Gilman, **The Yellow Wallpaper**		
Metaphor	- Comparing metaphors - Types of irony - Symbolism & motif - Language analysis	**Pattern**	- Noticing patterns in novels - How prose writers 'bind time'
Story	- Narratology - Perspective - Intertextuality	**Grammar**	- Multi-paragraph compositions - Review of all structures of learning
Argument	- Debate/thesis statements/structuring arguments: Arguments for equality - Ethos, pathos, logos - Comparing texts in relation to literary concepts, ideas and methods - Focus on the effects of the whole text & controlling ideas	**Context**	- Feminist literary theory - First, Second and Third Wave feminism - Embedding into essays

4.4 INTERLEAVING

Our curriculum is designed to link and interweave across the three years of KS3, and beyond. This is most obvious in the incremental progress in conceptual knowledge from Year 7 to Year 9, but there are also explicit thematic and textual links throughout. We've found that schools who take on the curriculum wholesale have particularly enjoyed highlighting and discovering these connections such as the rich comparisons between Oedipus and Odysseus, or that the 'Romance' unit in Year 7 lays the groundwork for Year 9's 'Women in Literature'.

Indeed, these connections go beyond our own curriculum and forward into KS4 and KS5: the clear parallels between *Journey's End* and *An Inspector Calls*, the fruitful comparisons between Desdemona and Othello's relationship with Macbeth and Lady Macbeth, as well as Romeo and Juliet. Studying tragedy lays the groundwork for critical study at A level, as does our approach to the sonnet and poetic form. There are also some inadvertent links which have become clear upon standing back and surveying the curriculum as a whole. For instance, flood myths pervade the curriculum from the flood in Gilgamesh, to the story of Noah's ark, the flood in Chaucer's 'The Miller's Tale' and the flood which wreaks such devastation on the characters of *Their Eyes Were Watching God*.

Throughout, the curriculum introduces and inducts students into the 'great conversation' of literature and empowers them to become active participants and critics.

Always a work in progress – as any curriculum should be – we hope you find these resources useful. However, everything we produce is always in beta and is regularly revised. If you find mistakes or can suggest improvements, we would be very glad to hear your feedback. Please feel free to use or adapt any of our materials under our creative commons license.[1]

4.5 THE KS4 CURRICULUM

If students are not prepared to begin their GCSE studies with confidence and enthusiasm, the KS3 curriculum has been a failure.

It's become something of a cliché to moan that English at KS4 has become a dry and tedious experience which puts students off taking Literature or Language at A level. As set out in

section 4.6, we have some suggestions for how English GCSEs could be reformed, but in the meantime, English teachers have to make the best of what we've got.

If students have followed our KS3 curriculum, if they have experienced the texts we have curated and mastered the concepts we have presented and progressed through the Couch to 5k writing programme, then they should be more than ready for the rigours of GCSE.

As discussed in section 1.4, English is a very different subject at KS3 and KS4. Whilst the texts students study during KS3 must merely be vehicles for mastering conceptual knowledge, for GCSE English Literature the texts themselves become important objects of study. This means it becomes worthwhile to ensure students learn the minutiae of character and plot, nuggets of contextual knowledge and lists of useful quotations. At the same time, the lack of any specified content for English Language means that it can be hard for teachers to know what to teach beyond the structure of the examination papers themselves. Thus, instead of the rich diet of reading and writing required to be successful, many KS4 courses are reduced to practising question types over and over.

As you can see in Figure 4.1, our KS4 curriculum is designed with the knowledge that most of our academies use the three most popular GCSE Literature set texts: *Macbeth*, *An Inspector Calls* and *A Christmas Carol*. We're also aware that many of our academies divide the teaching of English into separate and distinct Language and Literature lessons.[*]

Where we refuse to compromise is on the teaching of GCSE Language in Year 10. In too many cases, the KS4 curriculum has been reduced to two years of test preparation. One of the most depressing approaches to the English curriculum is to see a Year 10 programme of study beginning with students being taught 'Paper 1'. Not only is this tediously narrowing for students, it is also usually a joyless experience for English teachers. Instead, we have designed two modules for study in Year 10 which focus on how writers use language in a collection of linked extracts, focusing particularly on the ways in which gender and power relationships are explored. This is intended as a specific link to the content of A level Language courses as well as preparation for GCSEs.

---

* **NB.** This is not to say that we especially recommend either of these choices, rather we are simply acknowledging the reality of decisions made locally in our schools.

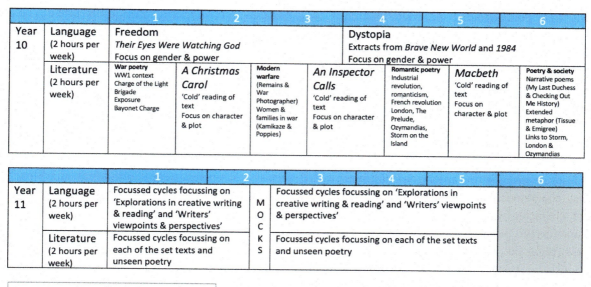

		1	2	3	4	5	6
Year 10	Language (2 hours per week)	**Freedom** *Their Eyes Were Watching God* Focus on gender & power			**Dystopia** Extracts from *Brave New World* and *1984* Focus on gender & power		
	Literature (2 hours per week)	**War poetry** WW1 context Charge of the Light Brigade Exposure Bayonet Charge	*A Christmas Carol* 'Cold' reading of text Focus on character & plot	**Modern warfare** (Remains & War Photographer) Women & families in war (Kamikaze & Poppies)	*An Inspector Calls* 'Cold' reading of text Focus on character & plot	**Romantic poetry** Industrial revolution, romanticism, French revolution London, The Prelude, Ozymandias, Storm on the Island	*Macbeth* 'Cold' reading of text Focus on character & plot	**Poetry & society** Narrative poems (My Last Duchess & Checking Out Me History) Extended metaphor (Tissue & Emigree) Links to Storm, London & Ozymandias

		1	2	3	4	5	6
Year 11	Language (2 hours per week)	Focussed cycles focussing on 'Explorations in creative writing & reading' and 'Writers' viewpoints & perspectives'	M O C K S	Focussed cycles focussing on 'Explorations in creative writing & reading' and 'Writers' viewpoints & perspectives'			
	Literature (2 hours per week)	Focussed cycles focussing on each of the set texts and unseen poetry		Focussed cycles focussing on each of the set texts and unseen poetry			

Year 11 Focussed cycle structure
Lesson 1: 45 min teaching + 15 mins planning
Lesson 2: 45 min teaching + 15 mins planning
Lesson 3: 45 min teaching + 15 mins planning
Lesson 4: Independent writing of planned essay
Lesson 5: Whole class feedback

NB. We are not recommending that schools adopt formally separate lessons for language and literature. This plan simply acknowledges that this is the reality in a number of our schools

FIGURE 4.1 OAT KS4 English curriculum

The focus of Literature lessons in Year 10 is on reading and enjoying the set texts. We recommend that texts are read quickly with a clear emphasis on character and plot. Each of the three set texts is very short: *Macbeth* is a little over 17,000 words in length, *An Inspector Calls* contains about 18,000 words and *A Christmas Carol* clocks in at 31,000 words. Both plays can be performed in not much more than two hours and Dickens' novella can be easily read in less than five hours. Why then do these texts often take weeks or months for students to complete in English lessons? The obvious answer is because teachers analyse the texts in microscopic detail and intersperse reading with written assignments. We believe that not only do these approaches undermine students' enjoyment of the stories, but that analysing, when students have only read a portion of a text, is hardly conducive to them developing a meaningful understanding of it.

That said, once students arrive in Year 11, it becomes increasingly important to begin preparing students for the examinations they will sit at the end of the year. To this end, we have designed a series of fortnightly teaching cycles which concentrate on specific aspects of either the texts on which students will have to write or on developing the language skills on which they will be judged.

If we assume five 60-minute English lessons per cycle, these cycles follow the same repeated pattern:

Lesson 1: 45 mins teaching + 15 mins planning
Lesson 2: 45 mins teaching + 15 mins planning
Lesson 3: 45 mins teaching + 15 mins planning
Lesson 4: Independent writing of planned essay
Lesson 5: Whole class feedback

Of course, these cycles can be adjusted to fit different timetable allocations but the basic expectation that students in Year 11 should write at least one piece of extended writing every week is necessary to ensure they will be thoroughly prepared when they sit their GCSEs.

This approach means that Year 11 students regularly revisit the key knowledge they learnt in Year 10, while the interleaved nature of the timetable allows revision alongside deeper teaching. As well as this, we know that there isn't a possibility that students won't revise a topic until a few weeks before their exams – we can manage their exposure to the knowledge and skills required and make sure that they are thoroughly practised on a regular basis.

Lessons can be used firstly to recall key knowledge but then elevate students' understanding by becoming more analytical and exploratory. The focus – right up until exams – should be on ensuring that students have the richest knowledge of the texts we can give them, while at the same time honing the way they are able to articulate this knowledge.

Rather than concentrating on exam technique or close analysis of extracts, this mode of sequencing can be used to help students meaningfully consider the texts in finer detail, rather than as an overwhelming list of things to remember. After all, the exams will require students to have a knowledge of whole texts, so it is important that their understanding is wide and fluid, rather than limited to quotations or basic plot points.

As an example of how this sequencing works, the first cycle of revisiting a text might be concerned with analysing characterisation: reading excerpts about a different character each lesson with a clear message that characters are constructs, not real people. The second cycle might be concerned with exploring themes throughout the text, reading selected extracts and considering how that theme develops. The third cycle might concern itself with writers' methods, again picking out quotations or passages from across the text and considering the symbols or motifs which emerge. The final run through could draw those threads together and link explicitly to the context during which the text was

written and considering the authors' intent. The regular reading of the texts is important; we can't expect students to be knowledgeable about a text they've only read once. The more they read the easier they'll find it to discuss and consider the ideas presented.

The most important part of these cycles of lessons, though, is the regular feedback which students are given. So much work goes into training students how to write each week, that it is only fair to offer feedback – not deep, individual marking – but instead whole class feedback which fixes one problem at a time. If students didn't embed quotations in cycle 1, then that is practised immediately in the first lesson of the next cycle and should (hopefully) not continue to be an issue in the essays written that week. It is much more useful to students and teachers to give regular feedback and address issues in this manner, than it is to wait until after a mock exam or other summative assessment.

Figure 4.2 shows a suggested plan as to what these cycles might consist of.

[OAT] OAT KS4 English curriculum overview

Year 11 Fortnightly cycles

		Lesson 1	Lesson 2	Lesson 3	Lesson 4	Lesson 5
Autumn 1	1	World War 1 - modernism links to AIC	Charge of the Light Brigade & Exposure	Bayonet Charge (CotLB & Exposure)	How to Compare	Essay
	2	Feedback / Poetry	Remains & War Photographer	Kamikaze & Poppies	Comparison	Essay
	3	Feedback: Poetry	Romanticism	London & Prelude	Ozymandias & Storm on the Island	Essay
	4	Feedback / Unseen	A Christmas Carol	A Christmas Carol	A Christmas Carol	Essay
	5	Feedback: A Christmas Carol	An Inspector Calls	An Inspector Calls	An Inspector Calls	Essay
	6	Feedback: An Inspector Calls	Language Paper 1	Language Paper 1	Language Paper 1	Essay
	7	Feedback: Language Paper 1	Macbeth	Macbeth	Macbeth	Essay

FIGURE 4.2 Year 11 Fortnightly cycles

OAT KS4 English curriculum overview

		Lesson 1	Lesson 2	Lesson 3	Lesson 4	Lesson 5
Autumn 2	1	Feedback / Macbeth	A Christmas Carol	A Christmas Carol	A Christmas Carol	Essay
	2	Mock Exams				
	3		Macbeth	Macbeth	Macbeth	Essay
	4	Feedback/ Macbeth	Language Paper 1	Language Paper 1	Language Paper 1	Essay
	5	Feedback Language Paper 1	An Inspector Calls	An Inspector Calls	An Inspector Calls	Essay
	6	Feedback: An Inspector Calls	Language Paper 2	Language Paper 2	Language Paper 2	Essay
Spring 1		Lesson 1	Lesson 2	Lesson 3	Lesson 4	Lesson 5
	1	Feedback: Language Paper 2	MLD & Checking Out Me History	The Emigree & Tissue	Links to Sotl, London, Ozymandias	Essay
	2	Feedback: Unseen	Language Paper 1	Language Paper 1	Language Paper 1	Essay
	3	Feedback: Language Paper 1	Unseen	Unseen	Unseen	Essay
	4	Feedback: Poetry	A Christmas Carol	A Christmas Carol	A Christmas Carol	Essay
	5	Feedback: A Christmas Carol	Macbeth	Macbeth	Macbeth	Essay
	6	Feedback: Macbeth	Unseen	Unseen	Unseen	Essay

FIGURE 4.2 (Continued)

[OAT] OAT KS4 English curriculum overview

<table>
<thead>
<tr><th></th><th></th><th>Lesson 1</th><th>Lesson 2</th><th>Lesson 3</th><th>Lesson 4</th><th>Lesson 5</th></tr>
</thead>
<tbody>
<tr><td rowspan="6">Spring 2</td><td>1</td><td>Feedback: Poetry</td><td>Revision</td><td>Revision</td><td>Revision</td><td>Revision</td></tr>
<tr><td>2</td><td colspan="5" align="center">Mock Exams</td></tr>
<tr><td>3</td><td>An Inspector Calls</td><td>An Inspector Calls</td><td>An Inspector Calls</td><td>An Inspector Calls</td><td>Essay</td></tr>
<tr><td>4</td><td>Feedback/ An Inspector Calls</td><td>Macbeth</td><td>Macbeth</td><td>Macbeth</td><td>Essay</td></tr>
<tr><td>5</td><td>Feedback/ Macbeth</td><td>Anthology Poetry</td><td>Anthology Poetry</td><td>Anthology Poetry</td><td>Essay</td></tr>
<tr><td>6</td><td>Feedback/Anthology Poetry</td><td>Language Paper 2</td><td>Language Paper 2</td><td>Language Paper 2</td><td>Essay</td></tr>
<tr><td rowspan="7">Summer 1</td><td></td><td>Lesson 1</td><td>Lesson 2</td><td>Lesson 3</td><td>Lesson 4</td><td>Lesson 5</td></tr>
<tr><td>1</td><td>Feedback: Language Paper 2</td><td>Macbeth</td><td>Macbeth</td><td>Macbeth</td><td>Essay</td></tr>
<tr><td>2</td><td>Feedback: Macbeth</td><td>A Christmas Carol</td><td>A Christmas Carol</td><td>A Christmas Carol</td><td>Essay</td></tr>
<tr><td>3</td><td>Feedback: A Christmas Carol</td><td>An Inspector Calls</td><td>An Inspector Calls</td><td>An Inspector Calls</td><td>Essay</td></tr>
<tr><td>4</td><td>Feedback: An Inspector Calls</td><td>Anthology Poetry</td><td>Essay</td><td>Unseen Poetry</td><td>Essay</td></tr>
<tr><td>5</td><td>Feedback: Poetry</td><td>Lang 1 Reading</td><td>Lang 1 Writing</td><td>Lang 1 Writing</td><td>Practice Paper</td></tr>
<tr><td>6</td><td>Feedback/Lang 2 Reading</td><td>Lang 2 Reading</td><td>Lang 2 Writing</td><td>Lang 2 Writing</td><td>Practice Paper</td></tr>
</tbody>
</table>

FIGURE 4.2 (Continued)

We recommend a thematic and chronological approach to the anthology poems. Teachers group the poems in pairs/clusters from the beginning, focusing on clear comparisons throughout, as well as giving students the wider contextual knowledge they need. The premise of this approach is to put comparison at the centre of what students study, instead of adding it on afterwards. Poems are not taught in minute depth but as a part of wider social and literary developments and always in connection to each other.

We are convinced that if students follow a KS4 curriculum similar to the one above that not only will they enjoy the subject more, but they are also more likely to perform better in exams.

4.5.1 Teaching AQA's Power and Conflict poetry cluster

As detailed in Figure 4.3, we recommend a chronological and thematic approach to teaching the poetry clusters.
War Poetry: Chronological approach

• Pre-teach/Recap: importance of the First World War for changing our perceptions of war but also completely changing society and literature (i.e. birth of modernism, rejection of pre-war values – clear links *to An Inspector Calls* here) – this doesn't need to be a whole lesson but is important core knowledge.

- 'The Charge of the Light Brigade' – the 'old' view of war as honourable, dying for your country, 'theirs not to question why', matched to meter and structure of the poem, Tennyson as Poet Laureate. Recommend use of reader's theatre and reading aloud together etc.
- 'Exposure' – **direct comparison for the energy/active nature of 'The Charge of the Light Brigade'** with 'nothing happens', how powerless the soldiers are, focus on weather and stillness (literally freezing).
- 'Bayonet Charge' – compare to **'The Charge of the Light Brigade'** and **'Exposure'**, focus on action/inaction, view of the soldiers in the following three quotes:
  1. Honour the light brigade/honour the charge they made/noble six hundred
  2. Dawn massing in the east her melancholy army/attacks once more in ranks on shivering ranks of grey/But nothing happens
  3. King, honour, human dignity etcetera/dropped like luxuries in a yelling alarm

NB. Methods reflect meaning (COTLB – active commands; Exposure – personification of the weather as enemy, repetition of 'nothing happens'; Bayonet Charge – greater level of abstraction shows the post-war interest in a) metaphorical language but also b) rejection of old values).

- **Modern warfare**: 'Remains' and 'War Photographer' – teach together, emphasis on internal struggle and suffering, mental health, different viewpoints of the war (soldier/civilian, active/passive, guilty/not guilty).
- **Comparison lesson**: compare 'War Photographer'/'Remains' with COTLB. Opportunity to model writing here as well.
- **Women and families in war**: 'Kamikaze' and 'Poppies' – what is the impact of war on society and those 'left behind'? Poems are becoming more abstract and no longer based on direct personal experiences (either the poets' or imagined). Focus on metaphorical language and symbolic meaning in both poems.
- **Mapping comparisons between the poems** (as appropriate for class with level of independence in choice).

Romantic Poetry

- Core knowledge: Industrial Revolution and impact on poetry, links to Romanticism as a movement, the pastoral, idealising the past/rural setting, French Revolution (mind forged manacles) – clear links to *A Christmas Carol* or *Jekyll and Hyde* here.
- 'London' by Blake – tracking his views on society and how he uses poetic methods to express this viewpoint.
- 'Prelude' by Wordsworth – **direct comparison with 'London'**, particularly in setting but also where the poet focuses our attention (Wordsworth on an individual's suffering, Blake on society as a whole, link to Romantic concerns with suffering and social commentary in general).
- 'Ozymandias' – **direct comparison to 'London'** by Blake, focusing on Shelley's social commentary on political power.
- 'Storm on the Island' – **direct comparison to 'Prelude' and 'London'**, how nature is presented, touch on possible interpretations of Northern Irish history if preferred.

Poetry and Society

- Teach **'My Last Duchess'** and **'Checking Out Me History'** together: narrative poems, direct address to reader, use of an imagined speaker in both poems, power of society – My Last Duchess in reputation/power over each other, presentation of women, commentary on own time; 'The Charge of the Light Brigade' power of history and race, drawing from own experiences, use of patois (power of language).
- Teach **'The Emigrée'** and **'Tissue'** together – focus on extended metaphor in both poems (the country in 'The Emigree', paper in 'Tissue'), recap/introduce tentative language in analysis.
- Make links to **'Storm on the Island'**, **'London'**, **'Ozymandias'** as also reflecting the power of society, poems.

4.6 A note about GCSE reform

The way in which English is examined at the end of KS4 exerts almost total control on the way the subject is taught. Whilst we must live with the reality of the current specifications, we can imagine a better future. With that in mind, this section briefly considers some possible alternatives to the way English is assessed.

The English Language GCSE is the most iniquitous of all the GCSEs children sit. In every other exam subject, children's results are dependent on their teachers teaching the content of the courses, but the fact that GCSE English Language has absolutely no specified content means that the broader students' cultural knowledge, the better they'll do. This means that children from advantaged backgrounds tend to do better regardless of what schools do. Students from more disadvantaged backgrounds are so dependent on schools bucking the trend and avoiding the trap of believing English is a 'skills-based' subject that they are statistically much less likely to succeed. The more you happen to know about the unfamiliar texts that pop up in the exam, the better you'll do. English teachers find themselves in a bind. Superficially, the endless treadmill of making students sit past papers and drilling them for a very narrow test seems like the best bet for exam success, but in fact it is the very narrowness of this approach that guarantees more socially advantaged children outperform their less fortunate peers.

Another consequence of the current GCSE is that because teachers know precisely the form questions will take, it seems logical to distil the curriculum into teaching 'Paper 1 question 3' or 'Paper 2 question 4' and away from sampling more broadly from the huge domain of English language.

Perhaps the quickest, simplest solution would be to start specifying content. If students were examined on what they'd actually been taught rather than on some vague, ill-defined 'skills', the playing field would be substantially levelled. Our suggestion is for exam boards to produce an anthology of texts to be studied and emulated. This should include material on the development of the English language and the ways in which it has changed in recent years. There could also be an opportunity to comment on grammatical and rhetorical choices made by writers. These changes might make it a more effective bridge to the subject as studied at A level.

To allay concerns about narrowing the curriculum and teaching to the text, the anthology could be made available mid-way through Year 11. This would still be far from perfect, but would at least allow students to be assessed on whether they have learned a body of knowledge.

Unlike English Language, the Literature GCSE follows clearly prescribed content. Here though the problem is, perhaps, one of too much rather than too little specification. Currently, students are assessed on whether they are able to respond to a narrow range of literary texts, arranged around such arbitrary groupings as 'modern texts', 'Victorian novels', poetry (which must include the Romantics) and, of course, a Shakespeare play. It's perfectly possible for students to perform well in such a course and yet know little about English literature.

Our suggestion is that the study of literature would be both more interesting and more rounded were it to include some of the concepts that underpin an expert knowledge of the subject. To this end, we propose that students should be assessed on their understanding of metaphor, their appreciation of narrative techniques, their ability to see the links between structure and content and the extent to which they understand the contexts in which a literary text was written and is read.

On top of this, the GCSE should introduce students to the broad sweep of literature. We should expect students to know something about the origins of literature in English as well as have a nodding familiarity with some of the great works and writers. Such a course should still retain some of the close analytic skills which are so inextricably associated with literary criticism, but by opening the subject out to the study of *literature itself*, rather than just individual works of literature, students would be exposed to a far broader – and arguably more useful – domain of knowledge.

Appendix 1

Glossary of agreed definitions

As discussed in section 2.7, effective teaching of subject terminology relies on agreed definitions which students learn and practise applying. The following list covers the conceptual terminology we cover in our KS3 curriculum. While some definitions are straightforward, others are the product of trial and error. The result is a list of definitions we have found to be most useful and practical in the classroom, along with their etymologies.

Adjective
Latin: *adjectivum* (something added to)
A word that modifies a noun

Adverb
Latin: *ad* (to) + *verb* (word)
A word that modifies a verb

Allegory
Greek: *allegoria* (speaking about something else)
A story containing another symbolic story or hidden meaning

Alliteration
Latin: *alliterationem* (to begin with the same letter)
The repetition of consonant sounds

Allusion
Latin: *ad* (near) + *ludere* (to play)
Calling something to mind without mentioning it explicitly – an indirect reference

Analogy
Greek: *analogia*
'proportion', 'from *ana* 'upon, according to'+ *logos* 'ratio', also 'word, speech, reckoning'
A thing which is comparable to something else

Anaphora
Greek: *ana* (back) + *phora* (carry or transport)
Repetition of words or phrases (often within the same sentence)

Antagonist
Greek: *anti* (against) + *agon* (struggle or contest)
The main rival of the main character (protagonist) of a story

Antithesis
Greek: *anti* (against) + *thesis* (to put or place)
To set opposing ideas in contrast (see juxtaposition)

Appositive
Latin: *apponere* (set near, give in addition)
Noun or noun phrase that renames another noun

Assonance
Latin: *assonantem* (to resound, respond)
The repetition of vowel sounds

Bildungsroman
German: *Bildung* (education) + *Roman* (novel)
A novel which follows a protagonist's formative years

Caesura
Latin: *caedere* (to cut)
A pause or break in the rhythm of a line of poetry

Catharsis
Greek: *katharsis* (purging, cleansing)
Emotions released as a result of reading literature

Characterisation
Greek: *kharacter* (engraved mark)
The process of creating a character

Chorus
Greek: *khorus* (group of dancers)
Person who comments on the action in a play

Clause
Latin: *clausa* (conclusion)
Part of a sentence

Comedy
Greek: *kōmōidia* 'amusing spectacle', from *kōmos*, 'revel, festival' + *aoidos* 'singer, poet'
A plot moving from disorder to order

Conjunction
Latin: *coniugare* (to join together)
A word used to connect clauses or sentences or to coordinate words in the same clause, e.g., *and*, *but*, *if*

Consonant
Latin: *con* (together) + *sonare* (sound)
Speech sound made using the tongue, lips or throat

Context
Latin: *con* (with) + *textere* (to weave)
The historical, social or literary background knowledge needed to understand a text

Convention
French: *convencion* (agreement)
The features of a text that define its genre

Couplet
French: *couple* (two of a kind)
Two rhyming lines of poetry

Denouement
French: *dénouer* (untie)
The winding up or resolution of a plot

Deus ex machina
Latin: god in the machine
A plot device which resolves a story improbably or unexpectedly

Diachronic change
Greek: Greek *dia* 'throughout' + *khronos* 'time'
The historical development of a language

Dialogue
Greek: *dialogos*, 'conversation', from *dia*, 'across, between' + *legein* 'speak'
Verbal exchanges between characters

Dramatic irony
When an audience knows more about events than the characters in a text

Enjambment
French: *enjamber* (to stride over, or to straddle)
Where the syntax of a phrase runs over two or more lines of poetry

Epic
Greek: *epos* (story)
A long poem, narrating the deeds and adventures of heroes and legendary figures

Epithet
Greek *epitheton* (something added)
Descriptive name for a person or thing

Ethos
Greek: *ethos* (moral character)
An appeal to the character of the speaker in an argument

Etymology
Greek: *etymologia* (study of the true sense) from *etymon*, (original meaning) + *-logia* (study of)
Study of the origin of words

Exposition
Latin: *ex* (from) + *positio* (placing)
Explanation, scene setting at the start of a story

Foreshadowing
Old English: *fore* (before) + *forescywa* (shadow)
Introducing an event or image that will recur later in a story

Genre
French: *genre* (kind or sort from Old French *gendre*)
A type of literary story and its conventions

Gothic
Greek: *gothoi* (of the goths)
Literary genre that uses medieval settings to suggest horror and mystery

Ground
Old English: *grund* (foundation)
The relationship between tenor and vehicle (what makes the metaphor work)

Hamartia
Greek: *hamartia* (an error of judgement)
A tragic flaw or mistake

Hero
Greek: *hērōs* (demi-god)
A man of superhuman strength or physical courage

Hyperbole
Greek: *hyper* (beyond) + *bole* (throwing)
Obvious and over-the-top exaggeration

In medias res
Latin: in the middle of things
To begin a story in the middle of the action

Intertextuality
Latin: *inter* (between) + *textus* (woven textile)
The 'conversation' between texts

Irony
Greek: *eironeia* (pretending to be ignorant)
When the opposite of what is meant is said

Juxtaposition
Latin: *iuxta* (beside, near to) + *positionem* (placing)
Placing objects or ideas together to contrast them

Logos
Greek: *logos* (word, reason)
An appeal to logic in an argument

Metaphor
Greek: *meta* (between) + *phor* (to carry or transport)
Language that transports meaning from one 'place' to another

Metonymy
Greek: *metōnymia* (to call by a new name) from *meta* (change) + *onyma* (name)
Trope in which an attribute is substituted for the thing meant, e.g., 'suit' to mean 'executive'

Metre
Greek: *metron* (to measure)
The basic rhythmic structure of a poem

Motif
Medieval Latin: *motivus* (moving, impelling)
Recurrent symbol, usually relating to a theme

Morpheme
Greek: *morphē* (form, shape)
Part of word which is the smallest unit of meaning

Narrative
Latin: *narratio* (telling or explanation)
The specific way a story is told

Noun
Latin: *nomen* (name)
Word used to identify a thing

Onomatopoeia
Greek: *onoma* 'word, name' + *poiein* 'compose, make'
A word which imitates a sound, e.g., 'buzz', 'drip'

Oxymoron
Greek: *oxymoron* (obviously stupid)
Combining opposites to make a point more strongly

Paradox
Greek: *para* (contrary to) + *dox* (opinion)
An idea contrary of beliefs or expectations

Parody
Greek: *parōidia* (funny song or poem)
A deliberately silly imitation of a style of writing

Pathos
Greek: *pathos* (pity, suffering)
An appeal to emotion in an argument

Personification
French: *personnifier* (to represent)
Where an idea or an object is given human characteristics

Phoneme
Greek: *phōnēma* (a sound made, voice)
The smallest unit of sound

Pragmatics
Greek: *pragmatikos* (fit for business) from *pragma* (a deed, act)
Branch of linguistics dealing with language in context

Prefix
Latin: *pre* (before) + *figere* (fasten)
A morpheme added to the beginning of a word

Prologue
Greek: *pro* (before) + *logos* (speech)
An introductory section to a literary work

Protagonist
Greek: *prōtagōnistēs* (actor who plays the chief part) from *prōtos* (first) + *agōnistēs* (competitor)
Main character in a literary text

Rhetoric
Greek: *rhētorike tekhnē* (art of an orator) from *rhetor* (speaker) + *techne* (art, or skill)
The art of persuasive argument

Satire
Latin: *satira* (mixed dish)
Literature intended to ridicule the powerful

Semantics
Greek: *semantikos* (significant) from *sema* (sign or mark)
Branch of linguistics concerned with study of the meaning of language

Sibilance
Latin *sibilantem* (hiss or whistle)
A hissing sound created by the repetition of 's' sounds

Simile
Latin: *similis* (of the same kind)
Type of metaphor where two things are compared, usually using 'like' or 'as'

Soliloquy

Latin: *soliloquium* (talking to oneself) from *solus* (alone) + *loqui* (to speak)

Character's thoughts spoken aloud for the benefit of an audience

Sonnet

Italian: *sonetto*, (little song) from Latin *sonus* (sound)

Fourteen-line poem, usually composed with regular metre and rhyme scheme

Subordinate clause

Latin: *sub* (under) + *ordinare* (arrange in order)

Part of a sentence that adds additional information but doesn't make sense on its own

Subordinating conjunction

A conjunction that introduces a subordinate clause

Syllable

Greek: *syllabē* (that which is held together)

A unit of pronunciation containing a single vowel sound

Symbol/ symbolism

Greek: *symbolon* (token, literally that which is thrown or cast together) from *syn-* (together) + *bole* (a throwing, or casting)

Use of an object to represent ideas or qualities

Stanza

Italian: *stanza* (room)

A section or verse of a poem

Suffix

Latin: *su(b)* (under) + *figere* (fasten)

A morpheme added to the end of a word

Tenor

Latin: *tenorem* (to hold)

The subject of the metaphor (the thing being described by the vehicle)

Theme

Greek: *thema* 'a proposition, subject'

Idea that runs through a literary work

Tone

Greek: *tonos* (use of voice)

Elements of a text which reveal the writer's attitude

Tragedy

Greek: *tragodia* (goat song) from *tragos* (goat) + *ōidē* (song)

Plot moving from order to disorder and disaster

Vehicle

Latin: *vehiculum* (means of transport)

The language used to described the subject (tenor) of the metaphor

Verb

Latin: *verbum* (word)

Word used to identify an action or state

Volta

Portuguese: *volta* (to turnaround)

Point in a poem where there is a change in mood or thought or both

Vowel

Old French: *voieul* (vocal letter)

Letters that represent sounds where air leaves the mouth without any blockage by the tongue, lips or throat

Appendix 2

Thirty creative sentence structures[1]

Follow the link in the QR code to find training videos on how to use each of these sentence types

1. The Comma Sandwich

Teach	Model	Write
Comma sandwiches add detail, increase tension and vary sentences. The 'sandwich' is a relative clause between two commas. Embedded relative clauses are easier to write with relative pronouns (which, whose, who). The relative clause splits the main clause between the subject and verb. Watch out for comma splices and fragments.	Cyclops, <u>whose eye was a mass of melted jelly</u>, screamed in agony. The monster, which no one had ever seen, roared in the distance.	The [subject], [embedded relative clause], [verb + predicate].

2. The More, The More, The More / The Less, The Less, The Less

Teach	Model	Write
Start with 2 × more (or less) = The more you learn, the more you'll earn. The more you give, the more you get. Make sure 'the' is repeated at the beginning of each clause. It's easier to write these sentences about characters rather than things. Choose active verbs rather than reflexive or modal verbs: action (screamed) + similar action (thrashed about) + consequence (he suffered).	The <u>more</u> Cyclops screamed, the <u>more</u> he thrashed about, the <u>more</u> he suffered. The <u>less</u> sound filtered into the chapel, the <u>less</u> his feet wanted to move forward, the <u>less</u> he wanted to find out the fate waiting for him inside. [In this example the final clause is more developed.]	The more [subject] + [verb], the more [pronoun] + [verb], the more {pronoun} + [verb]. The less _____, the less _____, the less _____.

3. Comparative More, More

Teach	Model	Write
First part of the sentence focuses on emotion, the second part focuses on an action associated with the emotion or an intensification of that emotion. Comparative clauses, separated by a comma, can go at the end of a sentence (examples 1 and 2) or at the start (example 3). Comparative adjectives show the state being described is growing more intense. This sentence is great for ramping up tension or heightening excitement. Additional comparative clauses can be added (Example 3). Opportunity to teach the effects of alliteration (Example 3).	Every step Gawain took towards the sinister chapel, the eerie green glow became <u>more</u> fearful, <u>more</u> overwhelming. With each step forward, the darkness grew deeper, <u>more</u> complete, <u>more</u> worrying. Becoming <u>more</u> fearsome, <u>more</u> formidable, <u>more</u> ferocious with every bone-crushing step, Grendel approached the trembling warriors.	Every _____ the _____, more [adjective], more [adjective]. With _____, _____, _____, more ____, more _____.

4. Semi-Colon Split

Teach	Model	Write
A semi-colon can be used to connect two main clauses that are closely related in meaning but not joined by a coordinating conjunction (such as 'and', 'but', or 'or'). A semi-colon indicates a stronger connection between the clauses than a full stop would, emphasising their relationship. The semi-colon performs the function of a conjunction. Readers pause for longer at a full stop so using a semi-colon speeds up the pace of writing. This can help inject a sense of urgency.	All signs of life were suddenly gone; even Gawain's breath seemed a distant intrusion. Beowulf was determined to slay Grendel's mother and avenge the fallen warriors; unhesitatingly, he dived into the treacherous depths of the murky lake.	_____; _____. The _____; there was _____.

5. Colon Clarification

Teach	Model	Write
Colons join two main clauses together. The second clause should clarify some ambiguity or further explain events in the first clause. A colon can also be used to: • **emphasise** or draw attention to a particular point or idea. It highlights the information that follows and indicates its significance • introduce a punchline or deliver a humorous effect • convey authority or expertise • create anticipation or build suspense • emphasise a dramatic reveal, or surprising information. It's important to use colons sparingly and appropriately to maintain their impact and effectiveness.	A huge figure suddenly stepped forward: it was the Green Knight. There was the faintest of sounds: it was my own breathing. The valiant and fearless Beowulf is the perfect warrior: his unwavering courage, unparalleled strength, and indomitable spirit inspire awe and admiration.	[main clause]: [main clause]. Character + action: it/there was/is_____: it is/was_____.

6. Three Verb Sentence

Teach	Model	Write
Verbs must agree – either all present (1st example) or all past tense (2nd example). It's also possible to use present continuous (___ing). Verbs can be synonyms or can show an arc of action (see 3rd example) Past participles are often irregular.	Beowulf <u>pivots</u>, <u>twists</u>, <u>dodges</u> in his charge towards the dragon. The crumbling rock of the walls <u>rose</u>, <u>loomed</u>, <u>towered</u> overhead. The Green Knight's axe <u>rose</u>, <u>paused</u>, <u>fell</u> with sudden terrifying speed.	[noun phrase] verb, verb, verb _____.

7. Not (Not) Nor Nor

Teach	Model	Write
This sentence is, despite its appearance, a single main clause. Start with the adverb 'not'. Commas are used to divide the list of noun phrases beginning with coordinating conjunction 'nor'. The final noun phrase must contain the subject of the sentence and a verb. The structure used in the sentence, with repeated clauses beginning with 'nor', creates a sense of emphasis and reinforces the idea of defiance and determination. The repeated negative clauses create a sense of escalation and intensifies the impact of the sentence. The structure also conveys a sense of completeness and exhaustiveness.	<u>Not</u> the homes of innocents, <u>nor</u> the public buildings of the forum, <u>nor</u> the whole of the Empire will be safe from his vengeance. <u>Not</u> the bonds of loyalty, <u>nor</u> the ties of kinship, <u>nor</u> the honour of Rome will sway my decision to protect the Republic. **Not** the flames of divine wrath, **not** the chains of imprisonment, **nor** the prayers of the righteous, **nor even** the armies of heaven can deter my insidious mission to sow chaos and rebellion throughout creation.	Not [noun phrase1], nor [noun phrase2]. nor [noun phrase 3] [verb] [noun phrase 4]. Not _____, not _____, nor _____, nor even _____ will _____.

8. Prepositional Push Off

Teach	Model	Write
Prepositions are words that show relationships between nouns, pronouns, or phrases to other words in a sentence, indicating location, direction, time, and other spatial or abstract relationships. Teach the most common prepositions (above, across, against, along, among, around, at, before, behind, below, beneath, beside, between, by, down, from, in, into, near, next, of, off, on, to, toward, under, upon, with and within). Sentence begins with a subordinate clause followed by a main clause. Comma as pivot point. Prepositions act as subordinating conjunctions.	<u>Beneath</u> the dark canopy of the forest, the world seemed to have come to an end. <u>Next</u> to offering Antony our throats, allowing him to speak at Caesar's funeral is as close to suicide as it's possible to imagine. <u>Between</u> the whispers of conspiracy and the knives of treachery, my presence at the Senate is as close to a defiant act of courage as mortal man can conceive.	[preposition] _____, _____. [preposition]+ [subordinate clause], [main clause].

9. Never Did, Than (So Much As)

Teach	Model	Write
'Never' is an adverb which, when used in conjunction with the verb 'did' introduces the main clause. 'Than' is used as a conjunction to connect a second clause. 'Than' can be swapped with alternative phrases such as 'as much as' (3rd example). Really useful for descriptive passages which explore emotions. No comma is needed as 'than' performs the pivoting role.	<u>Never did</u> a place fill me with a greater sense of wonder <u>than</u> this beautiful, sea-green world. <u>Never did</u> I feel so at peace <u>than</u> in the shade of those magnificent trees. <u>Never did</u> anyone frighten me <u>as much as</u> this cold, forbidding man.	Never did [noun phrase], than [noun phrase]. Never did _____ than _____. Never did [main clause] as much as [subordinate clause]. Never did _____ as much as _____.

10. The Writer's Aside

Teach	Model	Write
This is a variant of 1. The comma sandwich. An aside is a remark addressed to an audience outside the world of the text. In the embedded clause the writer directly addresses the reader, usually with direct pronouns. Parenthetic dashes intensify the tone, as if the speaker has raised their voice (brackets act like a lowered voice).	But – <u>and you might find this surprising</u> – although I was cut off and isolated, I felt at peace. The familiar world – <u>as you can imagine</u> – was a million miles away. However, when I attempted to speak – and you can surely understand my frustration – the only result was a series of grunts.	The [subject] – [embedded relative clause] – [verb + predicate].

11. So, So Sentence

Teach	Model	Write
Focus on an object and the overall idea you want to show. Use an initial adjective to describe it. Use two additional adjectives to intensify it. Use a verb linking to an action/state which shows it. Use commas to separate embedded clause from the main clause.	There was the faintest glimmer of light, <u>so</u> small, <u>so</u> distant, it didn't seem to exist. Anger grew in me, <u>so</u> hot, <u>so</u> destructive, that I had to leave the room.	The _____ (adjective) _____ (object), so _____ (adjective), so _____ (adjective), _____ (verb linking to an action or state).

12. The Big Because

Teach	Model	Write
'Because' is used as a subordinating conjunction. Object and related adjectives. Linked to verb (action or state). Use a comma to separate the subordinate clause from the main clause.	<u>Because</u> it was the first patch of sunlight, the relief I felt was edged with a little dismay. <u>Because</u> everyone loves his plays, he thinks he can treat me however he wants.	Because _____ (object), _____ (feeling caused by object). Because it was _____, the _____.

13. But No... More Than

Teach	Model	Write
'But' is acting as a coordinating conjunction (yes you *can* start a sentence with but!). Focus on an [object] to be described and the overall intention. 'More than' is a preposition phrase showing one amount is greater than another.	<u>But no</u> one <u>more than</u> me would put up with his rudeness! <u>But no</u> statue <u>more than</u> this immense idol could stand so tall. <u>But no</u> woman captivated Petrarch's heart <u>more than</u> the beautiful Laura.	But no (comparison) more than [subject] _____.

14. Past Participle Start

Teach	Model	Write
Sentence begins with a subordinate clause which uses a comma to pivot to main clause. The past participle must be followed by a preposition ('with', 'to' etc.) in a longer subordinate clause. Past participles are often irregular (2nd example). Subordinated clause may just be a single verb (3rd example) but for this to work, the past participle **must** be followed by the subject of the sentence (and it must be possible to insert 'was' between subject and verb). Beginning the sentence with a verb focuses attention on action.	<u>Filled</u> with the spirit of the Lord, David walked confidently towards Goliath. <u>Bound</u> to the pillars of the temple, Samson prayed for his strength to be restored. <u>Amazed</u>, I watched this puny boy make his way towards me.	[past participle] + [preposition] _____, _____. [past participle], [subject] _____.

15. Whoever, Whenever, Whatever

Teach	Model	Write
Sentence begins with three relative clauses followed by a main clause. The relative pronouns <u>whoever</u>, <u>whenever</u> and <u>whatever</u> (wherever) are used in the same way as subordinating conjunctions. Each relative clause provides additional information about the subject of the main clause. Sentence has the effect of suggesting the situation is **universal** and **inevitable**. The order of relative pronouns can be varied.	<u>Whoever</u> I pretended to be after Osborne's death, <u>whenever</u> the echoes of laughter subsided, <u>whatever</u> we had said to each other, I couldn't escape the relentless ache caused by the absence of my dearest friend. <u>Whoever</u> Stanhope appeared to others, <u>whenever</u> his leadership seemed uncertain, <u>whatever</u> flaws he possessed, <u>wherever</u> he led, I couldn't help but be in awe of his unwavering strength and unwritten heroism.	Whoever _____, wherever_____, whatever _____, _____. Whoever [subordinate clause], wherever [subordinate clause], whatever [subordinate clause], [main clause].

16. Adjective Attack

Teach	Model	Write
Double adjectives at the start of the sentence which add information to the object. 'And' needs to be placed between the two adjectives. Past participles and present particles can be used as adjectives. Using adjectives at the start of the sentences focuses readers' attention on description rather than action. Adjectives are often synonyms.	<u>Magnificent</u> and <u>proud</u>, I towered above him. <u>Angry</u> and <u>disappointed</u>, God unleashed a flood upon the world. <u>Patient</u> and <u>uncomplaining</u>, Noah waited for the flood to recede. <u>Soaring</u> and <u>swooping</u>, the doves spiralled away into the clouds.	[adjective] and [adjective], _____.

17. End Loaded Sentence

Teach	Model	Write
Sometimes called a periodic or left-branching sentence. The main clause comes after a long or multiple subordinate clause/s. Start clauses with subordinating conjunctions. The effect is to make the reader wait to find out the main thrust of the sentence. Can be used to build tension. Attention is focused on description and the writer's craft.	After listening to the drivelling idiot drone on about love this, beautiful that, I can tell you once and for all that <u>I've had enough of both poetry and men to last a lifetime</u>! As I plotted alongside Nicholas, cunningly deceiving John, and gleefully anticipating Absolon's humiliation, <u>I revelled in the chaos that ensued</u>. While rallying the women of Athens, tirelessly organising our plan to withhold our bodies from our husbands, and courageously defying societal norms, <u>I stood as the driving force behind our extraordinary revolution</u>.	[subordinate clause], [subordinate clause], [subordinate clause], [main clause].

18. Present Participle Start

Teach	Model	Write
Present participles *always* end in '_ing'. Present participles start a subordinate clause (Examples 1–3). Present participle can be a one-word subordinate clause (Example 4). Present tense action is foregrounded which makes the sentence feel immediate. Present Participle Start sentences can also be Adjective Attacks (Example 5).	<u>Speaking</u> for myself, I like a man who is practical and honest. <u>Having</u> no possibility of return, the way ahead seemed suddenly less daunting. <u>Dropping</u> to her knees in despair, tears rolled down her cheeks. <u>Gasping</u>, I suddenly realised what I had to do. <u>Simpering</u> and sappy, I can't stand that milksop Silvius.	___ing _____, _____. ___ing, _____. ___ing and _____, _____.

19. As If Pivot

Teach	Model	Write
'As if' denotes a simile – something imaginary is being described. The conjunctions 'as if' as a connective phrase which introduces a clause. Main clause focuses on concrete image. Although it's possible to use 'as if' as a simile start, it can be more effective if the sentence begins with a main clause and then *pivots* into a comparison.	Her face was seamed with wrinkles, <u>as if</u> she were an apple left to dry in sunlight for too long. <u>As if</u> a thousand meteors had suddenly struck the Earth, an explosion tore through the tower block.	[main clause], as if _____ _____. As if _____ _____.

20. As If Avalanche

Teach	Model	Write
'As if' is a conditional clause acting as a simile – must be preceded by 'It' and <u>past</u> participle verb (It was, it felt, it seemed etc.). The comparison in the initial main clause is extended and varied in a succession of subordinate clauses using <u>present</u> participle verbs (__ing). The subordinate clauses can be extended indefinitely to create an increasingly intense effect <u>as if</u> the reader is being buried by an <u>avalanche</u>.	It was <u>as if</u> the presence of the stranger had infused me with Heathcliff's wild energy and lent me his indomitable, brutish strength. It felt <u>as if</u> the marshland was dragging me into its depths, engulfing me with sadness, consuming me with grey misery, swamping me in despondency. It seemed <u>as if</u> the spectral figure was guiding me to her, reaching for me, bowing her head, dropping to her knees in sorrow.	It [past participle] _____, _____, _____, _____, _____.

21. Three Adjective Punch

Teach	Model	Write
This is very similar to 16. Adjective Attack except there is no use of 'and' to connect the adjectives. The use of commas makes the adjective more of a rapid onslaught of description.	<u>Desperate</u>, <u>frenzied</u>, <u>compelled</u>, I pounded and scratched at the wall. <u>Maddened</u>, <u>thwarted</u>, <u>confounded</u>, Heathcliff stormed away into the bleak landscape.	[adjective], [adjective], [adjective], [main clause] ___, ___, ___, _____.

22. Almost, Almost, When

Teach	Model	Write
This sentence is effective for building tension and creating cliff-hangers. Start with a main clause – the first 'almost' must come after the verb. The second almost can begin the first subordinate clause. Final subordinate clause must start with 'when'.	I had <u>almost</u> taken his hand in mine, <u>almost</u> felt the warm flesh of his hand, <u>when</u> he woke and retreated for ever out of my grasp. He was <u>almost</u> at the top, had <u>almost</u> reached safety, <u>when</u> the searchlight picked him out against the mountainside.	[subject] + [past participle] + almost _____, almost _____, when _____. _____ almost _____, almost _____, when _____.

23. Repeat and Reload

Teach	Model	Write
Sentence starts with a main clause containing two predicate adjectives. Colon indicates that the next clause will clarify or explain the first clause. Repeat adjectives in order they were used and explain or clarify their meaning. Using 'because', 'in that', 'due to', 'as' etc. makes it easier to *reload* the repeated adjectives.	My desire was <u>blind</u> and <u>insistent</u>: <u>blind</u> in that I had no real idea what drove me, <u>insistent</u> in that my passion could never be denied. Her laughter was <u>genuine</u> and <u>infectious</u>: <u>genuine</u> because it came from a place of pure happiness, <u>infectious</u> because it spread joy to everyone around her. His dedication was <u>unwavering</u> and <u>relentless</u>: <u>unwavering</u> as he faced every obstacle with steadfast determination, <u>relentless</u> in his pursuit of excellence.	[subject] + [verb] + [adjective 1] and [adjective 2]: [adjective 1] _____, [adjective 2] _____.

24. Let Loose Sentence

Teach	Model	Write
Begin with a simple main clause followed by a colon. Similarly to 20. The As If Avalanche, the intention is to 'let loose' a stream of clarification and exemplification in successive clauses. The more additional clauses students can use, they more they will have 'let loose'. Ideally, the final clause will echo the wording of the first clause.	The chaos had engulfed the city: the blaring sirens, the screeching tires, the frantic shouting, the smell of burning buildings, all becoming an unsettling backdrop to daily life in the city. It had all become normal: the constant thundering of the guns, the cold shivering into our bones, our bodies itching with filth and lice, the moaning of the wounded and the stench of the dead, all a normal part of life.	[main clause]: _____, _____, _____, _____, _____, [link back to first clause].

25. Simile Start

Teach	Model	Write
The vehicle of the simile must precede the tenor in a subordinate clause. The sentence must begin with the prepositions 'like' or 'as' which act like subordinating conjunctions. Comma pivots between the *vehicle* in the subordinate clause and the *tenor* in the main clause. Similes must be plausible and effective. (Avoid sentences like, 'Like a fast runner, she ran quickly.) Worth exploring abstract and concrete nouns to help students construct effective similes. Ensure verbs link to the effect of the simile.	<u>Like men dying of thirst</u>, we drank down every last moment of peace and comfort. <u>Like a spreading poison</u>, jealous thoughts ate through Othello's mind. <u>Like a bat out of hell</u>, I'll be gone when the morning comes*. <u>As corrosive as acid</u>, bitter thoughts tormented his soul. <u>Serpent-like</u>, a tendril of fear wormed in my stomach.	Like _____, _____. As _____ as _____, _____. _____-like, _____.

26. Or and Or

Teach	Model	Write
Start with a simple main clause. Think of two related actions using different verbs and clarifying adverbs. The subordinate clauses work best if they are complex and introspective. These sentences give the reader a sense of multiple possibilities, of viewing events from different possible angles.	Rain began to fall in stops and starts, **or** else it spattered onto the dry earth, and small drops trickled along cracks, **or** slowly seeped into everything, filling up the black, empty space that surrounded everything. Iago's mind schemed in twisted ways, **or** else it conjured up elaborate scenarios, envisioning a vengeful downfall for Othello, **or** relentlessly played out wicked manipulations, orchestrating a web of deceit that would entrap his unsuspecting victim. Okonkwo's heart weighed heavy with remorse, **or** sank into the depths of despair, regretting the irreversible consequences of his impulsive actions, **or** desperately yearned for a chance to turn back time and undo the damage he had caused.	[main clause] or _____ _____, or _____. [subject] (initial action), or (related action, or (related action).

27. Without, Without Sentence

Teach	Model	Write
Think of the overall idea you want to show. Think of feelings we would **not** associate with it. Think of an action you would use to demonstrate it. Think of an adverb to describe it in more detail. Use commas to separate the subordinate clauses from the main clause.	<u>Without</u> a hope, <u>without</u> any idea of where I was going, I wandered aimlessly but now with a lighter step. <u>Without</u> hesitation, <u>without</u> regard for the consequences, Marco seized Eddie's arm and drove the knife it clutched into his chest.	Without _____ (emotion), without any _____ (emotion), I _____ (adverb) _____ (verb). Without [subordinate clause], without [subordinate clause], [main clause].

28. Adverb Snap

Teach	Model	Write
Students may be familiar with this sentence as a 'fronted adverbial'. Sentence starts with a subordinate clause of a single adverb. Readers' attention is focused on *how* the events in the sentence play out. Not all adverbs end in '-ly'.	<u>Bitterly</u>, Okonkwo thought of the white men and their white god. <u>Agonisingly</u>, Othello thought of his hands squeezing the life from his beloved. <u>Soon</u>, he'd be back in her arms and the cares of this life would be over.	[Adverb], [main clause]. —ly, _____.

29. Double Adverb Snap

Teach	Model	Write
Sentence starts with two subordinate clauses of a single adverb. Adverbial phrase can connect the two adverbs with a conjunction (and, but etc.) Adverbial phrase can connect the two adverbs with a conjunction (and, but etc.) 'Quickly **but** clumsily'; 'Bravely **and** boldly'. Readers' attention is focused on *how* the events in the sentence play out. Not all adverbs end in '-ly'. Second adverb gives opportunity to reteach synonyms **or** look at alternative ways an action can be described.	<u>Slowly, carefully</u>, I scrambled down the sheer rockface. <u>Quietly</u>, <u>obsessively</u>, she descended further into madness, her mind unravelling amidst the confines of her secluded room. <u>Boldly</u> and <u>unabashedly</u>, the Wife of Bath embraces her sexuality and challenges societal norms, fearlessly asserting her autonomy and reclaiming her own narrative.	[adverb], [adverb], [main clause]. —ly, —ly, _____ _____. —ly [conjunction] —ly, _____.

30. Last Word, First Word

Teach	Model	Write
This is an example of *anadiplosis* – a rhetorical technique used to connect ideas. The repetition creates a cohesive, rhythmic effect. The last word of the first sentence must be repeated as the first word of the second sentence. The repeated word can be used as an adverbial phrase at the start of the second sentence. Technique can also be used *within* a sentence.	The end was <u>close</u>. <u>Close</u>, but still each minute seemed an eternity. Suddenly and miraculously, the knight was <u>transformed</u>. <u>Transformed</u>, yet still burdened by the weight of his past. I am trapped within these suffocating yellow walls, yearning for a glimpse of freedom <u>beyond</u>. <u>Beyond</u> lies the promise of liberation from this maddening confinement. With fiery determination, I refuse to be confined by society's <u>expectations</u>. <u>Expectations</u> be damned, I will forge my own path of liberation.	_____ [word]. [repeat word] _____.

* Yes, this *is* a lyric from Meatloaf's classic rock ballad

Appendix 3

Adapting the curriculum for alternative provision

In 2021, OAT welcomed four Alternative Provision (AP) academies into the Trust. Working out how best to support them in terms of providing an appropriate English curriculum has presented some challenges, both for the English Lead Practitioner team and for English teachers and leaders within our APs.

ADDRESSING MISCONCEPTIONS

The definition of Alterative Provision as education for young people unable to access mainstream schools[1] might encourage us to believe that the curriculum we have proposed requires complete and radical revision. This view if further reinforced if we consider DfE guidance that alternative provision does not have to follow the curriculum,[2] and confirmed by the common challenges teachers and students face in these settings. I certainly, at first, was somewhat sceptical whether our proposed curriculum fitted.

Speaking to staff and students, observing and teaching lessons has challenged this belief. It has become increasingly obvious that the central tenets of the curriculum we propose are not only well adapted but *vital* for students in alternative provision.

While there are challenges to overcome and logistical factors to be considered, it is undeniable that students in alternative provision require a curriculum that is broad and balanced, coherently sequenced, ambitious and delivered in a way where success precedes struggle.

KEY PRINCIPALS THAT REMAIN THE SAME

(a) Ambitious and challenging

Among the myriad reasons a student might attend alternative provision, lack of academic ability is not one of them. It is true that there is a higher likelihood that students are low prior attainers: however, this is often the result of low attendance or unrecognised needs. This might seem obvious but when we fail to provide students with an ambitious or challenging curriculum, we are implicitly treating them as if they are incapable or 'lower ability' and – crucially – failing to understand the complex reasons a student might have struggled to access mainstream education. This assumption is fundamentally unfair and, all too often, becomes a self-fulfilling prophecy.

If you've ever seen students in alternative settings, come alive reminiscing about performing as Lady Macbeth or argue determinedly for why they prefer *Othello* over *The Tempest*, you too might baulk at the suggestion that texts such as Shakespeare are too difficult. Students in alternative provision, like all students, deserve to be exposed to the best that English has to offer.

(b) Key conceptual knowledge

A curriculum which specifies key conceptual knowledge is crucial for students in alternative settings because of the greater likelihood of sporadic prior experience of education. Moreover, staff must rapidly build a picture of students' prior knowledge with limited to no reliable data.

If we do not specify the key conceptual knowledge students must know to read certain texts and write in certain styles (or fail to recognise this as knowledge) we risk confusing lack of understanding with lack of engagement. It also makes it harder for us to identify gaps in students' knowledge and take steps to close them.

I have seen this approach applied effectively with explicit vocabulary instruction, where teachers have used retrieval practice to teach ambitious vocabulary. I've been thrilled to see words such as equivocation, malevolent and disequilibrium appear in students' independent writing; students were able to use these words *because* teachers had specified them in the curriculum.

As we've seen, asking students to do something they have not been adequately prepared for, that has not been broken down into specific elements, is disempowering. This is especially so for students who often feel they have 'failed' at school. On the other hand, understanding the key knowledge students require and then asking them to practise allows them the opportunity to experience the success which is so essential for students who might have had limited or even negative prior experiences of education.

SPECIFIC CHALLENGES WE NEED TO MEET

(a) Time

The nature of alternative provision is that there are significant demands on teachers' and students' time. Teaching time is limited and precious. Often teachers are tasked with covering an enormous quantity of content in an impossibly short amount of time.

This means the balance between reading a broad range of extracts and reading whole texts is even more delicate. The key is to establish a balance and do so with intention. A specific and well-sequenced curriculum allows us to be clear about why we are reading certain texts and what we want students to get out of them.

The use of extracts may be necessary for revision in Year 11 and can be effective if these are selected to be generalisable and exemplify trends. That said, more time might be spent at KS3 and in Year 10 reading – and enjoying – texts in full should be given precedence. Prioritising reading over excessive writing tasks is important particularly as students may not have had the experience of reading a whole text before. Surely, if our curriculum achieves anything it should be that no student leaves us without having experienced a carefully curated canon of literature.

(b) Mixed year group classes

How do we plan a curriculum for KS3 if we have a class which includes students from Year 7 to 9? And what happens to this class if in the following year the same class is joined by new Year 7s? This is often the reality of AP.

Firstly, we must banish the impossibility of age-related expectations, replacing them with curriculum-related expectations. Secondly, we must create a three-year cycle which complicates our chronological model where each year builds on the next. One possible adaptation would be to favour the units which offer mini-chronologies.

Here is an example, considering the limited teaching hours and mixed year group classes:

Year	Autumn	Spring	Summer
1	Ancient Origins OR Links to Legends	The Art of Rhetoric	The Story of the Novel
2	The Sonnet Form	Comedy through Time	Women in Literature
3	War Writing	Tragedy through Time	Freedom

Bibliography

Adesope, O.O., Trevisan, D.A., & Sundararajan, N. (2017). Rethinking the use of tests: A meta-analysis of practice testing. *Review of Educational Research*, 87(3), 659–701.

Alexander, R. (2012, February). Improving oracy and classroom talk in English schools: Achievements and challenges. In *Extended and referenced version of a presentation given at a Department for Education seminar on Oracy, the National Curriculum and Educational Standards, London* (Vol. 20).

Alfieri, L., Brooks, P.J., Aldrich, N.J., & Tenenbaum, H.R. (2011). Does discovery-based instruction enhance learning? *Journal of Educational Psychology*, 103(1), 1–18.

Allen, R. (2018). What if we cannot measure progress? *Musing on Education Policy*. https://rebeccaallen.co.uk/2018/05/23/what-if-we-cannot-measure-pupil-progress/

Alloway, T.P., & Alloway, R.G. (2010). Investigating the predictive roles of working memory and IQ in academic attainment. *Journal of Experimental Child Psychology*, 106(1), 20–29.

Anderson, R.C., & Freebody, P. (1981). Vocabulary knowledge. In J.T. Guthrie (Ed.), *Comprehension and teaching: Research reviews* (pp. 77–117). International Reading Association.

Applebee, A.N. (2008). *Curriculum as conversation: Transforming traditions of teaching and learning*. University of Chicago Press.

AQA. (2019, June). *GCSE English Literature 8702/2: Modern texts and poetry. Report on the examination*. https://filestore.aqa.org.uk/sample-papers-and-mark-schemes/2019/june/AQA-87022-WRE-JUN19.PDF

Baker, S. (2018). Wait time and student engagement: How wait time affects classroom interactions. *Journal of the Scholarship of Teaching and Learning*, 18(4), 66–79. https://doi.org/10.14434/josotl.v18i4.22777

Bal, P.M. & Veltkamp, M. (2013). How does fiction reading influence empathy? An experimental investigation on the role of emotional transportation. *PLoS ONE*, 8(1): e55341. https://doi.org/10.1371/journal.pone.0055341

Barbash, S. (2012). *Clear teaching: With direct instruction, Siegfried Engelmann discovered a better way of teaching*. Education Consumers Foundation.

Barton, C. (2022). *Tips for teachers: 400+ ideas to improve your teaching*. John Catt Educational.

Beck, I.L., McKeown, M.G., & Kucan, L. (2013). *Bringing words to life: Robust vocabulary instruction*. Guilford Press.

Bennett, A., & Royle, N. (2015). *This thing called literature: Reading, thinking, writing*. Routledge.

Bernstein, B. (2003). *Towards a theory of educational transmissions*. Taylor & Francis Group. http://ebookcentral.proquest.com/lib/uea/detail.action?docID=214481

Bjork, E.L., & Bjork, R.A. (2011). Making things hard on yourself, but in a good way: Creating desirable difficulties to enhance learning. In M.A. Gernsbacher, R.W. Pew, L.M. Hough, & J.R. Pomerantz (Eds.), *Psychology and the real world: Essays illustrating fundamental contributions to society* (pp. 56–64). Worth Publishers.

Bjork, R.A., & Bjork, E.L. (1992). A new theory of disuse and an old theory of stimulus fluctuation. In A.F. Healy, S.M. Kosslyn, & R.M. Shiffrin (Eds.), *Essays in honor of William K. Estes, Vol. 1. From learning theory to connectionist theory; Vol. 2. From learning processes to cognitive processes* (pp. 35–67). Lawrence Erlbaum Associates, Inc.

Black, P., & Wiliam, D. (1998a). Assessment and classroom learning. *Assessment in Education: Principles, Policy & Practice*, 5(1), 7–74.

Black, P., & Wiliam, D. (1998b). *Inside the black box: Raising standards through classroom assessment*. Granada Learning.

Bloom, B.S. (1984). The 2 sigma problem: The search for methods of group instruction as effective as one-to-one tutoring. *Educational Researcher*, 13(6), 4–16.

Bourdieu, P. (1986). The forms of capital. In J. Richardson (Ed.), *Handbook of theory and research for the sociology of education* (pp. 241–258). Greenwood.

Brame, C.J. (2013). Effective educational videos: Principles and guidelines for maximizing student learning from video content. *CBE-Life Sciences Education*, 12(4), 342–348.

Brindley, S., Barron, P., & Kinnear, A. (2016). Hinge questions in geography: Exploring the potential for critical thinking. *Journal of Geography in Higher Education*, 40(3), 372–387.

Brophy, J. (1983). Research on the self-fulfilling prophecy and teacher expectations. *Journal of Educational Psychology*, 75(5), 631–661.

Bruner, J. (1977). *The process of education: Revised edition*. Harvard University Press.

Castles, A., & Coltheart, M. (2004). Is there a causal link from phonological awareness to success in learning to read? *Cognition*, 91(1), 77–111.

Cepeda, N.J., Pashler, H., Vul, E., Wixted, J.T., & Rohrer, D. (2006). Distributed practice in verbal recall tasks: A review and quantitative synthesis. *Psychological Bulletin*, 132(3), 354.

Cepeda, N.J., Vul, E., Rohrer, D., Wixted, J.T., & Pashler, H. (2008). Spacing effects in learning: A temporal ridgeline of optimal retention. *Psychological Science*, 19(11), 1095–1102.

Chi, M.T.H., & VanLehn, K. (2012). Seeing deep structure from the interactions of surface features. *Educational Psychologist*, 47(3), 177–188. doi: 10.1080/00461520.2012.695665

Christodoulou, D. (2017). *Making good progress? The future of assessment for learning*. Oxford University Press.

Clark, C. (2015). Using hinge questions to support online discussion forums in higher education. *International Review of Research in Open and Distributed Learning*, 16(3), 1–18.

Clark, C., & Douglas, J. (2011). *Young people's reading and writing: An in-depth study focusing on enjoyment, behaviour, attitudes and attainment*. National Literacy Trust. https://files.eric.ed.gov/fulltext/ED529480.pdf

Clark, C., & Rumbold, K. (2006). *Reading for pleasure and empowerment*. The National Literacy Trust. https://files.eric.ed.gov/fulltext/ED498447.pdf

Clark, J.M., & Paivio, A. (1991). Dual coding theory and education. *Educational Psychology Review*, 3(3), 149–210. doi: 10.1007/bf01320076

Coe, R. (2018, June 20) *But that's not an ASSESSMENT!* Centre for Evaluation and Monitoring. www.cem.org/blog/but-that-is-not-an-assessment

Coe, R. (2019, December 5). *Does research on retrieval practice translate into classroom practice?* Education Endowment Foundation. https://educationendowmentfoundation.org.uk/news/does-research-on-retrieval-practice-translate-into-classroom-practice/

Coe, R. (2020, June 29). Assessing learning in the new academic year (Part 1 of 2) – three key questions for school leaders to consider. *EEF Blog*. https://educationendowmentfoundation.org.uk/news/eef-blog-assessing-learning-in-the-new-academic-year-part-1

Considine, J. (2016). *The write stuff: Transforming the teaching of writing*. Training Space Ltd.

Counsell, C. (2018, April 7). *Senior curriculum leadership 1: The indirect manifestation of knowledge: (A) curriculum as narrative*. https://thedignityofthethingblog.wordpress.com/2018/04/07/senior-curriculum-leadership-1-the-indirect-manifestation-of-knowledge-a-curriculum-as-narrative/

Cromley, J.G., & Azevedo, R. (2007). Testing the cognitive theory of multimedia learning with eye tracking and near-infrared spectroscopy. *Educational Psychology Review*, 19(3), 297–314.

Crystal, D. (2017). English grammar in the UK: A political history. Supplementary material to *Making Sense: the Glamorous Story of English Grammar*. www.davidcrystal.com/Files/BooksAndArticles/-5247.doc

Cunningham, A.E., & Stanovich, K.E. (1998). What reading does for the mind. *Journal of Direct Instruction*, 1(2), 137–149.

Deane, P., Odendahl, N., Quinlan, T., Fowles, M., Welsh, C., & Bivens-Tatum, J. (2012). Improving the writing skills of at-risk students through explicit grammar instruction. *Journal of Educational Psychology*, 104(1), 193–206.

De Bellis, M.D., & Thomas, L.A. (2003). Biologic findings of post-traumatic stress disorder and child maltreatment. *Current Psychiatry Reports*, 5(2), 108–117.

Didau, D. (2014, June 19). Revisiting slow writing. *The Learning Spy*. https://learningspy.co.uk/literacy/revisiting-slow-writing-improving-writing-improves-thinking/

Didau, D. (2017, March 27). The problem with 'reading along'. *The Learning Spy*. https://learningspy.co.uk/reading/problem-reading-along/

Didau, D. (2019, March 3). What do students think about marking? *The Learning Spy*. https://learningspy.co.uk/featured/what-do-students-think-about-marking/

Didau, D. (2021). *Making meaning in English: Exploring the role of knowledge in the English curriculum*. Routledge.

Duke, N.K., & Pearson, P.D. (2002). Effective practices for developing reading comprehension. In A.E. Farstrup & S.J. Samuels (Eds.), *What research has to say about reading instruction* (3rd ed., pp. 205–242). International Reading Association.

Dunlosky, J., Rawson, K.A., Marsh, E.J., Nathan, M.J., & Willingham, D.T. (2013). Improving students' learning with effective learning techniques: Promising directions from cognitive and educational psychology. *Psychological Science in the Public Interest*, 14(1), 4–58.

Elliott, V., Baird, J.A., Hopfenbeck, T.N., Ingram, J., Thompson, I., Usher, N., Zantout, M., Richardson, J., & Coleman, R. (2016). *A marked improvement? A review of the evidence on written marking*. Education Endowment Foundation. doi:10.13140/RG.2.1.2224.7280

Ellis, N.C., & Beaton, A. (1993). Psycholinguistic determinants of foreign language vocabulary learning. *Language Learning*, 43(4), 559–617.

Emerson, R.W. (2001). *The American scholar*. Virginia Tech.

Engelkamp, J., & Zimmer, H.D. (1989). Motor programs and their use in verbal learning. *Journal of Memory and Language*, 28(3), 214–231. doi: 10.1016/0749-596x(89)90046-2

Engelmann, S. (1993). The curriculum as the cause of failure. *Oregon Conference Monograph Journal*, 5(2), 3–8.

Ericsson, K.A., Krampe, R.T., & Tesch-Römer, C. (1993). The role of deliberate practice in the acquisition of expert performance. *Psychological Review*, 100(3), 363–406.

Fearn, H. (2019, July 1) Busting the 'intent' myth. *Ofsted Blog*. https://educationinspection.blog.gov.uk/2019/07/01/busting-the-intent-myth/

Fordham, M. (2017, March 4) The curriculum as progression model. *Clio et cetera*. https://clioetcetera.com/2017/03/04/the-curriculum-as-progression-model/

Fullan, M. (2001). *Leading in a culture of change*. Jossey-Bass.

Furedi, F. (2015). *Power of reading: From Socrates to Twitter*. Bloomsbury Publishing.

Gathercole, S.E., & Alloway, T.P. (2008). Working memory and classroom learning. In C.M. Evertson & C.S. Weinstein (Eds), *Handbook of classroom management: Research, practice, and contemporary issues* (pp. 243–258). Routledge.

Graesser, A.C., Singer, M., & Trabasso, T. (1994). Constructing inferences during narrative text comprehension. *Psychological Review*, 101(3), 371–395.

Graff, G., & Birkenstein, C. (2018). *They say / I say: The moves that matter in academic writing* (4th ed.). W.W. Norton & Company.

Graham, S., & Perin, D. (2007). A meta-analysis of writing instruction for adolescent students. *Journal of Educational Psychology*, 99(3), 445–476.

Graham, S., MacArthur, C.A., Fitzgerald, J., Weigle, S.C., & Goldenberg, C. (2017). An evaluation of a comprehensive writing program for high-poverty elementary schools. *Journal of Writing Research*, 9(3), 251–277.

Guo, J., Li, W., Liang, X., Bi, Y., & Hu, Y. (2020). The production effect in memory: A meta-analysis. *Memory*, 28(3), 280–292. doi: 10.1080/09658211.2019.1643212

Gupta, R., Kar, B.R., & Srinivasan, N. (2014). Enhancement of cognitive control by approach and avoidance motivational states. *PLoS One*, 9(10), e109847. doi: 10.1371/journal.pone.0109847

Haladyna, T.M., Downing, S.M., & Rodriguez, M.C. (2002). A review of multiple-choice item-writing guidelines for classroom assessment. *Applied Measurement in Education*, 15(3), 309–333.

Hattie, J., & Timperley, H. (2007). The power of feedback. *Review of Educational Research*, 77(1), 81–112.

Hillocks Jr, G. (1986). *Research on written composition: New directions for teaching*. ERIC Clearinghouse on Reading and Communication Skills.

Hirsch, E.D. (1987). *Cultural literacy: What every American needs to know*. Houghton Mifflin.

Hirsch, E.D. (2003). Reading comprehension requires knowledge of words and the world. *American Educator*, 27(1), 10–13.

Hirsch, E.D. (2019). *Why knowledge matters: Rescuing our children from failed educational theories*. Harvard Education Press.

Hochman, J., & Wexler, N. (2017). *The writing revolution: A guide to advancing thinking through writing in all subjects and grades*. Jossey-Bass.

Horvath, J.C. (2020). *10 things schools get wrong (and how we can get them right)*. John Catt Educational.

Jones, G., & Macken, B. (2015). Questioning the role of long-term memory in the production effect. *Journal of Experimental Psychology: Learning, Memory, and Cognition*, 41(3), 915–924. doi: 10.1037/xlm0000069

Jussim, L., & Harber, K.D. (2005). Teacher expectations and self-fulfilling prophecies: Knowns and unknowns, resolved and unresolved controversies. *Personality and Social Psychology Review*, 9(2), 131–155.

Kalyuga, S. (2007). Expertise reversal effect and its implications for learner-tailored instruction. *Educational Psychology Review*, 19(4), 509–539.

Kalyuga, S. (2014). The expertise reversal principle in multimedia learning. In R.E. Mayer (Ed.), *The Cambridge handbook of multimedia learning* (2nd ed., pp. 566–584). Cambridge University Press.

Kane, M.T. (2013). Validating the interpretations and uses of test scores. *Journal of Educational Measurement*, 50(1), 1–73. doi: 10.1111/jedm.12000

Karpicke, J.D., & Blunt, J.R. (2011). Retrieval practice produces more learning than elaborative studying with concept mapping. *Science*, 331(6018), 772–775.

Kidd, D.C., & Castano, E. (2013). Reading literary fiction improves theory of mind. *Science*, 342(6156), 377–380.

Kirschner, P.A., Sweller, J., & Clark, R.E. (2006). Why minimal guidance during instruction does not work: An analysis of the failure of constructivist, discovery, problem-based, experiential, and inquiry-based teaching. *Educational Psychologist*, 41(2), 75–86.

Koedinger, K.R., Carvalho, P.F., Liu, R., & McLaughlin, E.A. (2023). An astonishing regularity in student learning rate. *Proceedings of the National Academy of Sciences*, 120(13), e2221311120.

Komarraju, M., & Nadler, D. (2013). Self-efficacy and academic achievement: Why do implicit beliefs, goals, and effort regulation matter? *Learning and Individual Differences*, 25, 67–72.

Kornell, N., & Bjork, R.A. (2008). Learning concepts and categories: Is spacing the 'enemy of induction'? *Psychological Science*, 19(6), 585–592.

Lakoff, G., & Johnson, M. (1980). *Metaphors we live by*. University of Chicago Press.

Laming, D. (2003). *Human judgment: The eye of the beholder*. John Wiley & Sons.

Latham, D. (2002). *How children learn to write: Supporting and developing children's writing in school*. Sage.

Lemov, D. (2021). *Teach like a champion 3.0: 63 techniques that put students on the path to college*. John Wiley & Sons.

MacLeod, C.M., Gopie, N., Hourihan, K.L., Neary, K.R., & Ozubko, J.D. (2010). The production effect: Delineation of a phenomenon. *Journal of Experimental Psychology: Learning, Memory, and Cognition*, 36(3), 671–685. doi: 10.1037/a0018785

Mar, R.A., Oatley, K., Djikic, M., & Mullin, J. (2011). Emotion and narrative fiction: Interactive influences before, during, and after reading. *Cognition & Emotion*, 25(5), 818–833.

Mason, L. (2005). Expertise and feedback for learning. In J.H. McMillan (Ed.), *The Sage handbook of research on classroom assessment* (pp. 181–199). Sage Publications.

Mayer, R.E. (2014). Cognitive load theory. In J.A.C. Hattie & E.M. Anderman (Eds.), *International handbook of student achievement* (pp. 181–183). Routledge.

McNamara, D.S., & Kintsch, W. (1996). Learning from texts: Effects of prior knowledge and text coherence. *Discourse Processes*, 22(3), 247–288.

Mundelsee, L., & Jurkowski, S. (2021). Think and pair before share: Effects of collaboration on students' in-class participation. *Learning and Individual Differences*, 88, 102015.

Nagy, W.E. and Anderson, R.C. (1984). How many words are there in printed school English? *Reading Research Quarterly*, 19, 304–330. http://dx.doi.org/10.2307/747823

Nagy, W.E., Herman, P.A., & Anderson, R.C. (1985). Learning words from context. *Reading Research Quarterly*, 20(2), 233–253.

Nation, K., & Snowling, M.J. (1998). Semantic processing and the development of word-recognition skills: Evidence from children with reading comprehension difficulties. *Journal of Memory and Language*, 39(1), 85–101. doi: 10.1006/jmla.1998.2578

National Reading Panel. (2000). *Teaching children to read: An evidence-based assessment of the scientific research literature on reading and its implications for reading instruction*. National Institute of Child Health and Human Development.

Nist, S.L., & Holschuh, J.P. (1983). Study skills instruction in introductory psychology: An experimental evaluation. *Teaching of Psychology*, 10(1), 14–19.

Nussbaum, E.M., & Dweck, C.S. (2008). Defensiveness versus remediation: Self-theories and modes of self-esteem maintenance. *Personality and Social Psychology Bulletin*, 34(5), 599–612.

Nuthall, G. (2007). *The hidden lives of learners*. New Zealand Council for Educational Research Press.

Ofqual. (2019, August 22). *Variability in GCSE results for schools and colleges 2017–2019*. https://assets.publishing.service.gov.uk/government/uploads/system/uploads/attachment_data/file/826695/Variability_in_GCSE_results_for_schools_and_colleges_2017-2019_v3.pdf

Ofsted. (2015). *Key Stage 3: The wasted years?* www.gov.uk/government/publications/key-stage-3-the-wasted-years

Ofsted (2019). *Education inspection framework (EIF)*. www.gov.uk/government/publications/education-inspection-framework

Ofsted. (2022). *School inspection handbook.* www.gov.uk/government/publications/school-inspection-handbook-eif/school-inspection-handbook

Paas, F., Renkl, A., & Sweller, J. (2003). Cognitive load theory and instructional design: Recent developments. *Educational Psychologist*, 38(1), 1–4.

Patel, V., & Jasani, R. (2020). The effects of reading on stress reduction: A systematic review. *Journal of Mental Health*, 29(6), 715–721.

Pekrun, R., Elliot, A.J., & Maier, M.A. (2009). Achievement goals and achievement emotions: Testing a model of their joint relations with academic performance. *Journal of Educational Psychology*, 101(1), 115–135.

Pelham, W.E., Gnagy, E.M., Greiner, A.R., Hoza, B., Hinshaw, S.P., Swanson, J.M., Simpson, S., Shapiro, C., Bukstein, O., Baron-Myak, C., & McBurnett, K. (2000). Behavioral versus behavioral and pharmacological treatment in ADHD children attending a summer treatment program. *Journal of Abnormal Child Psychology*, 28(6), 507–525.

Pellegrino, J.W., Chudowsky, N., & Glaser, R. (Eds.). (2001). *Knowing what students know: The science and design of educational assessment.* National Academy Press.

Purves, M. (2018, December 16) Data in the context of the curriculum. *Ofsted News.* www.youtube.com/watch?v=zcrp5N6c334&ab_channel=Ofstednews

Putnam, A.L., & Roediger III, H.L. (2018). Does the testing effect scale to high-stakes exams? *European Journal of Psychology of Education*, 33(2), 263–277.

Rasinski, T. (2017). *The fluent reader: Oral reading strategies for building word recognition, fluency, and comprehension* (2nd ed.). Scholastic.

Rayner, K., Well, A.D., & Pollatsek, A. (1980). Asymmetry of the effective visual field in reading. *Perception & Psychophysics*, 27(6), 537–544.

Readers' Theatre. (2021). *Improving literacy in KS2.* Education Endowment Foundation. https://d2tic4wvo1iusb.cloudfront.net/eef-guidance-reports/literacy-ks2/KS2-Lit-Readers-theatre.pdf?v=1678461696

Renkl, A., & Scheiter, K. (2017). The expertise reversal effect: Cognitive load and instructional design in learning and problem solving. *Educational Psychologist*, 52(2), 107–121.

Rhead, S., Black, B., & Pinot de Moira, A. (2018). *Marking consistency metrics: An update.* Ofqual.

Richards, I.A., & Constable, J. (2018). *The philosophy of rhetoric.* Routledge.

Rijlaarsdam, G., Braaksma, M., Couzijn, M., Janssen, T., & Van der Kamp, M. (2017). Grammar instruction embedded in content-rich writing tasks: Effects on second language writing. *Journal of Second Language Writing*, 35, 19–36.

Rohrer, D., Dedrick, R.F., Hartwig, M.K., & Cheung, C.N. (2019). A randomized controlled trial of interleaved mathematics practice. *Journal of Educational Psychology.* doi: 10.1037/edu0000367

Rosen, Y., & Beck-Hill, D. (2012). Improving reading comprehension and fluency through the use of repeated reading. *Reading & Writing Quarterly*, 28(1), 23–46.

Rosenshine, B. (2012). Principles of instruction: Research-based strategies that all teachers should know. *American Educator*, 36(1), 12–19.

Rosenthal, R., & Jacobson, L. (1968). *Pygmalion in the classroom: Teacher expectation and pupils' intellectual development.* Holt, Rinehart and Winston.

Rowe, M.B. (1986). Wait time: Slowing down may be a way of speeding up! *Journal of Teacher Education*, 37(1), 43–50. https://doi.org/10.1177/002248718603700110

Rubie-Davies, C.M. (2010). Teacher expectations and perceptions of student attributes: Is there a relationship? *British Journal of Educational Psychology*, 80(1), 121–135.

Ryan, R.M., & Deci, E.L. (2000). Intrinsic and extrinsic motivations: Classic definitions and new directions. *Contemporary Educational Psychology*, 25(1), 54–67.

Schneider, M., & Chein, J.M. (2003). Cognitive processes underlying context effects in intelligence tests. In R.J. Sternberg, J. Lautrey, & T.I. Lubart (Eds.), *Models of intelligence: International perspectives* (pp. 379–397). American Psychological Association.

Schoenbaum, S. (Ed.). (2015). *Macbeth: Critical essays.* Routledge.

Schools Week Reporter. (2017, November 28). Interview with Christine Counsell. *Schools Week.* https://schoolsweek.co.uk/christine-counsell-director-of-education-inspiration-trust/

Schunk, D.H., & Zimmerman, B.J. (2012). *Motivation and self-regulated learning: Theory, research, and applications.* Routledge.

Sedova, K., & Sedlacek, M. (2023). How vocal and silent forms of participation in combination relate to student achievement. *Instructional Science*, 51, 343–361. https://doi.org/10.1007/s11251-022-09609-1

Shanahan, T., & Shanahan, C. (2012). Teaching disciplinary literacy to adolescents: Rethinking content-area literacy. *Journal of Adolescent and Adult Literacy*, 56(6), 471–478.

Shavelson, R.J., & Ruiz-Primo, M.A. (1999). On the measurement of learning progressions. *Educational Researcher*, 28(5), 4–16. doi: 10.3102/0013189X028005004

Sherwood. (2020, October 15). Just how reliable are exam grades? *Rethinking Assessment.* https://rethinkingassessment.com/rethinking-blogs/just-how-reliable-are-exam-grades/

Smith, M.A., Karpicke, J.D., & Roediger III, H.L. (2013). Retrieval practice with short-answer, multiple-choice, and hybrid tests. *Memory*, 21(7), 784–802.

Snowling, M.J., & Hulme, C. (2011). Evidence-based interventions for reading and language difficulties: Creating a virtuous circle. *British Journal of Educational Psychology*, 81(1), 1–23.

Soderstrom, N.C., & Bjork, R.A. (2015). Learning versus performance: An integrative review. *Perspectives on Psychological Science*, 10(2), 176–199.

Spielman, A. (2018, June 6). Speech at the Bryanston Education Summit. www.gov.uk/government/speeches/amanda-spielman-at-the-bryanston-education-summit

Stahl, R.J., & Davis, E.A. (2010). The role of wait time in enhancing EFL classroom discourse. *TESOL Quarterly*, 44(2), 300–319. https://doi.org/10.5054/tq.2010.221825

Stahl, S.A., & Nagy, W.E. (2006). *Teaching word meanings.* Lawrence Erlbaum Associates.

Stice, E., & Barrera, M. (1995). A longitudinal examination of the reciprocal relations between perceived stress and eating disorder symptoms: A test of the stressor vulnerability model. *Journal of Abnormal Psychology*, 104(1), 84–89.

Sullivan, A., Parsons, S., Green, F., Wiggins, R.D., & Ploubidis, G. (2018). The path from social origins to top jobs: Social reproduction via education. *British Journal of Sociology*, 69(3), 776–798. https://doi.org/10.1111/1468-4446.12314

Swanborn, M.S.L., & de Glopper, K. (1999). Incidental word learning while reading: A meta-analysis. *Review of Educational Research*, 69(3), 261–285.

Swanson, H.L., & Sachse-Lee, C. (2001). A meta-analysis of single-subject-design intervention research for students with LD. *Journal of Learning Disabilities*, 34(2), 114–136.

Sweller, J. (1988). Cognitive load during problem solving: Effects on learning. *Cognitive Science*, 12(2), 257–285.

Sweller, J. (1999). *Instructional design in technical areas*. ACER Press.

Sweller, J., Kalyuga, S., & Ayres, P. (2011). *Cognitive load theory*. Springer.

Tinker, M.A. (1963). *Legibility of print*. Iowa State University Press.

Tomsett, J. (2019, June 17). This much I know about… helping students avoid making nonsensical interpretations of poems. https://johntomsett.com/2019/06/17/this-much-i-know-about-students-avoid-making-nonsensical-interpretations-of-poems/

Treadaway, M. (2015). Why measuring pupil progress involves more than taking a straight line. *Education Datalab*. https://ffteducationdatalab.org.uk/2015/03/why-measuring-pupil-progress-involves-more-than-taking-a-straight-line/

Troia, G.A., & Olinghouse, N.G. (2013). The Common Core State Standards and evidence-based educational practices: The case of writing. *School Psychology Review*, 42(3), 343–357.

Vaid, J., & Lal, D. (2012). The impact of text layout on reading performance and impressions of credibility: Does skimming improve evaluation? *Journal of Technical Writing and Communication*, 42(3), 245–265.

van de Pol, J., Volman, M., & Beishuizen, J. (2010). Scaffolding in teacher–student interaction: A decade of research. *Educational Psychology Review*, 22(3), 271–296. https://doi.org/10.1007/s10648-010-9127-6

van Gog, T., Kester, L., Nievelstein, F., & Giesbers, B. (2011). Self-explanation and the expertise reversal effect in multimedia learning. *Journal of Educational Psychology*, 103(1), 218–228.

van Gog, T., & Sweller, J. (2015). Not new, but nearly forgotten: The testing effect decreases or even disappears as the complexity of learning materials increases. *Educational Psychology Review*, 27, 247–264.

Vansteenkiste, M., Simons, J., Lens, W., Sheldon, K.M., & Deci, E.L. (2004). Motivating learning, performance, and persistence: The synergistic effects of intrinsic goal contents and autonomy-supportive contexts. *Journal of Personality and Social Psychology*, 87(2), 246–260.

Vivanti, G., Dissanayake, C., Zierhut, C., Rogers, S.J., & Victorian Autism Specific Early Learning and Care Centre (2013). Brief report: Predictors of outcomes in the Early Start Denver Model delivered in a group setting. *Journal of Autism and Developmental Disorders*, 43(7), 1717–1724.

Weinstein, R.S. (2002). *Reaching higher: The power of expectations in schooling*. Harvard University Press.

Westbrook, J., Sutherland, J., Oakhill, J., & Sullivan, S. (2019). 'Just reading': The impact of a faster pace of reading narratives on the comprehension of poorer adolescent readers in English classrooms. *Literacy*, 53(2), 60–68.

Wilson, M. (2013). Seeking coherence between principles of learning, assessment and measurement. *Assessment & Evaluation in Higher Education*, 38(6), 750–762. doi: 10.1080/02602938.2012.690049

Woelfel, J., & Fink, E.L. (1980). Newspaper column width and type size: Legibility and reader preference. *Journalism & Mass Communication Quarterly*, 57(1), 112–117.

Wolf, M. (2018). *Reader, come home: The reading brain in a digital world*. HarperCollins.

Yorke, J. (2013). *Into the woods: How stories work and why we tell them*. Penguin.

Young, M. (2009). What are schools for? In H. Daniels & L.J. Porter (Eds.), *Knowledge, values and educational policy: A critical perspective* (pp. 10–18). Routledge.

Zimmaro, D.M. (2010). Hinge-point questions in a statistics course. *Journal of Statistics Education*, 18(3), 1–16

Notes

1. INTENT

1. Spielman (2018)
2. Fearn (2019)
3. Ofsted (2022)
4. Engelmann (1993, p. 3)
5. Discussed in *Making Meaning in English* (Didau, 2021, pp. 315–329) and taken from an argument made by Arthur Applebee in *Curriculum as Conversation* (2008).
6. Ofsted (2015)
7. Pierre Bourdieu (1986) discusses how individuals and groups possess different types of capital, which they can use to gain social and economic advantages. Bourdieu identifies three types of capital: economic capital, which refers to money and other financial resources; cultural capital, which includes knowledge, skills and education; and social capital, which encompasses networks of relationships and social connections. He argues that these forms of capital are not independent but are interrelated and reinforce each other, and that individuals with more capital have greater power and advantage in society. Additionally, Bourdieu notes that the possession of cultural and social capital can be used to convert economic capital into other forms of capital. Bourdieu's theory highlights the importance of understanding the multiple forms of capital and how they are used in social interactions and hierarchies.
8. The Way of the Dodo. Available at www.satspapers.org/SATs%20papers/2016%20onwards/2016%20Reading/2016_ks2_Englishreading_readingbooklet_26012016_PDFA.pdf
9. This idea is explored in Bernstein (2003) and Sullivan et al. (2018). Bernstein examines how poverty affects education and suggests strategies for addressing the issue. Bernstein highlights how poverty can create disadvantages for students, including inadequate nutrition, lack of access to healthcare, and limited access to learning resources. These factors can lead to cognitive and developmental delays, as well as emotional and behavioural problems. Bernstein recommends a holistic approach to education that addresses the physical, emotional and social needs of students in addition to academic ones. This approach involves building partnerships with families and communities, providing access to health and social services, and creating supportive learning environments that are sensitive to the diverse backgrounds and needs of students. By focusing on the whole child, Bernstein argues, educators can help to mitigate the effects of poverty and promote equitable learning opportunities for all students. Sullivan et al. investigate how social origins affect access to top jobs in the UK. The authors use data from the 1958 National Child Development Study and examine the role of education in mediating the relationship between social class and occupation. They find that children from high socio-economic backgrounds are more likely to achieve educational success, which in turn increases their chances of securing top jobs. Furthermore, they find that the relationship between social origins and educational success has strengthened over time, resulting in greater social stratification in the labour market. The authors argue that the educational system plays a key role in perpetuating social inequality and call for policies that address the root causes of inequality, such as improving access to high-quality education and reducing the socio-economic gaps in educational outcomes.
10. The concept of powerful knowledge was first proposed by Michael Young (2009) and its relevance to English is explored in *Making Meaning in English* (Didau, 2021, pp. 83–85).
11. These descriptors are all taken from AQA mark schemes for GCSE English Literature or Language but the same limitations are apparent in all such descriptors whether compiled by exam boards or put together within schools.
12. We have found that our curriculum mutates most lethally where these principles are least well understood.
13. Emerson (2001, p. 296)
14. Lakoff & Johnson (1980)
15. Yorke (2013, pp. 138–139)
16. Didau (2021)
17. Our mapping of English concepts may not be optimal but as far as we're aware, no one else seems to have attempted to organise the conceptual understandings of English in this way.
18. Bruner (1977, p. 33)
19. Hirsch (2019, p. 67). Hirsch contends that the Bruner Principle neglects the role of prior knowledge in learning. He argues that knowledge builds upon itself, and students who lack the necessary background knowledge will struggle to understand new concepts. This lack of foundational knowledge is a significant contributor to the achievement gap between students from different socio-economic backgrounds. Therefore, Hirsch emphasises the importance of a broad-based, content-rich curriculum that provides students with the background knowledge they need to succeed in school and beyond.

20. Research has consistently shown that children with working memory deficits can benefit from instructional techniques that carefully sequence information and break it down into manageable chunks. Alloway & Alloway (2010) found that working memory capacity was a strong predictor of academic achievement across several subjects, including maths and reading. The authors suggest that this is because working memory helps children to hold and manipulate information in their minds, which is critical for learning. Gathercole & Alloway (2008) summarise a range of studies that have investigated the relationship between working memory and classroom learning. The authors also conclude that children with working memory deficits can benefit from instructional techniques that carefully sequence information and break it down into smaller chunks. They suggest that teachers can use strategies like repetition, visualisation and scaffolding to support these students. Swanson & Sachse-Lee's (2001) meta-analysis of 85 studies found that instructional techniques that carefully sequenced information and broke it down into manageable chunks were particularly effective for students with learning disabilities, including those with working memory deficits. The authors suggest that these techniques help to reduce cognitive load, allowing students to focus on the most important information.

21. Phonics instruction helps to develop phonological awareness and other key skills needed for reading, leading to improved reading fluency and comprehension for all children. Snowling & Hulme (2011) examined a range of interventions for reading and language difficulties, including dyslexia. The authors conclude that systematic synthetic phonics instruction is a highly effective approach for teaching reading, and that this approach benefits both children with dyslexia and those without. Castles & Coltheart (2004) found that phonological awareness, which is a key component of phonics instruction, is a strong predictor of reading success for both children with dyslexia and those without. The authors suggest that phonics instruction can help to develop phonological awareness, leading to improved reading skills. The National Reading Panel (2000) conducted a comprehensive review of the scientific literature on reading instruction and found that systematic synthetic phonics instruction is highly effective for teaching reading, particularly for children with dyslexia. The authors recommend that phonics instruction should be followed by extensive exposure to a broad range of texts, which helps to develop reading fluency and comprehension.

22. Attachment disorder: De Bellis & Thomas (2003) suggests that children with attachment disorders may benefit from a structured environment, consistent rules and professional distance from caregivers. This can help them to develop a sense of security and stability, which can in turn support their emotional and behavioural development. Autism spectrum disorder: Vivanti et al. (2013) found that children with autism spectrum disorders benefit from structured, predictable routines and a calm learning environment. This can help them to feel more comfortable and secure and can support their engagement and learning. ADHD: Pelham et al. (2000) found that children with ADHD benefit from clear boundaries and consistent, proportional consequences. This can help them to understand expectations and develop self-control, leading to improved behaviour and academic performance. While these studies suggest that students with SEND benefit from specific approaches, these approaches will also be beneficial for other children. For example, a struc-

tured environment and consistent rules can help all children feel safe and supported, while clear boundaries and consequences can help all children understand expectations and develop self-control.

23. Counsell (2018)

24. Cunningham & Stanovich (1998) detail the cognitive benefits of reading. Their article summarises research on how reading can improve a person's vocabulary, cognitive skills and empathy, and even help prevent cognitive decline in later life. It also discusses the importance of developing good reading habits and provides suggestions for parents and educators on how to encourage children to read. Mar et al. (2011) explore how reading narrative fiction can affect emotional and cognitive responses before, during and after reading. Kidd & Castano (2013) found that reading literary fiction can improve a person's 'theory of mind', or their ability to understand and empathise with others' mental states. In addition, Bal & Veltkamp (2013) found that reading fiction can improve emotional regulation and reduce symptoms of depression.

25. Clark & Rumbold (2006) examined the research on the benefits of reading for pleasure and reader engagement and found that reading for pleasure can have a positive impact on language development, cognitive development, educational attainment and personal well-being. The authors also discuss the factors that influence reader engagement, such as the availability of reading materials, the social context of reading, and the individual's motivation to read. Overall, the article suggests that reading for pleasure and promoting reader engagement can have significant benefits for individuals and society as a whole. In addition, Clark & Douglas (2011) investigated the relationship between young people's reading behaviours, attitudes and attainment levels. The research found that young people who enjoy reading and who read for pleasure are more likely to perform better academically, have higher levels of empathy and possess greater emotional intelligence. How frequently children read, and how much they enjoy reading correlates closely with academic attainment.

26. Some of our schools have struggled to 'get through' modules in the time we expected. The main reason for this is that they spent too long on analysing and low-quality writing practice.

27. Contrary to popular opinion, this is the correct formulation of the proverb. An early recording of the phrase is in a letter on 14 March 1538 from Thomas, Duke of Norfolk, to Thomas Cromwell, as 'a man can not have his cake and eat his cake'.

28. Schools Week Reporter (2017)

29. Ofsted (2019)

30. Lemov (2021, p. xxiv)

31. This is the profile for one of our secondary academies in Norfolk but is broadly representative of all our school communities.

32. 2018 AQA GCSE writing task.

33. AQA (2019)

2. IMPLEMENTATION

1. Exciting recent research has lent considerable weight to this proposition. Koedinger et al. (2023) explored the question of 'Can anyone learn to be good at anything they want?' In response, they write, 'Our evidence suggests that given favorable learning conditions for deliberate practice and given

the learner invests effort in sufficient learning opportunities, indeed, anyone can learn anything they want' (p. 26). The idea that the only excuse for students performing poorly is either a failure to make learning conditions favourable enough or an inability to inspire them to try hard enough is both daunting and tantalising.

2. Engelmann (1993, p. 8)

3. This a paraphrase of Graham Nuthall in *The Hidden Lives of Learners*: 'Ability appears to be the consequence in differences of what children learn from their classroom experience' (2007, p. 84).

4. A useful introduction to Engelmann's ideas about flawless, or faultless, instruction can be found in *Clear Teaching* by Shepard Barbash (2012): 'Try this experiment. Make up a nonsense word for a familiar concept and try teaching the concept to someone without using its regular name. Engelmann holds up a pencil and says, "This is glerm". Then he holds up a pen and says, "This is glerm". Then he holds up a crayon – also glerm. So what is glerm? A student responds: "Something you write with". Logical, but wrong, Engelmann says. Glerm means up. The student learned a misrule – Engelmann's examples were deliberately ambiguous, exemplifying both the concepts for up and for writing implements, and the student came to the wrong conclusion. This is one of the exercises Engelmann uses to teach instructional design. His point is to make us aware of the minefield teachers must navigate to avoid generating confusion in their students. Next he wanders around the room giving examples of the concept "graeb", without success. At last he opens the door, walks out and shouts: "This is not graeb". Graeb means in the room. To show what something is, sometimes you have to show what it's not. He points to a cup on his desk and says, "That's glick". Then he holds up a spoon and says, "Not glick". He points to a book on a student's desk – glick – then raises a pen – not glick. What's glick? No one is sure. Finally he puts the spoon on his desk – that's glick – lifts it – not glick – puts the pen on the student's desk – glick – and lifts it – not glick. Everyone gets it: glick means on' (p. 19).

5. Ericsson et al. (1993) discuss the role of deliberate practice in the development of expertise. They argue that expert performance is not simply the result of innate talent or innate ability, but rather the product of extensive and deliberate practice. Deliberate practice is defined as practice that is focused, effortful and involves challenging oneself with tasks that are just beyond one's current level of ability. The authors review evidence from various domains, including music, sports and chess, to support the idea that deliberate practice is the key to developing expertise. They also discuss the importance of feedback, motivation and goal setting in the development of expertise. Overall, the article provides strong support for the idea that expertise is developed through sustained and focused effort, rather than innate ability or talent. More specifically, Rosen & Beck-Hill (2012) examined the effectiveness of repeated reading (i.e., reading the same text multiple times) in improving reading comprehension and fluency in school children. The results showed that deliberate practice of repeated reading led to significant improvements in both reading comprehension and fluency, and that these improvements were maintained over time.

6. Komarraju & Nadler (2013) found that self-efficacy (i.e., a student's belief in their ability to succeed) was a strong predictor of academic achievement. However, the relationship between

self-efficacy and achievement is moderated by the level of challenge presented by the task. Specifically, when tasks were too easy or too difficult, the relationship between self-efficacy and achievement weakened. This suggests that balancing the level of challenge with a student's sense of self-efficacy is important for promoting academic achievement. Nussbaum & Dweck (2008) found that students who were presented with tasks that were too difficult or beyond their current skill level were more likely to adopt a defensive self-theory, in which they attributed failure to their own lack of ability. In contrast, students who were presented with moderately challenging tasks were more likely to adopt a remedial self-theory, in which they viewed failure as an opportunity to learn and improve. This suggests that balancing the level of challenge with a student's sense of self-efficacy can influence their attitudes towards failure and their willingness to persist in the face of challenges. Additionally, Schunk & Zimmerman (2012) argue that finding the optimal level of challenge for students is important for promoting self-regulated learning, which involves students actively monitoring their own learning and adapting their strategies based on feedback. When tasks are too easy or too difficult, students are less likely to engage in self-regulated learning, as they may not feel the need to monitor their progress or adjust their strategies. However, when tasks are moderately challenging, students are more likely to engage in self-regulated learning, which can lead to greater learning and skill acquisition.

7. Our definition is taken from that used by Soderstrom & Bjork (2015) in which they say, 'instruction should endeavor to facilitate learning, which refers to the relatively permanent changes in behavior or knowledge that support long-term retention and transfer' (p. 176).

8. Opportunity cost refers to the value of the next best alternative that must be foregone in order to pursue a certain action or decision. It is the cost of choosing one option over another and involves comparing the benefits and drawbacks of each possible choice. Essentially, opportunity cost is what you give up in order to do something else. Understanding opportunity cost helps teachers and school leaders to make more informed and efficient decisions by considering the potential costs and benefits of different options.

9. Rob Coe (2019) discusses the research on retrieval practice. While there is overwhelming evidence that retrieval practice has a positive impact on learning across a variety of subjects and age groups, he highlights the importance of implementing retrieval practice effectively in the classroom, including providing clear guidance and feedback to students, using appropriate timing and spacing of practice, and ensuring that retrieval practice is integrated into the overall curriculum.

10. Bjork & Bjork (1992) propose a new theory of disuse, which explains how memories fade over time due to lack of use, and suggest that the process of retrieval can actually strengthen memories. The authors also discuss an old theory of stimulus fluctuation, which suggests that fluctuations in environmental cues can cause memories to fade. They propose that these two theories can be integrated to provide a more comprehensive understanding of how memories are formed, maintained and forgotten.

11. A study by Kornell & Bjork (2008) found that practising retrieval of information through testing led to better long-term retention compared to restudying the same information. However, when

participants were tested on related but not identical information, those who had restudied the original material performed better, indicating that retrieval practice may have reduced storage strength for related information. Similarly, a study by Cepeda et al. (2006) found that distributed practice, where learning is spread out over time, leads to better long-term retention compared to massed practice, where learning occurs in a single session. However, when participants were tested immediately after learning, those who had engaged in massed practice performed better, indicating that massed practice may have enhanced retrieval strength in the short term at the expense of storage strength.

12. The term 'desirable difficulties' was first introduced by Robert Bjork & Elizabeth Bjork (2011) In which the Bjorks discussed how introducing certain challenges or difficulties during learning can actually enhance long-term retention and transfer of knowledge, rather than hinder it.

13. Dunlosky et al. (2013, p. 32)

14. Evidence on the benefits of retrieval practice for more complex tasks is mixed. Karpicke & Blunt (2011) demonstrate that students' reading of educational texts on science topics followed by free recall results in successful retrieval. Also, Adesope et al. (2017) found that free recall had a slightly higher effect size (0.62) than cued recall (0.58). However, van Gog & Sweller (2015) argue that 'the testing effect decreases as the complexity of learning materials increases... the effect may even disappear when the complexity of learning material is very high' (p. 247), while Rohrer et al. (2019) note 'benefits of retrieval practice have yet to be demonstrated for mathematics tasks other than fact learning' (p. 3).

15. Cepeda et al. (2008) investigated the spacing effect in learning, which refers to the finding that learning is better when studying is spread out over time compared to massed study. They conducted a meta-analysis of 184 studies and found that spacing improves retention of information and that the effect is greater for longer retention intervals. They also identified a temporal ridgeline, which is the optimal spacing interval for retention, and found that the ridgeline shifted to longer intervals as the retention interval increased. The optimal spacing interval depends on the length of the retention interval, and it shifts to longer intervals as the retention interval increases. For example, for a retention interval of a day, the optimal spacing interval might be a few hours; for a week or longer, the optimal spacing interval might be days or weeks. Longer spacing intervals are generally more effective for long-term retention. Therefore, for a retention interval of one year, optimal spacing intervals might range from several weeks to several months, depending on the material being learned.

16. Smith et al. (2013) compared the effectiveness of short-answer, multiple-choice and hybrid tests for promoting long-term retention. They found that retrieval practice using short-answer or hybrid tests was more effective than multiple-choice tests.

17. Putnam & Roediger (2018) investigated the effects of stakes on the benefits of retrieval practice for learning foreign language vocabulary. They found that retrieval practice improved vocabulary retention for both high- and low-stakes conditions, but the effect was stronger for low-stakes conditions.

18. Research has consistently shown a strong relationship between vocabulary and reading, with vocabulary knowledge being an important predictor of reading comprehension (Cunningham & Stanovich, 1998; Nagy & Anderson, 1984). Vocabulary size is positively correlated with reading comprehension, and students with a larger vocabulary tend to have better reading comprehension skills (Cromley & Azevedo, 2007; Nation & Snowling, 1998). Also, students with larger vocabularies are more likely to learn more new vocabulary from their reading (Hirsch, 2003). Vocabulary knowledge has been found to be a better predictor of reading comprehension than other factors such as decoding ability or background knowledge (Stahl & Nagy, 2006). Direct vocabulary instruction can lead to improved reading comprehension. Effective vocabulary instruction involves teaching specific words, as well as strategies for learning new words (Beck et al., 2013). Providing students with opportunities to read a wide variety of texts can help improve vocabulary knowledge. Research has shown that students who read more widely tend to have larger vocabularies (Swanborn & de Glopper, 1999). Vocabulary instruction should not be limited to elementary grades. Research has shown that older students can also benefit from vocabulary instruction, particularly instruction that focuses on academic vocabulary (Duke & Pearson, 2002).

19. *Bringing Words to Life* by Isabel L. Beck, Margaret G. McKeown and Linda Kucan (2013) advocates for robust vocabulary instruction in order to help students acquire a deep understanding of words. The authors argue that effective vocabulary instruction should go beyond simply teaching definitions, and instead should focus on teaching students how to use new words in context, how to spell and pronounce them correctly and how to understand their nuanced meanings. They provide practical strategies for teaching vocabulary, including using graphic organisers, engaging in word play and creating a word-rich classroom environment. The authors also emphasise the importance of selecting and prioritising high-utility words that students are likely to encounter in multiple contexts. The goal of robust vocabulary instruction is to enable students to become more proficient readers and writers by giving them the tools to comprehend and express complex ideas.

20. There is evidence to suggest that providing definitions, pronunciation practice and opportunities for recognition can help boost the chances of retaining new vocabulary. Definitions can help learners to understand the meaning of a new word and to relate it to their existing knowledge. Research has shown that providing explicit definitions of new words can improve comprehension and retention (see for example, Nagy et al., 1985). Pronunciation can help learners to correctly pronounce the word and to remember it more accurately. Research has shown that providing explicit instruction on the pronunciation of new words can improve retention (see for example, Ellis & Beaton, 1993). Recognition can help learners to recognise a new word in different contexts and to consolidate it in their long-term memory. Research has shown that providing opportunities for learners to practise recognising new words can improve retention and transfer to new contexts (see for example, Nation & Snowling, 1998).

21. Research suggests that saying something aloud can make it more memorable by engaging multiple sensory modalities, such as hearing, speech production and proprioception. When we say something aloud, we create a stronger association between the verbal information and the context in which it was presented, leading to better retention and recall. Additionally,

saying something aloud can also enhance our emotional connection to the information, which further reinforces our memory. See MacLeod et al. (2010), Engelkamp & Zimmer (1989), Gupta et al. (2014), Clark & Paivio (1991), Guo et al. (2020) and Jones & Macken (2015).

22. As a Trust, OAT encourages academies to implement Lexonik Advance as an intervention for students with below-average reading scores. The process is very much based on teaching morphology. You can read an interview with David Didau on Lexonik here: https://lexonik.co.uk/case-studies/a-morally-right-intervention-with-david-didau-and-ormiston-academies-trust

23. Daisy Christodoulou, in *Making Good Progress? The Future of Assessment for Learning* (2017), argues that you wouldn't train for a marathon by trying to run 26.2 miles in every training session. And in the same way, you shouldn't prepare for an exam by doing exam-style activities in every lesson.

24. Considine (2016, p. 43)

25. Didau (2014)

26. There is no clear consensus in the evidence base on how best to teach grammar. On the one hand, Deane et al. (2012) found that explicit grammar instruction led to improvements in students' writing skills, particularly in the areas of sentence structure, sentence combining and punctuation, while Graham et al. (2017) found that an integrated approach that combines grammar instruction with opportunities for writing practice and feedback was more effective than grammar lessons taught in isolation. Hillocks (1986) argues that an effective approach to writing instruction involves a combination of modelling, guided practice, and independent writing opportunities, and Troia & Olinghouse (2013) suggest that effective writing instruction should be comprehensive and cover multiple aspects of writing, including grammar, vocabulary and writing processes. Rijlaarsdam et al. (2017) found that incorporating grammar instruction into writing tasks that aligned with the curriculum content led to greater improvements in students' writing quality than teaching grammar in isolation. Finally, Shanahan & Shanahan (2012) suggest that teaching disciplinary literacy, including grammar, in the context of the students' content area improves students' writing skills and motivation to write. Overall, while there is evidence to suggest that aligning grammar instruction with curriculum content can be more effective, more research is needed to fully understand the best ways to integrate grammar instruction into content-based instruction. In the meantime, we are persuaded by the approach set out in *The Writing Revolution* by Judith Hochman and Natalie Wexler (2017). Their approach is based on the principles of cognitive science, which emphasise the importance of building knowledge and practising skills in order to improve learning outcomes. Students need to master the building blocks of writing, such as sentence structure, grammar and vocabulary, before they can effectively express their ideas in writing. Hochman and Wexler also emphasise the importance of content knowledge in writing, arguing that students need to have a deep understanding of the subject matter they are writing about in order to express their ideas clearly and effectively. To this end, they advocate for the incorporation of content-rich texts and materials into the curriculum.

27. These questions derive from David Crystal (2017, pp. 27–28).

28. Westbrook et al.'s (2019) study investigated the impact of faster reading pace on the comprehension of poorer adolescent readers in Year 8 classrooms. The study involved 162 students from three schools in England, and the students were divided into two groups: one group read at a faster pace, while the other group read at a normal pace. The study found that students who read at a faster pace showed significant improvements in their comprehension of narrative texts, particularly in their ability to make inferences and understand the plot. The faster pace also helped to maintain students' attention and engagement throughout the reading task. The study suggests that increasing the pace of reading in English classrooms may be a useful strategy for improving the comprehension skills of struggling readers. The authors note, however, that this strategy should be used in conjunction with other effective teaching practices, such as explicit instruction in comprehension strategies and vocabulary development. We should probably treat the finding that progress is doubled for less advantaged students with caution.

29. Furedi (2015, p. 209)

30. Reading can improve cognitive function, vocabulary and general knowledge (Cunningham & Stanovich, 1998). Reading literary fiction has been shown to improve theory of mind, or the ability to understand others' thoughts and feelings (Kidd & Castano, 2013). Reading has been shown to reduce stress levels. (Patel & Jasani, 2020) and a longitudinal study found a reciprocal relationship between perceived stress and eating disorder symptoms, supporting the stressor vulnerability model (Stice & Barrera, 1995).

31. In *Reader, Come Home*, Marilyn Wolf (2018) argues that the rise of digital media has led to a decline in deep reading and critical thinking skills, which are essential for understanding complex information and developing empathy. She distinguishes between screen and print literacy, arguing that screen literacy is more geared towards scanning and browsing, while print literacy is better suited for sustained attention and comprehension. Wolf encourages readers to cultivate their print literacy skills and balance their digital media consumption with other forms of reading and engagement with the world.

32. David Didau (2017) presents evidence that 'following along' is likely to reduce comprehension.

33. According to Rasinski (2017), echo reading helps students improve their fluency and comprehension by providing them with a model of fluent reading and allowing them to hear their own reading aloud. Rasinski emphasises that echo reading should be used as a temporary strategy and that students should gradually transition to independent reading as their fluency and confidence improve.

34. Readers' Theatre (2021)

35. Emerson (2001, p. 5)

36. Bennett & Royle (2015, p. 16)

37. Didau (2021, pp. 97–8)

38. Here's a sample of some of the body of research that supports the idea that novices tend to learn more effectively when provided with explicit instruction. A meta-analysis of 71 studies found that explicit instruction was more effective than other types of instruction, such as inquiry-based learning, for improving students' conceptual understanding and procedural skills (Alfieri et al., 2011). A study of college-level introductory psychology classes found that students who received explicit instruction on how to study effectively (e.g., note-taking, active reading) performed better on exams than those who did not receive such instruction (Nist & Holschuh, 1983). More specifically to English, in

a study of teaching methods for teaching writing to elementary school students, students who received explicit instruction on specific writing skills (e.g., organisation, sentence structure) showed greater improvements in their writing ability than those who did not receive such instruction (Graham & Perin, 2007).

39. Cognitive Load Theory is a theoretical framework that explains how working memory capacity limits the amount of information that can be processed and learned by an individual. The theory proposes that learning is optimised when the cognitive load of a task is managed to ensure that it does not exceed the individual's working memory capacity. Here are some key findings of the Cognitive Load Theory: 1) Working memory has a limited capacity, which constrains the amount of information that can be processed at any given time. 2) There are two types of cognitive load: intrinsic load, which is inherent to the task, and extraneous load, which is caused by the way the task is presented or structured. 3) The optimal learning environment minimises extraneous cognitive load, which contributes to the construction of schemas in long-term memory. 4) Cognitive load can be managed through instructional design, such as breaking complex tasks into smaller, manageable components, and using worked examples to provide learners with a model of problem-solving. John Sweller (1988) conducted a seminal study that explored the effects of cognitive load on learning. The study found that when learners were presented with a problem-solving task that exceeded their working memory capacity, they were unable to solve the problem successfully, and their learning was impaired. Sweller (1999) extended his work by applying Cognitive Load Theory to instructional design. He argued that instructional materials should be designed to manage cognitive load by reducing extraneous cognitive load and increasing germane cognitive load. This can be achieved through techniques such as providing worked examples, reducing the complexity of tasks, and using instructional supports to guide learners. Paas et al. (2003) reviewed recent developments in Cognitive Load Theory and instructional design. They emphasised the importance of considering the expertise of learners when designing instruction, as experts have more efficient schemas in long-term memory and require less instructional support. Kirschner et al. (2006) challenged the constructivist approach to learning, which emphasises student discovery and exploration. They argued that this approach can lead to excessive cognitive load and impair learning, and instead advocated for a more guided approach to instruction that minimises extraneous cognitive load. Mayer (2014) provided an overview of Cognitive Load Theory, emphasising the importance of managing cognitive load in instructional design. He discussed techniques such as reducing the complexity of materials, using worked examples and scaffolding instruction to support learners. He also highlighted the importance of considering the expertise of learners and providing appropriate levels of support to manage cognitive load.

40. The expertise reversal effect refers to a phenomenon where instructional methods that are effective for novice learners become less effective or even detrimental for more advanced learners. In other words, as learners become more knowledgeable and skilled in a particular area, the optimal way to teach them may change. This effect can occur due to several reasons, such as increased cognitive load as learners become more advanced, changes in the type of knowledge and skills

needed, and the use of different learning strategies. It highlights the importance of considering learners' expertise level when designing instructional methods and strategies. Kalyuga (2007) provides an overview of the expertise reversal effect and its implications for learner-tailored instruction. The author discusses different factors that contribute to this effect and proposes strategies for optimising instructional methods for learners with varying levels of expertise. Kalyuga (2014) explores the expertise reversal principle in multimedia learning. The chapter discusses how the effect applies to different types of multimedia learning materials and how instructional design can be tailored to learners' expertise level to optimise learning outcomes. Sweller et al. (2011) provide a comprehensive overview of Cognitive Load Theory, which is closely related to the expertise reversal effect. The authors discuss how cognitive load affects learning and problem-solving and provide practical guidelines for instructional design based on this theory. van Gog et al. (2011) investigate the expertise reversal effect in the context of self-explanation as a learning strategy. The study examines how self-explanation affects learning outcomes for novices and experts and provides insights into the cognitive processes underlying this effect. Renkl & Scheiter (2017) discuss the expertise reversal effect in relation to instructional design for learning and problem-solving. The authors provide an overview of different strategies for managing cognitive load and tailoring instructional methods to learners' expertise level to optimise learning outcomes.

41. Black & Wiliam (1998b, p. 11)

42. Recent research from Sedova & Sedlacek (2023) found that high internal behavioural engagement did not guarantee student achievement if the engagement was not accompanied by talk.

43. Latham (2002, p. 40)

44. Alexander (2012, p. 6). He goes on to say, 'Of course, confidence is a precondition for articulating ideas in front of others, but so too is the acquisition of ideas to articulate, so confidence cannot be pursued in isolation. We all know people who talk rubbish with supreme confidence! Yet note that most of the attainment target levels for Speaking and Listening in the current National Curriculum orders for English make heavy and repeated use of the words "confident", "confidently" and "carefully": "pupils talk confidently... pupils listen carefully". These repeated social or behavioural modifiers say nothing about the *structure*, *content*, *quality* or *manner* of talk, and indeed they deflect attention away from such attributes'.

45. The recommendations for how long teachers should wait before expecting students to answer questions is based on the complexity of the question and the needs of the students. For instance, a study by Rowe (1986) found that when teachers waited for at least three seconds after asking a question, students were more likely to provide complete and accurate responses. However, for complex questions, students needed even more time to think before answering. In this study, Rowe found that waiting for ten seconds or more led to more thoughtful and higher quality student responses. Similarly, a study by Stahl & Davis (2010) suggested that extended wait times can be particularly beneficial for English language learners who need more time to process and translate the question before answering. Both Baker (2018) and van de Pol et al. (2010) conclude that waiting for around ten seconds is most likely to lead to better participation in discussion.

46. Recent research from Mundelsee & Jurkowski (2021) provides good evidence in support of Think-Pair-Share as a strategy for increasing students' willingness to participate in classroom discussion.

47. This can obviously be a risky strategy that will be much more likely to work with students who know and trust you.

48. Tomsett (2019)

49. It will be essential to teach the meaning of these words in almost all cases.

50. Barton (2022, p. 57)

51. Richards & Constable (2018, p. 94)

52. Richards & Constable (2018, p. 94)

53. The benefits of whole class feedback are: 1) Whole class feedback is a more time-efficient approach to providing feedback, as it allows teachers to address common errors and misconceptions in a single session. 2) WCF ensures that all students receive the same feedback, which promotes consistency and fairness in assessment. 3) It encourages students to participate in the learning process, as they can reflect on their own work in the context of the whole class. 4) WCF provides an opportunity for students to learn from their peers, as they can see examples of good practice and identify areas for improvement in their own work. 5) Reduced workload: WCF can help reduce the workload for teachers, as it allows them to provide feedback to a larger group of students in a more streamlined way. Overall, whole class feedback is a valuable teaching approach that can benefit both teachers and students, as it promotes efficiency, consistency, engagement, peer learning and reduced workload. In addition, Elliott et al. (2016) found no evidence to suggest that writing feedback on students' work provided any additional benefit to providing feedback in other ways.

54. Evidence on the motivational power of feedback is overwhelming. Black & Wiliam (1998a), Ryan & Deci (2000), Vansteenkiste et al. (2004), Hattie & Timperley (2007) and Pekrun et al. (2009) all suggest that when teachers provide feedback that is personalised and supportive, it can help students feel cared for and invested in their success. However, there is almost no research specifically on the effects of marking students' work. Elliott et al. (2016) conducted a review of the evidence on written marking in order to investigate whether marking improves student learning. They analysed ten studies that examined the effects of written marking on student achievement and found that the evidence was mixed. Some studies suggested that marking had a positive impact on student achievement, while others found no effect or even negative effects. The authors also noted that there was a lack of consistency in the way marking was carried out and that the studies used different methods and measures to assess student achievement. The review makes clear that the current state of evidence is insufficient to make any claims about the efficacy of marking.

55. David Didau (2019) argues that although students say they really value teachers' comments they don't tend to read them. In fact, there appears to be an inverse relationship between the length of the comment and the likelihood that it will be read. Also, students say they value their work being ticked (and especially double-ticked) almost as much as they appreciate teacher comments.

56. See here for more details about Carousel: www.carousel-learning.com/teaching-and-learning/carousel-english-launch%21

57. *Getting Started with Reading Progress in Teams*: https://support.microsoft.com/en-gb/topic/getting-started-with-reading-progress-in-teams-7617c11c-d685-4cb7-8b75-3917b297c407#IDOEDD=Students

58. There are various sources of evidence to suggest that text presented in columns can be easier to read than text presented in a single block of text. Here are a few examples: Eye movement studies: Rayner et al. (1980) found that readers tend to make fewer fixations and shorter saccades (i.e., movements of the eyes) when reading text in columns compared to text in a single block. This suggests that readers can more easily navigate through the text in columns. Comprehension: Tinker (1963) has shown that readers can comprehend text more easily when it is presented in columns. Vaid & Lal (2012) found that participants were able to answer comprehension questions more accurately and quickly when reading text in two columns compared to a single block. Preference: Readers overwhelmingly prefer text presented in columns. In a study of newspaper layouts, participants overwhelmingly preferred layouts with columns of text rather than a single block (Woelfel & Fink, 1980).

59. The 2015 Department for Education (DfE) workload survey was conducted in England to investigate the workload of teachers and school leaders in primary and secondary schools. The survey was completed by 43,000 respondents, including classroom teachers, middle leaders, senior leaders and headteachers. The survey found that workload was a major concern for teachers and school leaders, with a significant number of respondents reporting that they were working long hours, including evenings and weekends. The workload was driven by a variety of factors, including curriculum changes, assessment requirements, administrative tasks, and the need to provide individualised support to students. The survey also found that workload was having a negative impact on teacher well-being and job satisfaction, with many respondents reporting high levels of stress and anxiety. The impact of workload was felt across all career stages, with newly qualified teachers and experienced teachers alike reporting high levels of workload-related stress. The DfE made a number of recommendations in response to the survey, including simplifying administrative tasks, reducing the frequency of assessment, and improving communication between schools and the government. The survey has been influential in shaping policies aimed at reducing teacher workload and improving teacher well-being in England.

60. Fullan (2001). Fullan emphasises that dips in performance are a normal and expected part of the change process. Here are the key points made in the book regarding dips in performance during change implementation: 1) Change is a process: Fullan emphasises that change does not occur smoothly and continuously. Instead, it involves a series of stages and phases, and performance may dip temporarily during these transitions. 2) Resistance and uncertainty: When organisations undergo change, resistance and uncertainty are common reactions. People may resist the new initiatives due to fear of the unknown, loss of control, or scepticism about the benefits. This resistance can lead to a temporary decline in performance. 3) Cultural clashes: Change often disrupts established norms, values and practices within an organisation. When a new culture clashes with the existing one, it can create confusion, conflicts and a decline in performance. 4) Learning curve: Implementing change requires individuals and teams to acquire new skills, knowledge and ways of working. This learning process can initially lead to a drop in performance as people adapt to the changes and

develop proficiency in the new methods. 5) Monitoring and support: Fullan stresses the importance of monitoring performance during the change process. It is crucial to identify areas where performance is dipping and provide necessary support, resources and training to help individuals and teams overcome challenges and improve their performance. 6) Persistence and resilience: Fullan encourages leaders to remain persistent and resilient during periods of performance dip. They should communicate the importance of the change, provide clarity, support and resources, and maintain a positive attitude to help the organisation navigate through the challenges.

61. See the EEF guidance report in improving literacy in KS2 here: https://educationendowmentfoundation.org.uk/education-evidence/guidance-reports/literacy-ks2

3. IMPACT

1. Purves (2018)
2. Rob Coe (2018) says, 'It has become common, although I still find it surprising, to hear teachers use the word "data" as if it were a bad thing. "Data drops" have come to epitomise a pointless exercise in collecting meaningless numbers and feeding them into a system that can have no possible benefit for learners. People even say that Ofsted is "too reliant on data", as if a judgement process could – or should – rely on anything other than data. The problem is that data is often not actually data. The numbers that are typed into spreadsheets or tracking systems every six weeks don't signify anything; they have no informational content, so cannot really be described as data'.
3. Nicholas Soderstrom and Robert Bjork (2015) have explored the distinction between performance and learning, and how we can optimise learning by prioritising long-term memory over short-term performance. Bjork argues that traditional approaches to learning often focus on immediate performance and reinforcement, rather than promoting long-term retention and transfer of knowledge. For example, students may cram for exams and perform well in the short term, but quickly forget what they learned. Instead, Bjork suggests that we should focus on creating 'desirable difficulties' in learning that promote long-term retention, even if they may temporarily hinder performance. One way to create desirable difficulties is through the use of spaced repetition, or interleaved practice, where learners are presented with material at intervals, rather than all at once. This helps prevent overlearning and strengthens long-term memory. Other desirable difficulties include testing, elaboration and generation, which require learners to actively engage with the material and create connections between concepts. Bjork's work suggests that while short-term performance may be important, focusing too heavily on it can actually hinder long-term learning and retention. By creating desirable difficulties and prioritising long-term memory, we can optimise learning and ensure that knowledge is retained and transferred to new situations.
4. Fordham (2017)
5. Michael Purves (2018) from Ofsted discusses data in the context of the curriculum.
6. Treadaway (2015)
7. Ofqual (2019)
8. Horvath (2020, p. 40)
9. Coe (2018)
10. Bloom (1984) discusses a problem in education where students receiving one-to-one tutoring consistently outperform those receiving traditional classroom instruction, with an average difference of two standard deviations (2-sigma). Bloom analyses research studies and suggests that the use of mastery learning, which involves frequent assessments, feedback and individualised instruction, can help close this gap and achieve similar learning outcomes to those of one-to-one tutoring. Bloom also emphasises the importance of adopting innovative and effective teaching methods to enhance student learning in group settings.
11. Coe (2020)
12. A responsive curriculum is one that responds to students' struggles by identifying and eliminating gaps in instructional sequences.
13. Construct validity refers to the degree to which an assessment measures the intended construct, such as reading comprehension or writing proficiency. A valid assessment of reading comprehension should measure the specific skills and abilities involved in understanding written texts, while a valid assessment of writing proficiency should measure the specific skills and abilities involved in producing effective written communication. To establish construct validity we might use the following: Content validity: ensuring that the assessment items are representative of the content and skills that students are expected to know, such as vocabulary, sentence structure, and comprehension strategies; Criterion validity: comparing the assessment scores to other established measures of the same construct, such as other reading or writing assessments or teacher ratings; Convergent validity: comparing the assessment scores to other measures of the same construct, such as classroom performance or work in books; Discriminant validity: comparing the assessment scores to measures of other constructs that are not related to the intended construct, such as handwriting or creativity. Establishing construct validity in assessments is important because it helps ensure that the assessment accurately measures the skills and abilities that are relevant to reading and writing proficiency. This, in turn, helps teachers make informed decisions about student learning and instructional practices, and helps ensure that students are being assessed fairly and accurately.
14. This comes from the insert to AQA's November 2019 English Language GCSE (AQA, 2019)
15. The ability to comprehend a text is strongly linked to prior knowledge of the topic being discussed. Readers who have prior knowledge of the topic are more likely to comprehend the text effectively. ED Hirsch Jr is a prominent proponent of this idea. He argues that readers who possess a broad and deep knowledge of the world are better able to understand and interpret what they read. In his book *Cultural Literacy: What Every American Needs to Know* (1987), Hirsch contends that a shared cultural knowledge base is necessary for effective communication and understanding across different communities and contexts. He suggests that without a common understanding of important historical, literary and cultural references, readers may struggle to comprehend the intended meaning and implications of a text. There are various sources that add weight to this position. McNamara & Kintsch (1996) found that prior knowledge influences how much information a reader can extract from a text, and that readers with relevant

prior knowledge are better able to remember and comprehend a text than readers without such knowledge. Graesser et al. (1994) argue that readers use their prior knowledge to construct inferences, or connections between the information presented in a text and their own knowledge and experiences. The authors contend that readers with more relevant prior knowledge are better able to generate inferences and comprehend a text. Anderson & Freebody (1981) argue that vocabulary knowledge is closely linked to prior knowledge. They contend that readers must have sufficient knowledge of a word's referent in order to understand its meaning in a text, and that readers with greater background knowledge are better able to infer word meanings from context.

16. Rosenshine (2012, p. 17)
17. Rosenshine (2012, p. 17)
18. Several studies have investigated the effectiveness of hinge point questions in various settings, and the evidence generally supports their use. One study conducted by Black & Wiliam (1998b) found that using hinge point questions in a classroom setting helped teachers identify students' misunderstandings and adjust their teaching methods accordingly. A study by Brindley et al. (2016) found that using hinge point questions in geography education helped students retain information better and improve their critical thinking skills. Brame (2013) conducted a literature review of the use of hinge point questions and found that they can be effective in a range of educational settings. Brame noted that hinge point questions can be particularly useful in large lecture-style courses, where it can be challenging for instructors to gauge students' understanding of course material. Clark (2015) investigated the use of hinge point questions in an online learning environment and found that they were effective in promoting critical thinking and student engagement. Clark noted that hinge point questions can help students stay focused on the most important material and can provide opportunities for students to apply their knowledge. Haladyna et al. (2002) conducted a study on the use of hinge point questions in standardised tests and found that they were effective in improving the quality of test questions. The authors noted that hinge point questions can help ensure that tests are measuring students' understanding of key concepts rather than just their ability to memorise facts. Also, Zimmaro (2010) investigated the use of hinge point questions in a university-level statistics course. The study found that using hinge point questions was effective in promoting student engagement and understanding of key concepts. In particular, the study found that hinge point questions were helpful in identifying misunderstandings and guiding further discussion and explanation of difficult topics. The study also found that students appreciated the use of hinge point questions and felt that they were beneficial for their learning.
19. Allen (2018)
20. Article II. Laming (2003, p. 51)
21. This is a phenomenon often called 'expertise blindness'. Expertise blindness in assessment refers to the tendency of experts to overlook important details or make assumptions about the knowledge and abilities of others when evaluating their work. Research in this area has shown that expertise blindness can have significant implications for the fairness and accuracy of assessments. See Chi & VanLehn (2012), Mason (2005), Schneider & Chein

(2003), Kane (2013), Pellegrino et al. (2001), Shavelson & Ruiz-Primo (1999) and Wilson (2013).
22. By analysing the data in Ofqual's November report (Rhead et al., 2018), we can work out that the average reliability for Combined English Language and Literature is about 52%. What this suggests is that 'if the 6 million scripts, as typically submitted for each summer's exams, were to be re-marked by a senior examiner, some 4.5 million (about 75%) of the originally-awarded grades would be confirmed, and around 1.5 million (about 25%) would be changed, approximately half upwards and half downwards. Or, in simple terms, on average, 1 exam grade in every 4 is wrong' (Sherwood, 2020).
23. The halo effect is a cognitive bias where a person's overall impression of a person, product or organisation influences their evaluation of specific traits or characteristics associated with that entity. Research on the halo effect has shown that people are more likely to evaluate a person or object positively if they have a favourable overall impression of them, even if they have little or no direct evidence to support their evaluation. For example, studies have found that people who are considered attractive are often perceived as being more intelligent, competent and trustworthy, even when these qualities are not related to their physical appearance. Similarly, people who are perceived to have a high status or social standing are often evaluated more positively than those who are perceived to be of lower status, even if their actual performance or achievements are the same. Research on the halo effect in education includes Brophy (1983), Jussim & Harber (2005), Rosenthal & Jacobson (1968), Rubie-Davies (2010) and Weinstein (2002).

4. THE CURRICULUM IN DETAIL

1. Under the terms of our license you can share (copy and redistribute the material in any medium or format) and adapt (remix, transform and build upon the material). In return, we ask that **you** give appropriate credit, provide a link to the license and indicate if changes were made. You may do so in any reasonable manner, but not in any way that suggests the licensor endorses you or your use. You may not use the material for commercial purposes. If you remix, transform or build upon the material, you must distribute your contributions under the same license as the original. You can read the full licence here: https://creativecommons.org/licenses/by-nc-sa/4.0/

APPENDIX 2

1. Many of these sentence types are taken from the work of English teacher Peter Ahern.

APPENDIX 3

1. Alternative provision (www.gov.uk)
2. Additional health needs guidance (publishing.service.gov.uk)

Index

Page numbers in *italics* denote a figure, **bold** a table, n an endnote